European Models of Bilingual Education

Multilingual Matters

Alsatian Acts of Identity
  LILIANE M. VASSBERG
Attitudes and Language
  COLIN BAKER
Breaking the Boundaries
  EUAN REID and HANS H. REICH (eds)
Citizens of This Country: The Asian British
  MARY STOPES-ROE and RAYMOND COCHRANE
Community Languages: A Handbook
  BARBARA M. HORVATH and PAUL VAUGHAN
Continuing to Think: The British Asian Girl
  BARRIE WADE and PAMELA SOUTER
Cultural Studies in Foreign Language Education
  MICHAEL BYRAM
Education of Chinese Children in Britain and the USA
  LORNITA YUEN-FAN WONG
Immigrant Languages in Europe
  GUUS EXTRA and LUDO VERHOEVEN (eds)
Key Issues in Bilingualism and Bilingual Education
  COLIN BAKER
Life in Language Immersion Classrooms
  ELIZABETH B. BERNHARDT (ed.)
Linguistic and Communicative Competence
  CHRISTINA BRATT-PAULSTON
Linguistic Minorities, Society and Territory
  COLIN H. WILLIAMS (ed.)
Migration and Intercultural Education in Europe
  U. PÖRNBACHER (ed.)
Minority Education: From Shame to Struggle
  T. SKUTNABB-KANGAS and J. CUMMINS (eds)
Multilingualism and Nation Building
  GERDA MANSOUR
One Europe - 100 Nations
  ROY N. PEDERSEN
Opportunity and Constraints of Community Language Teaching
  SJAAK KROON
Sociolinguistic Perspectives on Bilingual Education
  CHRISTINA BRATT PAULSTON
The World in a Classroom
  V. EDWARDS and A. REDFERN

Please contact us for the latest book information:
Multilingual Matters Ltd,
Frankfurt Lodge, Clevedon Hall, Victoria Road,
Clevedon, Avon BS21 7SJ, England

MULTILINGUAL MATTERS 92
Series Editor: Derrick Sharp

European Models of Bilingual Education

Edited by

Hugo Baetens Beardsmore

MULTILINGUAL MATTERS LTD
Clevedon • Philadelphia • Adelaide

Library of Congress Cataloging in Publication Data

European Models of Bilingual Education/Edited by Hugo Baetens Beardsmore
p. cm. (Multilingual matters: 92)
Includes bibliographical references and index
1. Education, Bilingual–Europe. 2. Education–Social aspects–Europe.
3. Education and state–Europe.
I. Baetens Beardsmore, Hugo. II. Series: Multilingual Matters (Series): 92.
LC3736.A2E97   1993
371.97'0094—dc20

British Library Cataloguing in Publication Data

A CIP catalogue record for this book is available from the British Library.

ISBN 1-85359-183-1 (hbk)
ISBN 1-85359-182-3 (pbk)

Multilingual Matters Ltd

UK: Frankfurt Lodge, Clevedon Hall, Victoria Road, Clevedon, Avon BS21 7SJ.
USA: 1900 Frost Road, Suite 101, Bristol, PA 19007, USA.
Australia: P.O. Box 6025, 83 Gilles Street, Adelaide, SA 5000, Australia.

Printed and bound in Great Britain by the Longdunn Press, Bristol.

Contents

Introduction

'*L'Europe sera multilingue ou elle ne sera pas.*'

Europe has a history of some form of bilingual education going back over several millennia (cf. Glyn Lewis, 1976) and the continent's experience with multilingual diversity has often been taken somewhat for granted. Linguistic homogeneity has rarely coincided with national geographic boundaries, though from the end of the eighteenth century there has been a tendency for most European nations to view themselves from a more or less linguistically homogeneous perspective, particularly as widespread public education became prevalent in this century. This perception has led to the development of monolingual education systems coinciding at times with national boundaries, as in the United Kingdom and France, at times with regional sub-divisions, as in Belgium and Switzerland, on generally accepted assumptions that monolingual education was the most natural form to propagate. It is only in recent decades that such assumptions have been called into question and it is the purpose of this book to help activate the querying of beliefs about the link between language and education.

Although general assumptions about the monolingual norm in educational provision have long held sway, this does not mean that alternative forms have not co-existed. Usually these alternatives have tended to be low-profile or else considered as special, marginal, remedial, compensatory, peripheral, experimental or exotic. As such, alternative bilingual forms of education have simply got on with their business outside the mainstream of consciousness, accumulating experience and expertise which have failed to reach out to the relevant research or academic spheres, let alone the wider public. The result has been that, in spite of history and experience, the impetus for innovation in bilingual education has not come from Europe but from North America, and particularly from Canada with its impressive commitment to research on immersion programmes, leading to the neglect and lack of awareness of alternative approaches based on European experience. What this book tries to show is that immersion is only one form of bilingual education that can be developed.

1

The well-deserved strength of the Canadian immersion phenomenon is due to the solidity of research which backs it up, and which perhaps accounts for the lesser impact of alternative models. Cummins (1991: 191) indicates that there are approximately a thousand studies on immersion education in Canada. No European form of bilingual education has anything approaching this Canadian investment in research, and it is this factor which has determined the selection of contributions to the present volume. Purely descriptive accounts of variegated forms of bilingual education abound, yet they fail to get taken up because they are interpreted as interesting case studies in how to overcome specific educational needs but are not considered relevant or applicable to broader segments of the population. Given the smaller research background behind the European models it was decided to compensate for their potential lack of credibility or extension by restricting this volume along several criteria.

The chapters that follow devote themselves exclusively to well-established, publicly funded and relatively widespread networks of schools, in the hope that such restriction helps compensate for the relative lack of research and adds credibility to their value. This is not to say that there is no research evidence behind the papers presented here, as will be clear from their presentation. In fact, with regard precisely to this research evidence, the contents go beyond descriptions of recently-established, or privately-run, or experimental bilingual schools which can be found, often with exciting and interesting features. To include reports on these would have run the risk of dismissive, 'So what?' type arguments from the dominant monolingual-school frame of thinking. A relatively new bilingual programme leads to a wait-and-see reaction, a privately-run one provokes sentiments of elitism, while any experimental programme is open to the accusation that it succeeds precisely because it is experimental.

The reports involve publicly-funded bilingual schools, most of which have had a long existence, and all of which form parts of networks; they are not unique examples whose success may depend on specific local contingencies. This is considered important in a volume devoted to analysing model programmes, since the duplication of specific formats across several schools is an important factor in their credibility. Moreover, all models are open to expansion within their specific catchment areas, except for the European Schools, which are regulated by international treaty restricting their expansion. The fact that the schools are publicly-funded is important, given the frequently-held conception that bilingual education is an expensive alternative which should only be provided with parsimony. The general literature on bilingual education across the world never addresses the cost factor, so there is no data on this aspect. Although some programmes are expensive, such as the European School model, due to its complexity, the recruitment of temporary foreign staff, the amount of extra or special materials required, etc. (one reason why its expansion is restricted), the majority of schools presented here fit into normal budgetary limitations with no or little extra cost attributable to their specific bilingual nature.

The types of schools described cover bilingual education for linguistic majorities, as in Luxembourg where the whole school population is involved, minorities, for example in the Danish–German border area, and migrants, as in the Brussels Foyer project. Many of them have multiple outcome goals which encompass the range of possibilities schematised by Fishman (1976) into maintenance, transitional and enrichment programmes; in fact all programmes included here are essentially different forms of enrichment programmes and contain elements which,

> . . . aim toward language maintenance, strengthened cultural identity and the affirmation of ethnic groups' civil rights in the national society (Hornberger, 1991: 222)

The nature of the enrichment programme depends on the specific circumstances of the population involved and the location, though in no case is there any attempt at rapid-exit transitional outcomes as a deliberate goal which is so prevalent in the United States.

The selection of models has also tried to cover the major types of circumstances prevailing in Europe, from the maintenance and expansion of a threatened linguistic patrimony as in Wales, the revival and expansion of smaller regional languages as in Catalonia and the Basque country, the accommodation of cross-border minorities as in Schleswig, the promotion of neighbouring languages across national frontiers as in the German model, the provision of high-level multilingual proficiency as in Luxembourg and the European Schools, and the integration of immigrant populations into mainstream society as in the complex Brussels environment.

The least productive model included in this collection is that of the European Schools, given that it is not destined for expansion, is expensive to operate and could be taxed with elitism. Nevertheless, the immense practical experience gained from this complex form of multilingual education and the many insights it offers on how to handle mixed populations on an equal footing should provide elements of inspiration. As a model it is unlikely to be adopted elsewhere. It differs significantly from many so-called international schools, however, in that, unlike the latter, it is genuinely multilingual both in programme and in outcome, whereas most so-called international schools are only international in population make-up, to some extent in curriculum, but rarely so in languages on offer.

There are obviously other specific population categories whose linguistic and educational needs could be addressed, e.g. Gypsies or refugees, but these have not been incorporated because of the lack of well-established, publicly-funded networks of schools able to serve as models.

An important issue in bilingual education, as in all education, is the role of ideology, and it is naive to presume that models, programmes and outcomes can be analysed without reference to some politico-historical ideological basis. All examples presented here are clearly contextualised from their ideological stance, ranging from the pan-European bias of the European School and German models to the somewhat intriguing case of the Danish–German border schools, whose pedagogic strategy appears anachronistic and yet who continue to represent attractive alternatives to mainstream unilingual education. It is this peculiar situation, explicable only in ideological terms, which justifies the mirror-image presentation of the Schleswig case in two separate papers.

Intimately linked to ideological questions is the issue of culture, an area which can easily degenerate into a veritable quagmire of platitudinous generalities in debates about bilingualism in education. Although not specifically addressed from a European perspective in this volume, it is clear that the promotion of Europe's linguistic and cultural diversity (also taking into account the non-European immigrant dimension) is a thread that runs throughout the collection. It is specifically illustrated in the last three contributions to this book, where more practical aspects are touched upon.

Most of the chapters present models and programmes from the traditional academic perspective. The last three contributors present some of the concrete issues involved in developing bilingual education. The paper on bilingual geography from a teacher's perspective reveals how to overcome inherent cultural incompatibilities in teaching-style, materials, and examination criteria, without in any way diluting the bilingual outcome or sacrificing certain national characteristics. Other papers incidentally touch on such questions, but it is felt that a practical description of the 'nitty-gritty' of how to cope in the front-line of the classroom is worth far more to the practitioner than a volume of academic rhetoric.

The German model presented from an administrator's perspective closely ties in with the teacher's viewpoint since although it describes a type of programme, it also goes into concrete issues of how to implement and expand the model, while also concentrating heavily on the cultural implications of propagating bilingual education in Europe. The final paper dealing with the adaptation of computer terminology to Welsh classroom needs is a highly significant contribution which counters the potentially insidious homogenisation of 'modern' linguistic development by coming to terms with the audio-visual technological age with which we are confronted.

The self-imposed limitations on the selection of models might well provoke criticism of the neglect of Eastern Europe. The former Soviet Union has considerable experience with high quality specialist language schools and with bilingualism in general. Hungary is developing different forms of specialist foreign language schools providing instruction through the medium of German, French, English, Italian, Spanish and Russian, while Czechoslovakia is also developing bilingual programmes. Given the fundamental changes and uncertainties these countries are undergoing and the recency of many of the programmes it was decided to restrict contributions to those that have been stabilised within the European Community.

The European Commission is instrumental in promoting the development of multilingualism, both through its *Lingua* programme for secondary education and its *Erasmus* programme for higher education. European integration within the Community by no means implies linguistic and cultural homogenisation; on the contrary, greater human mobility and equality of opportunity throughout the member states can only imply an increase in multilingual proficiency. This book is a modest attempt to give some indications as to how this can be achieved.

Hugo Baetens Beardsmore
Visiting Professor, National University of Singapore.
June 1992

References

CUMMINS, J. 1991, The politics of paranoia: reflections on the bilingual education debate. In O. GARCÍA (ed.) *Bilingual Education: Focusschrift in Honor of Joshua A. Fishman*. Amsterdam–Philadelphia: Benjamins. 183–99.

FISHMAN, J. 1976, *Bilingual Education: An International Sociological Perspective*. Rowley, Mass.: Newbury House.

GLYN LEWIS, E. 1976, Bilingualism and bilingual education: The ancient world to the renaissance. In J. FISHMAN *Bilingual Education: An International Sociological Perspective*. Rowley, Mass.: Newbury House. 151–200.

HORNBERGER, N. 1991, Extending enrichment bilingual education; Revisiting typologies and redirecting policy. In O. GARCÍA (ed.) *Bilingual Education: Focusschrift in Honor of Joshua A. Fishman*. Amsterdam–Philadelphia: Benjamins. 215–34.

1 Bilingual Education in Wales

COLIN BAKER

Introduction

To understand the current philosophy, policy provision and practice of bilingual education in Wales, it is essential to contrast the fate of the Welsh language this century with the growth of bilingual education in Wales. This reveals the opposite movement of language decay and the continuing development of bilingual education. The growth in bilingual education is viewed as a gentle revolution away from a formal education system where the Welsh language as a subject, and especially as a medium of instruction, was rarely visible in the curriculum. Thus the chapter commences by briefly portraying the historical context of modern bilingual education in Wales. The recent growth and present composition of bilingual education indicates a reversal from Anglicised education. Welsh has increasingly become a medium throughout the curriculum and is increasingly being used in formal examinations, an important indicator of the currency and market value of Welsh. While the statistics of the growth of bilingual education provide clear evidence of a gentle revolution, they do not convey the movement as having vision, ideas and drive from within and without. Therefore, the chapter proceeds to show how institutional growth of bilingual education has been supported by a wide variety of agencies, voluntary movements, initiatives and commitments. In conclusion, the chapter briefly examines the extent to which the growth of education has contributed to the balance sheet of the fortunes of the Welsh language.

The Welsh Language and Bilingual Education

If the fate of Welsh medium education had followed the fate of the Welsh language in the last 100 years, it would have shown a pattern of decline and diminution. Rather than paralleling the decline of the language, Welsh medium education has recently grown and flourished. This is the paradox which this chapter initially seeks to portray.

The growth of Welsh medium education in relation to the decline in the absolute number of Welsh speakers and their relative numerical dominance in the population can be illustrated by two sets of figures. First, the following graph (see Figure 1.1) provides evidence from Census data (1891 to 1991) of the decline in the absolute number and percentage distribution of Welsh speakers in the population of Wales.

The following graph (see Figure 1.2) provides a second set of data revealing a positive relationship between year and the increase in numbers of Designated Bilingual Schools. Such Designated Bilingual Schools have been established in mainly urban, English-speaking areas. They contain pupils from Welsh-speaking homes and from English language backgrounds; a mixture of 'heritage language' and 'immersion' children. Apart from the Designated Bilingual Schools, the revolution in the place of Welsh in education is also found in 'natural' Welsh schools, that is, schools in predominantly Welsh speaking areas where the main medium of instruction is Welsh.

It is clear from these two figures that bilingual schooling has not reflected Welsh language Census trends. On the contrary, the possibility of a reaction to language trends is one major explanation of the development of bilingual education. In this sense, bilingual education has become a main engineer of attempted language reversal.

If a reaction thesis is tenable, the immediate question is the cause

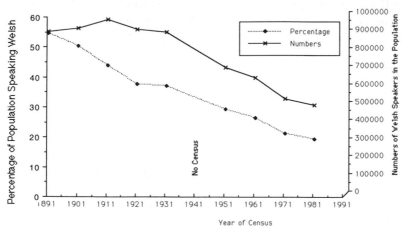

FIGURE 1.1 *Welsh speakers in the population of Wales.*

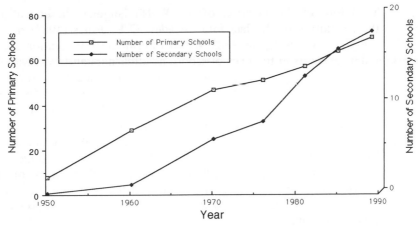

FIGURE 1.2 *The increase in Designated Bilingual Schools by Year.*

of the reaction. Locating and defining the origins of the development of bilingual education can never rest with simple influences. The development is likely to be the result of complex educational, political, economic and social factors. Reactions to developing transport systems and mass communication systems, industrialisation and urbanisation, in-migration and out-migration, the growth of mass media and a decline in religious attendance may each have an effect. The growth of nationalistic political consciousness, a reaction to the authoritarian imposition of the English language and Anglophone culture are similarly important external effects on the development of Welsh bilingual education. That is, the development of bilingual education in Wales is not a purely educationally derived phenomenon. It does not develop from simple arguments about the educational virtues of bilingual education. Rather, such growth is both an action and reaction in the general growth of consciousness about the virtues of preserving an indigenous language and culture. Such growth cannot be viewed in simple, functional terms. Conflicts with authority, protests, non-violent but militant action all have been a part of the equation of change.

The Gentle Revolution

The growth of bilingual schools is one major indicator of a gentle revolution that has occurred in schools in Wales in the last four decades. That a revolution and not evolution has occurred is demonstrated by brief illustrations of the position of the Welsh language in education before the revolution of the last four decades. G.E. Jones (1982) notes that in the years following the 1889 Welsh Intermediate Education Act, Welsh had little status in the eyes of school headteachers and was 'widely regarded as an inferior language and certainly an unnecessary one; it was of no help in "getting on" . . . [a] low-status irrelevancy' (p. 18). When the Board of Education produced a report on 'Welsh in Education and Life' (1927), of the 135 secondary schools surveyed, in none was Welsh the everyday language of the school and no Welsh language textbooks were available for the school or Higher Certificate stages in History and Geography (Jones, 1982). Upward social mobility often dominated the ideas and priorities of parents and teachers, and thus the English language was perceived as the route to vocational progression and relative prosperity.

It is worthy of note that, despite a gentle revolution in bilingual education in Wales, problems identified in the first two decades of the century (by The Report on Welsh in Education and Life, 1927) as surrounding the indigenous language, are still issues of debate today in Wales and many minority language European contexts: the comparative economic and utilitarian value of Welsh and English, examination syllabuses and the expectations of higher education constraining the implementation of a full Welsh cultural curriculum, the apathy of certain groups of Welsh speakers to their own language and culture, the presence of monolingual English speakers in the Welsh speaking heartlands, the 'brain-drain' of Welsh speakers (especially teachers) to England, the unequal distribution and availability of media in the two languages, debates about literary, classical Welsh and living, colloquial Welsh, concerns that bilingualism has negative effects on 'intelligence' and school attainment, debates about the value of a minority language as opposed to fostering major European languages, the role of the organic community in the health of the Welsh language, debates as to the relative power of government in Cardiff and London, and the depopulation of small 'Welsh' villages (Board of Education, 1927). *L'histoire, qu'est-ce autre chose qu'une analyse du présent, puisque c'est dans le passé que l'on trouve les éléments dont est formé le présent?* (attributed to Durkheim).

The beginning of the revolution in bilingual education in Wales cannot and should not be dated. Before structural change there needs to be change in public opinions or in dominant philosophy and policy. In 1939, the first bilingual (Welsh) school was opened in Aberystwyth, this being a primary school in the private sector. As Edwards (1984) noted, 'Despite scornful opposition from Welsh as well as non-Welsh speakers, it thrived and in time became the pattern for many similar primary bilingual schools (5–11 years old), all of which were subsequently established and supported by local education authorities' (p. 250). The establishment in 1956 of Ysgol Glan Clwyd as the first designated bilingual secondary school marks the beginnings of secondary school change in Welsh education.

The current statistics (Welsh Office, 'Statistics of Education', 1976–1990) show that:

(1) Approximately one in every four primary school children in Wales are mostly or partly taught through the medium of Welsh. Under the National Curriculum, all children will be taught Welsh as a first or a second language. Thus, from Welsh being excluded from the curriculum in the early decades of this century, it has now become virtually compulsory in schools throughout Wales.

(2) There are 417 Welsh-speaking (bilingual) primary schools and 42 Welsh-speaking (bilingual) secondary schools in Wales. In terms of the total number of schools, this is respectively 24.1% of primary schools and 17.7% of secondary schools. A Welsh-speaking (bilingual) school is currently defined under the 1988 Education Reform Act as a school where a half or more subjects (other than English and Welsh) are taught wholly or partly in Welsh.

(3) There has been a substantial rise in the percentage of secondary schools offering certain subjects through the medium of Welsh. This is illustrated in the figures below:

	Maths	French	PE/Games
1979	6.1%	6.1%	6.6%
1990	17.7%	14.3%	17.3%
change	+11.6%	+8.4%	+10.7%

	Physics	Chemistry
1982	7.1%	3.7%
1990	9.5%	9.1%
change	+2.4%	+5.4%

(4) There has also been a rise in the number of examination subjects offered and entered. The figures below (see Figure 1.3) concern Welsh medium subjects offered to 16 year olds (at the Ordinary level).

From the small acorn planted some four decades ago, still young but sturdy oak trees have developed. In the last decade, the central girth of those trees has expanded, with an increasing percentage of pupils being

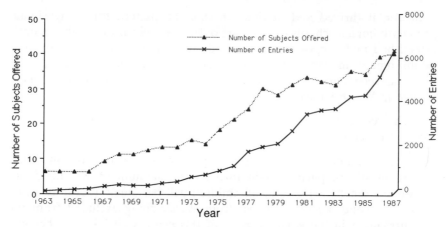

FIGURE 1.3 *Examination subjects offered through the medium of Welsh.*
Note: In 1988, with the introduction of the General Certificate of Secondary Education, 71 subjects were offered throught the medium of Welsh. The number of entries was 8886.

taught Welsh as a first or second language. That the seeds of change are slowly being planted elsewhere in the system is evident from the increasing number of secondary schools using Welsh as a medium of transmission in the curriculum. Particular growth has recently occurred in the Mathematics and Science curriculum. History, Geography and Religious Education have been 'natural' subjects for Welsh-medium teaching due to their obvious Welsh cultural links, relative lack of problems with terminology and a partial availability of suitable curriculum material. Since the inception of bilingual secondary education, these tended to be the first subjects taught in Welsh. For opposite reasons, Maths and Science have tended to be among the last subjects to use Welsh as the medium of communication.

One of the best and clearest indicators of growth in bilingual education is the linear increase in 'Ordinary' level subjects (taken at the age of 16) offered through the medium of Welsh and the take-up by pupils and schools of these exams. In a quarter of a century, both 'Ordinary' level entries and subjects in Welsh increased by more than sixfold. This statistic is important because such examinations are prime symbols of the currency value of bilingual education as perceived by pupils, parents and employers. The market-value of Welsh-medium examinations appears both to have risen in recent years and is currently regarded as a desirable commodity. Such examinations are also good reflectors of the status of Welsh-medium courses in schools. Such status has both grown and is yet to peak. However, one Achilles heel of bilingual education in Wales has been post-school bilingual provision. Higher education and further education have sometimes failed to keep pace with changes in bilingual education. This can decrease the intrinsic value of Welsh-medium examinations. A related problem has been to retain bilingually educated pupils within the Welsh higher education system. Many pupils from bilingual secondary education exert their freedom of choice of University by selecting a University or College in England. While this provides evidence that bilingual education does not impede the ability to participate and compete favourably with monolingually educated pupils, it also causes anxiety that Welsh speakers will emigrate permanently to England, thereby reducing the stock of able Welsh speakers working in Wales.

It is important to view the growth of bilingual education as not occurring in a vacuum. Such growth has been promoted and sustained by a wide and complexly interacting variety of formal and informal support systems. It is important for an understanding of the gentle revolution in the place of Welsh in education to consider briefly such support mechanisms.

Regional Variations

Wales is divided into eight counties each with its own Educational Authority. Each county has thus been able to devise its own bilingual educational policy, provision and practice. As Baker (1985) documented, growth in the use of Welsh has not only varied from county to county, but also cannot be simply explained by language demographics. A comparison of the counties of Clwyd and West Glamorgan, for example, reveals differences of language policy and provision not accounted for by densities of Welsh speakers in the population. One of the most developed and detailed bilingual education policies derives from the county of Gwynedd which contains substantial heartland areas of Welsh-speakers. This county's policy is to develop the ability of pupils and students so that they can be full members of the bilingual society of which they are a part (Gwynedd County Council, 1986). All pupils are expected to become thoroughly bilingual, to be able to speak, read and write fluently and confidently in both English and Welsh by the age of eleven.

In a response to in-migrant monolingual English pupils, the county of Gwynedd created Language Reception Centres in the mid 1980s to aid the transition of such children into bilingual classrooms. In-migrant children spend about 14 weeks in such a Centre before transferring to mainstream schools. The activity of the Centre is focused on Welsh language communicative competence. This is in contrast to the situation in major cities of England where Reception Centres for non-English speaking in-migrants has been abandoned to maximise early integration. The important difference is that in England the now discredited Reception Centres were for minority ethnic groups. In Wales, the Reception Centres are for majority language speakers (English) in the context of preserving a minority language (Welsh). The county of Gwynedd has also been one of the bodies ensuring that developments in Computer Based Learning have been translated into Welsh (and created in Welsh) to give the Information Technology revolution a Welsh dimension (Humphreys, 1987 & 1988).

In comparison with Gwynedd, developments in bilingual education in the county of Clwyd were early in the gentle revolution and have since tended to become less adventurous. Although not having the same concentration of Welsh speakers as Gwynedd, the county of Dyfed also contains Welsh language heartland areas. Like Gwynedd, it has been one of the areas where a recent small backlash against Welsh-medium education has occurred. This serves to illustrate that bilingual schooling is a political as well as an educational event. The development of bilingual education regionally and nationally cannot be properly understood except through the political economy.

Overall, this discussion has indicated that there are regional variations in bilingual education policy and practice in Wales. This is now further explored by considering types of bilingual school.

Typologies of Bilingual Education in Wales

There exists a wide variety of bilingual educational provision in Wales. For example, in some primary schools in the North-West of Wales, all, or almost all the curriculum is delivered through the medium of Welsh. Such schools tend to be in heartland areas where a large percentage (e.g. over 70%) of the population is Welsh speaking. The philosophy of such schools is that children need to have their education in the minority language; there being enough opportunities to learn English in the community, through the mass media and when experiencing

Anglo-American culture that particularly dominates the teenage years. These schools will mostly be populated by first language Welsh speakers. However, a varying proportion (e.g. 5% to 30%) of each class will be from English-speaking homes. In some areas, such children will be recent in-migrants into rural areas. It is rare to find a class full of first language Welsh speakers.

At the other end of the language dimension there are schools in predominantly English speaking areas of Wales (e.g. Gwent, Pembroke, border areas with England) where Welsh is taught as a second language in primary and secondary schools for half an hour or so per day. Such second language teaching produces relatively few fluent Welsh speaking children. In between basically monolingual Welsh and monolingual English schools in Wales, there is the widest variety of practice of bilingual education. The kaleidoscopic variety of bilingual educational practice in Wales makes the production of a simple typology inherently dangerous. The balance of first language Welsh and first language English children in a classroom varies considerably as does the amount of Welsh-medium teaching. Such wide variations occur due to such factors as the language skills of available teachers, Local Education Authority policy, and the preferences of Headteachers and Governors of individual schools. The language of the hidden curriculum and the playground can differ from the language of the formal and pastoral curriculum and the managerial language of the classroom. A Welsh-medium school usually contains a mixture of first language Welsh pupils, relatively fluent second language Welsh speakers, plus those whose out-of-school language is English (i.e. 'immersion' pupils). While lessons may be mostly in Welsh, there will sometimes be dual-language episodes between teachers and pupils as well as English-only conversations between pupils.

The Official Typology

The Government (Welsh Office) categorisation of bilingual education in Wales can be summarised as follows:

(1) Primary schools having classes where Welsh is the sole or the main medium of instruction of first and second language pupils.
(2) Primary schools having classes of first and second language pupils where some of the teaching is through the medium of Welsh.
(3) Primary schools having classes of second language pupils where some of the teaching is through the medium of Welsh.

(4) Primary schools having classes where Welsh is taught as a second language but not used as a teaching medium.
(5) Secondary schools where Welsh is taught as both a first and second language.
(6) Secondary schools where Welsh is taught as a first language only.
(7) Secondary schools where Welsh is taught as a second language only.
(8) Schools where Welsh is not taught at all.

This official typology does not take into account the variations among schools in the range of subjects which are available through the medium of Welsh, through the medium of English and sometimes available (in secondary schools) through both languages.

Apart from the official typology, various other typologies exist (e.g. Faculty of Education, Aberystwyth, 1988). Two counties in Wales have, for policy-making and practical purposes, established categorisations of bilingual schools. The county of Dyfed divides its primary schools into three categories: schools in traditionally Welsh heartland areas where Welsh is to be the dominant language of the curriculum; bilingual schools where the use of Welsh and English in the curriculum will vary according to demand and resources; and schools with English as the language of the classroom and Welsh is taught as a second language.

The county of Gwynedd has developed a sixfold model of its bilingual secondary schools:

1.   Schools Initially Established to Provide Bilingual Education

Such schools contain a mixture of first language Welsh speakers and those from partly or mostly English language backgrounds who have elected to take their education through the medium of Welsh. These schools normally exist in an area where there is an alternative English-medium school. All the staff are bilingual and a substantial part of the curriculum is taken through the medium of Welsh. At least 70% of the curriculum (from the age of 11 to 16) will be through the medium of Welsh. However terminology is taught bilingually (e.g. in Science, Maths, 'Control, Design and Technology', Geography, Civics). At the same time, such schools provide for those less fluent in Welsh. While seeking to improve their Welsh competence, a typical pattern is for such pupils to take 30% of their curriculum through the medium of Welsh, 20% through the medium of English and 50% in classes where both languages are used side by side. The culture of the school will aim to be dominantly Welsh.

2. Schools of Over 600 Children in Welsh Areas

Such schools contain a children from a wide range of language backgrounds: from first language Welsh speakers to varying levels of fluency and literacy in Welsh and to recent English-only in-migrants. Such schools serve nearly all the secondary children in the catchment area. All teachers are bilingual. In terms of language contact time, up to four types of provision may be found within a school. First, for fluent Welsh speakers and writers, 70% or more of the curriculum taken in Welsh. Second, for those less fluent but still capable enough to follow subjects in Welsh, 50% of the curriculum may be through the medium of Welsh. Third, for those whose Welsh is still developing, 30% of the curriculum is taken in Welsh. Fourth, separate provision may need to be provided for recent in-migrants. In practice, classes may need to operate bilingually. Because the schools contain a wide variety of Welsh language competence, bilingual presentations (oral and written resources) may exist alongside individual, pupil-centred learning strategies.

3. Schools of Over 600 Children in Linguistically Mixed Catchment Areas

Such schools exist in areas that were formally predominantly Welsh but are now Anglicised. There are similarities with the second type (see above). The differences are in the teaching staff not all speaking Welsh and in the specification of the percentage of Welsh in the curriculum. Those who are less fluent in Welsh may either take around 30% of their subjects in Welsh with some subjects being taught bilingually. Alternatively, those with lower ability in Welsh may take around 20% of the 'practical' curriculum in Welsh to strengthen their second language. When such pupils reach the fourth year in Secondary schooling (about 14 years old), English-medium teaching tends to prevail as examination syllabuses determine method and medium of teaching.

4. Schools of Under 600 in Welsh Speaking Catchment Areas

Such schools are found in small towns and rural heartland areas, often being the only choice for parents. The small size of such schools constrains choice of language teaching medium. While teachers will all be bilingual, teaching is at two levels: for fluent Welsh speakers and writers, 70% or more of the curriculum taken in Welsh; for Welsh learners an attempt is made to immerse them in Welsh in the first two years so that a substantial number of subjects may be taken through the medium of Welsh afterwards. Special arrangements are promised for in-migrants (e.g. transport to neighbouring English-medium provision).

5. Schools of Under 600 Pupils in Linguistically Mixed Areas

Such schools are located in Anglicised areas where there is no close alternative state schooling. First language Welsh speakers form a minority of the intake of such schools. Not all teachers will be Welsh speaking; some that are Welsh speaking may not be linguistically competent enough to teach in Welsh. Where possible, 'separate class' provision is made for fluent Welsh speakers with 70% or more of the curriculum delivered through Welsh. For the less fluent, around 30% of the curriculum is expected to be provided in Welsh, increasing to around 50% for those close to fluency in Welsh. Practical necessities mean that classes sometimes operate bilingually to cater for different levels of competence in Welsh. The language balance of the classroom, the availability of suitable and up-to-date learning materials and the preferred teaching style of an individual teacher are some of the major determinants of how policy is interpreted and finely tuned in the classroom. In the movement from a philosophy of bilingual education through the layers of politics, policy, planning, provision and practice, adjustments and departures naturally occur.

6. Large Schools with Very Few First Language Welsh Speakers

Such schools of over 1000 pupils exist in urban, relatively densely populated, Anglicised areas. Almost all pupils speak English as a first language but have been taught Welsh as a second language in the Primary school. A substantial proportion of teachers in the school will not be able to teach in Welsh. English-medium lessons prevail with the expressed Gwynedd ideal being for 20% of the curriculum being in Welsh or delivered bilingually. Fluent Welsh speakers are requested to receive 30% of the curriculum in Welsh. The County policy for such schools with regard to administration and organisation reveals the missionary approach:

> In order to nurture a new tradition in the early years, the schools in this Model need to reflect Welshness in their administration and organisation. The co-operation of the staff will be all important in order to support the lead given by the school's headteacher. A clear policy on the model of using Welsh and English in the school's administration and organisation is required. This policy should

give direction on use of noticeboards, signs, memoranda, letters, information for teachers, morning services, publications, reports, organisation and discipline. (Gwynedd County Council, 1986: 29).

No existing typology of bilingual education in Wales captures the full kaleidoscope of colours that exist. The existing categorisations also lack empirical backing. It is a straightforward procedure to collect information on bilingual schools in Wales which can be statistically analysed (cluster analysis) to produce empirically based categorisations. Simple, neat, uni-dimensional models could then be replaced by a more sophisticated, complex and grounded classification of bilingual education. Such a categorisation would need to show that the formal subject curriculum, the pastoral and classroom management curriculum and not least, the hidden curriculum, have complex bilingual dimensions with considerable variation from school to school. Such a categorisation is also needed to reflect recent government reforms in the curriculum. It is such reforms that are now considered.

The National Curriculum and Bilingual Education in Wales

The 1988 Education Reform Act divides up curriculum subjects into core and foundation subjects. The core subjects are Mathematics, English and Science. The foundation subjects are History, Geography, Technology, Music, Art, Physical Education and a modern foreign language such as French and German. The place of Welsh as a core or foundation subject varies according to type of school. In a Welsh speaking school, Welsh becomes a core subject. In all other schools in Wales, with a very small number of exemptions, Welsh becomes a foundation subject. Thus the National Curriculum recently instituted in England and Wales tends to raise the status of the Welsh language in the Principality by Welsh becoming a compulsory subject for almost all pupils from 5 to 16 years of age. The national assessment which occurs at the ages of 7, 11, 14 and 16 is also being made available through the medium of Welsh. This contrasts with community languages in England (e.g. Bengali, Urdu, Punjabi, Chinese, Greek, Turkish) for which there is no provision in the National Curriculum for such languages as a teaching medium. Such languages can only be introduced as a modern language into the secondary curriculum so long as a European modern language is also taught to these pupils. Assessment materials are not available in these Community languages.

One major problem in the delivery of Welsh as a teaching medium and as a second language in the National Curriculum is the shortage of Welsh speaking teachers. For example, in the 1989 Secondary School Staffing Survey (Welsh Office Statistics of Education, 1990), 20.8% of teachers in Wales were categorised as fluent in oral and written Welsh. Another 30.1% rated themselves as having limited Welsh. Therefore, imaginative solutions have been proposed and implemented to enable monolingual English teachers to teach Welsh as a second language in the classroom. A recent innovatory project is entitled Parablu. Parablu is a series of 48 sequentially structured television programmes directly usable in the classroom. An accompanying resource pack includes a bilingually produced teacher handbook, audio tapes (songs and language practice), graded reading books and musical scores. Parablu is designed for teachers who are not Welsh speakers or who are learners of Welsh and have no experience of teaching Welsh as a second language. With approximately 2000 videos and well over a 1000 resource packs sold to primary schools in Wales, Parablu is currently targeted at the 5–7 year old age group, but is also being used for ages beyond this group. The videos integrate education and entertainment in a lively way having been produced by a major independent television company in Wales (HTV). Parablu centres on the activities of a group of touring actors who live in a caravan and put on shows for children. In the family atmosphere of the caravan, language about meals, daily living and retiring to bed can be enacted using simple vocabulary and concepts. The actors and actresses put on plays and performances. This leads to various activities such as dancing, games and jokes. More importantly, it leads to rehearsing, the learning of parts and coaching, providing an opportunity for repetition and consolidation in second language learning.

The Role of School Inspectors

Not only at the visible and formal level, but also in an informal manner, Her Majesty's Inspectors of Education (HMI) in Wales have supported and influenced the post-War bilingual education movement from the early Primary bilingual education beginnings to the recent compulsory publication of their inspections of schools. For example, such publications contain implicit assumptions of the cross-curricula validity of the use of the indigenous language, perceptive and considered advice for the progressive evolution of bilingualism throughout the school, not just in the formal curriculum, but also in the culture and ethos of the school. It is easy to underestimate the legitimisation process effected by

HMI on the growth of bilingual education in the last two or three decades. Baker (1985) and Rawkins (1987) have argued that Welsh language policy lacks integration, cohesion and synthesis, laying blame with the government's piecemeal and reactive approaches to language planning. However, specifically in terms of Welsh language education, central government agencies have played neither a neutral nor an uninterested role. Particularly through HMI (though not ignoring the role of civil servants and politicians), central policy has often been positive to change. While it is popular and probably psychologically and strategically necessary to claim that not enough is being achieved in education in Wales to preserve the heritage language, there is evidence that central policy has frequently encouraged developments in bilingual education.

Alongside HMI's needs to be added the contribution of Local Education Authority Advisers to developments in bilingual education. These local education officers inspect and advise schools within their region and often have influence in the determination of local provision and policy. In the counties of Wales, such Advisers have made key contributions at various levels of the county system: policy, planning, provision, and not least at the sharp ends of educational politics and classroom practice.

The Role of Parents

Despite such official support, without the pressure, enthusiasm, commitment and interest in bilingual education of groups of parents and teachers, it is unlikely that bilingual education would have begun or advanced as it has. While local authority officers in Flintshire were of paramount influence in the opening of Ysgol Glan Clwyd in 1956, the growth of Designated Bilingual Schools in South Wales owes much to parental endeavour. Through the activity of Rhieni Dros Addysg Gymraeg (Parents for Welsh Medium Education) and through informal networks of local parents and language activists, Local Education Authorities (often as a reaction to sustained pressure and persuasion) have responded to market preferences. Such parental groups have naturally contained Welsh speaking parents who wish the language to be reproduced in their children with the essential help of formal education. However, the pressure for such bilingual schooling has also come from non-Welsh speaking parents. Merfyn Griffiths, headteacher of such a Designated Bilingual school (Ysgol Gyfun Llanhari) commented that, in 1986, there are Welsh-medium schools, at both primary and secondary levels, where over 90% of the pupils come from homes where the language is not spoken. By now it is non-Welsh-speaking parents and learners who are often the most ardent advocates of Welsh medium education and who apply most pressure on local education authorities to establish more Welsh-medium schools. Without their support, faith and enthusiasm, further progress will not be possible. (p. 5)

The willingness and enthusiasm of non-Welsh speaking parents to opt for bilingual education, particularly where there is a choice of school, is a positive feature of recent trends. Such enthusiasm tends to have regional variations. Growth rates in pupil admissions are evident in Mid Glamorgan, for example, whereas in much of North Wales there has been a comparative lack of growth.

Motivations

Motivations for choosing bilingual education in Wales (where there is a choice of English-medium or bilingual education) are often discussed, but rarely researched. While Khleif (1980) suggests a naked economic motive (i.e. the Welsh language increasing opportunities for entry and promotion in the jobs market), such attributions are both simplistic and ill-founded, as Reynolds (1982) has rightly noted. The researches of Bush *et al.* (1984) and Davies (1986) have indicated that motivations within a person can be varied and complex. Integrative motivations as well as instrumental orientations frequently exist and co-exist. Parents and pupils alike are often positive to the Welsh language, not only for its utilitarian value, but also for cultural, affiliative and social reasons (Baker, 1988 & 1992).

Part of the motivation of parents opting for bilingual education is likely to be the perceived success of the target school. Popular belief tends to be that Designated Bilingual schools in particular, are more successful than their Anglicised counterparts. The meagre statistics available to support or refute this claim (e.g. external examination results) while used by supporters, require other differences between schools (e.g. social class composition, material resources) to be taken into account in such a comparison (Baker, 1991).

School Ethos

The perceived success of bilingual schools can never be demonstrated solely by hard statistical indicators. Part of the reputation of the schools, whether real or mythical, is in terms of more indefinable qualities such as ethos, esprit de corps and purposefulness. A contrastive, research-based analysis of bilingual schools suggests that such perceived success is partly, if not largely, based on the relatively greater commitment and dedication of the teachers (and pupils) in such schools (Roberts, 1985). One function of the school, to promote the Welsh language and culture, appears to provide teachers with increased motivation, commitment and sense of direction. This research finding allows an essential notion to be added to an analysis of the development of bilingual education. Apart from central and Local Education Authority policy and provision, bilingual education is ultimately dependent for its success on grounded activity in classrooms. Any history of the growth of bilingual education needs to take into account the growth in reputation, particularly of Designated Bilingual Schools, such that perceived success has itself been a contributory and direct cause of expansion. Such perceived success derives from pioneering Headteachers and a great many devoted and committed teachers.

However, the commitment of many Welsh medium teachers which has contributed to the perceived success of Designated Bilingual Schools is a factor causing current concern. The supply of Welsh speaking teachers is likely to be outstripped by the demand, despite bursaries to attract recruits. In many curricula areas under the National Curriculum, a shortage of Welsh speaking teachers threatens at the least, to stem the growth of bilingual education in the different types of school. A mere supply of teachers is a low baseline to achieve; a supply of good quality teachers is an important, and in a long-term view, a possibly more important issue.

On a more positive note, curricula support for teachers in Wales has been a remarkable part of the growth of bilingual education. As reviews by Webster (1982), Prys Owen (1985), I.W. Williams (1987), T.P. Jones (1987), H.G. Roberts (1987) and G.E. Humphreys (1988) show well, the provision of curricula materials across most ages, subjects and ability levels has lent considerable support to the growth from acorns to blossoming trees. In the progression from a complete dearth of Welsh language material in the 1950s (Ministry of Education, 1953) to the still insufficient but eminently improved availability three decades later (T.P. Jones, 1987), various institutions have played important innovatory and supportive roles by commissioning, funding or publishing. Such institutional support of the curriculum is now considered.

Institutional Support

One major institution in the creation of curriculum materials has been the Schools Council Committee in Wales (later called the Schools Curriculum Development Committee in Wales) (B. Jones, 1986). This body established 'Gorwelion' to facilitate the teaching of Welsh as a first language in secondary schools, and the Bilingual Education Project to satisfy the needs of second language pupils with above average proficiency in Welsh entering secondary schools. The development of major resources at the Primary level (e.g. the language materials of Cyfres y Ddraig, Cynllun y Porth), Special Education level (Cynllun y Canllaw) as well as at the secondary level depended much on innovatory, pioneering educationists who worked on those projects with visible success in dissemination and take-up.

Alongside the major input by the Schools Council for the Development of the Curriculum in Wales, bilingual education has also flourished due to the contribution of Welsh language resources from the central Cardiff-based Welsh Joint Education Committee. Through its Welsh Language and Culture Committee, the Publications Advisory Panel, and not least by its willingness to provide examinations in any subject through the medium of Welsh, the WJEC has provided a central co-ordinating function in an educational system in Wales that is more often noted for its county variations in policy and provision. One example of the WJEC's contribution has been the Welsh Textbook Scheme, with its principle of guaranteed sales. With increased help from the Specific Grant terms of the 1980 Education Act, the WJEC has maintained an oversight of the cross-curricula provision of Welsh readers and Welsh textbooks. Despite such co-ordinated activity, T.P. Jones (1987) still finds 'that the need for Welsh curricular materials is probably as acute now as it has ever been because of the increasing awareness among parents of the value of Welsh medium education, coupled with the necessity to keep up to date with contemporary pedagogic innovations' (p. 25). Such a task faces the recently constituted Committee for the Development of Welsh Medium Education, with its advisory supervision of the overall development of bilingual education in Wales.

Other institutions have also supported the development of bilingual education. The University Colleges at Bangor and Aberystwyth and the teacher training Colleges at Carmarthen and Bangor have increasingly responded to the need to provide teacher-education at initial and in-service levels for Welsh medium school teachers. Aberystwyth's contribution through the Welsh Textbooks Project, the co-ordinating work of its Resources Centre, publication of 'Cyfres Mathemateg Cambria' and a comprehensive catalogue of Welsh medium educational resources has been complemented by Bangor's contribution to Welsh medium Science, Religious Education (through the Welsh National Centre for Religious Education) and Special Education. As Owen's (1985) survey of Welsh medium resources found, there are needs for further resources across the curriculum (e.g. Modern Languages, Drama, Music), for updating material to fit recent movements and evolution within all subjects, and for a response to the demands of the National Curriculum.

Educational Research

The provision of Welsh medium curriculum resources has followed the provision of Welsh-medium education and imperfectly helped to sustain such expansion. In contrast, it is dubious whether educational research, however widely defined, has played much more than a minimal role in this expansion. As Reynolds' (1982) seminal 'state of the art' paper and Baker's books (1985, 1988) revealed, research into bilingual education in Wales has been meagre. The paradox is that, up to the 1960s, Wales had an international reputation for research into bilingualism (e.g. Saer, 1923; Barke & Parry-Williams, 1938; Smith, 1923; W.R. Jones, 1966). Such research, however, cast doubt on bilingual education, connecting bilinguals with 'mental confusion' and relatively lower school achievement compared to monolinguals (J.L. Williams, 1960). At the time of expansion of bilingual education in Wales, foundational educational research in Wales generally failed to respond. There are exceptions, the most notable being the Attitudes and Attainment research of Sharp *et al.* (1973), and the evaluation of the Schools Council Bilingual Project (Dodson, 1985).

The overall failure of research to respond to the expansion of bilingual education in Wales needs to be traced to a variety of interacting factors such as lack of personnel, decreasing financial support of educational research, and foundational research being given decreasing priority. An initiative to reverse this trend has been the institution of the Committee for the Development of Welsh Medium Education and the remit of three geographically separate agencies (Aberystwyth, Bangor, Cardiff) to engage in both research and curriculum development activity. If this political manoeuvre to become translated into activity that is genuinely supportive of, and responsive to long term bilingual education in Wales, one or more Centres will need to engage in research and not just circulate curriculum materials.

The failure of research to support bilingual education in Wales is to be contrasted with the success of research in supporting the various Canadian immersion and heritage language programmes that have blossomed since the 1960s (see Baker, 1988). Evaluations of these experiments in bilingual education and research on the cognitive advantages of balanced bilingualism, by outcome and not by intention, provided the positive publicity for such education to expand rapidly. If objective evaluations, for example of Designated Bilingual Schools, had demonstrated their relative success, it is not unlikely that doubting Welsh-speakers and agnostic monolingual English-speakers would have increasingly chosen this form of education. With current protests (e.g. in Gwynedd and Dyfed) regarding Welsh medium education and repeated threats of court action, the failure of educational research in Wales to address bilingual issues is starkly illuminated.

Conclusions: The Balance Sheet

Bilingual education derives its *raison d'être* not only from a concern to save the Welsh language from further diminution, but also from educational, economic, social, cultural and political reasons. Perceived success in public examinations, the beliefs of some in the extra commitment of bilingual teachers and relatively pleasant ethos of such bilingual schools, the utilitarian hopes that Welsh language skills will enhance job opportunities (a remarkable reversal of nineteenth century and early twentieth century beliefs in the lack of economic value of Welsh for employment and mobility), and the concern to preserve a variety of Welsh cultural forms, are some of the reasons for the continuing growth of bilingual education. Indeed, the rationale of such schools needs increasingly to be built on the *varied and multiple* advantages of bilingual education.

The growth of the bilingual education movement has also needed to contend with a variety of constraints, particularly a decentralised decision making system allowing for wide county by county variation. A similar constraint may occur in the future with the recent reforms in terms of the local management of schools and an imposed National Curriculum. A combination of local school management and a compulsory curriculum will be crucial issues in the future health and development of bilingual education.

If the relationship between the Welsh language and bilingual education can be artificially isolated, bilingual education in Wales has gathered momentum and strength due to its relationship with the plight of the Welsh language. If there is such a strong relationship, a key question is how bilingual education has contributed to the fate of the language. Initially such a question must be framed in a wider collage of positive and negative effects. In the balance sheet of the fate of the Welsh language this century, there are factors possibly connected with the downward trend revealed in Census figures: the in-migration of English monolinguals, the emigration of Welsh speakers, mass communications, information technology, increased communication links (e.g. railways, roads, air travel), tourism, urbanisation and industrialisation, decline in religious attendance and the influence of Anglo-American culture. There are also factors other than bilingual education which need placing on the credit side of the balance sheet; for example, Mudiad Ysgolion Meithrin (Welsh Medium Nursery School Movement), Yr Urdd (The Welsh League of Youth—a strong and well organised national youth organisation), language activists in a variety of public, private and 'pressure group' organisations, and figure-heads among politicians, administrators and educationists who have promoted policy and provoked publicity.

The central question is whether the Welsh language would have any chance of survival without the growth of formal primary and bilingual secondary education in Wales. It appears likely that, despite all the elements on the credit side of the balance sheet, without such growth in bilingual education, the Welsh language would have almost no chance of survival as a living language of the people. Simply stated, without the growth of bilingual education, there is good reason to believe the Welsh language would not survive. Yet, the danger is in placing too much reliance on formal bilingual education as the salvation of the heritage language. In a minor sense, this reflects the half-truth of a famous Welsh writer, Saunders Lewis, who argued that bilingualism is the chief killer of the Welsh language. This view is that bilingualism is a half-way house on the road to majority language monolingualism. It is a debatable point whether there needs to be heritage language education rather than 'balanced' bilingual education to achieve 'balanced' bilingualism in children. Informal influences within school and pervading Anglicising influences out of school (e.g. TV, 'pop' culture, the information technology revolution) soon provide skills in the majority language and enculturation into English and American value-systems (Baker, 1992). In a major sense, bilingual education alone cannot reverse language trends. There needs to be other support mechanisms for the language, from cradle to grave, from high culture to lowly kerbstone. To live, a language needs an economic basis. For children to leave bilingual education and find the Welsh language has no market value will only, in time, create language disaffection and decay. There is also the current danger of Welsh becoming the language of the school, and English the language of the street, screen and shop. Rather than Welsh being a school-only phenomenon, it needs to penetrate an individual's whole way of life, and be present in everyday active, participatory culture.

In the balance sheet of the Welsh language, bilingual education in Wales is a crucial investment. Bilingual education cannot by itself guarantee a final profit balance. At the same time, without the growth of bilingual education, it is likely the Welsh Nation would soon have become bankrupt in its heritage language and culture.

References

BAKER, C. 1985, *Aspects of Bilingualism in Wales*. Clevedon: Multilingual Matters.
— 1988, *Key Issues in Bilingualism and Bilingual Education*. Clevedon: Multilingual Matters.
— 1991, The effectiveness of bilingual education, *Journal of Multilingual and Multicultural Development*, 11, 4, 269–77.
— 1992, *Attitudes and Language*. Clevedon: Multilingual Matters.
BARKE, E.M. and PARRY-WILLIAMS, D.E. 1938, A further study of comparative intelligence of children in certain bilingual and monolingual schools in South Wales. *British Journal of Educational Psychology*, 8, 63–7.
BOARD OF EDUCATION, 1927, *Welsh in Education and Life*. London: HMSO.
BUSH, E., ATKINSON, P. and READ, M. 1984, A minority choice: Welsh medium education in an Anglicised area—Parents characteristics and motives. *Polygot* 5, Fiche 1 (April).
DAVIES, J.P. 1986, Dadansoddiad o Nodau Graddedig Ar Gyfer Oedolion Sy'n Dysgu'r Gymraeg fel Ail Iaith. Unpublished Ph.D. thesis, University of Wales.
DODSON, C.J. 1985, Schools council project on bilingual education (Secondary Schools) 1974–1978: Methodology. In C.J. DODSON (ed.) *Bilingual Education: Evaluation, Assessment and Methodology*. Cardiff: University of Wales Press.
EDWARDS, D.G. 1984, Welsh-medium education. *Journal of Multilingual and Multicultural Development* 5, 3 & 4, 249–57.
FACULTY OF EDUCATION, UNIVERSITY OF WALES ABERYSTWYTH, 1988, *Report on*

Secondary Education in Rural Wales, University of Wales, Aberystwyth: Faculty of Education.

GRIFFITHS, M. 1986, Introduction. In M. GRIFFITHS (ed.) *The Welsh Language in Education*. Cardiff: WJEC.

GWYNEDD COUNTY COUNCIL, 1986, Language Policy. Caernarfon: Gwynedd County Council.

HUMPHREYS, G.E. 1987, Polisi Iaith Awdurdod Addysg Gwynedd—Adolygu a Gweithredu ym 1986. *Education for Development* 10, 3, 7–23.

— 1988, *Bilingual Education in Wales. Facing the Future with Confidence*. Newport: National Eisteddfod Publications.

JONES, B. 1986, The work of the schools council in Wales 1964–1984. In M. GRIFFITHS (ed.) *The Welsh Language in Education*. Cardiff: WJEC.

JONES, G.E. 1982, *Controls and Conflicts in Welsh Secondary Education 1889–1944*. Cardiff: University of Wales Press.

JONES, T.P. 1987, Thirty years of progress. A brief outline of the development of Welsh language teaching materials. *Education for Development* 10, 3, 24–39.

JONES, W.R. 1966, *Bilingualism in Welsh Education*. Cardiff: University of Wales Press.

KHLEIF, B.B. 1980, *Language, Ethnicity and Education in Wales*. New York: Mouton.

MINISTRY OF EDUCATION, 1953, *The Place of Welsh and English in the Schools of Wales*. London: HMSO.

OWEN, P. 1985, *Welsh Language Exploratory Survey*. Cardiff: School Curriculum Development Committee.

RAWKINS, P.M. 1987, The politics of benign neglect: Education, public policy, and the mediation of linguistic conflict in Wales. *International Journal of the Sociology of Language* 66, 27–48.

REYNOLDS, D. 1982, A state of ignorance? *Education for Development* 7, 2, 4–35.

ROBERTS, C. 1985, Teaching and learning commitment in bilingual schools. Unpublished Ph.D. thesis, University of Wales.

ROBERTS, H.G. 1987, Microelectronics—the Welsh connection. *Education for Development* 10, 3, 55–62.

SAER, D.J. 1923, The effects of bilingualism on intelligence. *British Journal of Psychology*, 14, 25–38.

SHARP, D., THOMAS, B., PRICE, E., FRANCIS, G. and DAVIES, I. 1973, *Attitudes to Welsh and English in the Schools of Wales*. Basingstoke/Cardiff: Macmillan/University of Wales Press.

SMITH, F. 1923, Bilingualism and mental development. *British Journal of Psychology*, 13, 271–82.

WEBSTER, J.R. 1982, Education in Wales. In L. COHEN, J. THOMAS and L. MANION (eds) *Educational Research and Development in Britain 1970–1980*. Slough: NFER-Nelson.

WELSH OFFICE, 1976–1990, *Statistics of Education in Wales*. Cardiff: Welsh Office.

WILLIAMS, I.W. 1987, Mathematics and science: The final frontier for bilingual education. *Education for Development* 10, 3, 40–54.

WILLIAMS, J.L. 1960, Comments on articles by Mr. D.G. Lewis and Mr. W.R. Jones. *British Journal of Educational Psychology*, 30, 271–2.

2 Catalan and Basque Immersion Programmes

JOSEP MARIA ARTIGAL

[Translated from Catalan by Jacqueline Hall]

The present article deals with the immersion programmes currently in operation in the Catalan and Basque countries, i.e. in the regions of Spain and France whose indigenous historical language is either Catalan or Basque.

After a brief description of the social and political background against which these programmes have been implemented the concept of 'immersion' is defined with reference to the political, linguistic and pedagogical situations specific to Catalonia and the Basque Countries. An overall description of the development of the Catalan and Basque immersion programmes outlines their development from their inception around 1980 to the present day. Finally, certain aspects of these programmes will be highlighted for their relevance to other European contexts.

At the outset a word of caution is called for. For reasons of internal coherence the present article seeks common factors and general criteria in describing Catalan and Basque immersion programmes. Nevertheless, it is vital to bear in mind, that both the historical evolution of the Catalan and Basque Countries and their current status present appreciable differences in political, linguistic and even pedagogical terms.

Societal Framework

Several regions have Catalan as their language: Catalonia (5,978,000 inhabitants), the region of Valencia (3,831,000 inhabitants), the Balearic Islands (681,000 inhabitants) and the Roussillon (located in France with 331,000 inhabitants). Basque is the language of the Basque Autonomous Community (2,136,000 inhabitants), the Community of Navarre (501,000

30

inhabitants) and of Iparralde (also located in France with 249,000 inhabitants).

In all these territories a contact language has been present for a long time and has gradually acquired the status of dominant or High language (as defined by Ferguson, 1959), with Catalan and Basque relegated to a Low language status in their respective historical territories. In Catalonia, the region of Valencia, the Balearic Islands, the Basque Autonomous Community and the Community of Navarre, Spanish (or Castilian) has acted as the dominant language, while in the Roussillon and Iparralde the same role has been played by French.

Though these diglossic processes were set in motion a long time ago, especially in the case of Basque, they have intensified as mechanisms of language substitution have been at work during the present century. In the regions belonging to France the so-called Catalan and Basque 'patois' began to be regarded with considerable scorn in comparison with French at the beginning of the twentieth century, as French was officially promoted as the sole language of social promotion and prestige. As a result of a policy of systematic and continuous aggression over a period of well over a hundred years, the levels of competence and social use of Basque, and especially of Catalan, in France were confined to restricted environments, notably rural populations and/or the elderly and militant resistance groups. In Spain, on the other hand, the major trend towards language substitution got underway towards 1950 and was due to three main factors. The first was the massive influx of immigrants from Spanish-speaking areas of Spain seeking employment in the industrialised Catalan and Basque-speaking regions (the population of Catalonia, for instance, leapt by 75% between 1950 and 1975). The second factor was the appearance of modern mass media in which only the use of Spanish was allowed. The media thus become a powerful social instrument exerting considerable pressure on the Basque and Catalan languages, which were already in a weak sociolinguistic position. The third factor was the all-out policy of cultural and linguistic homogenisation implemented by successive Spanish governments under the Franco dictatorship between the end of the Civil War (1939) and the death of General Franco (1975). The imposition of Spanish was not presented in subtle terms, as in France, by claiming it to be a means of social promotion; instead all Catalan and Basque signs of identity were subjected to crude and brutal aggression.

Consequently, the Catalan and Basque countries are now facing a situation with distinctly diglossic levels of competence and use of their own languages. The first reason for this is that, while practically 100%

TABLE 2.1 *Knowledge of Catalan (in %)*

	Understand 1981	Understand 1986	Speak 1986	Read 1986	Write 1986
Catalonia	79.2	90.2	63.9	60.3	31.4
Region of Valencia		77.1	49.4	20.8	7.0
Balearic Islands		89.6	70.9	46.1	16.5

Source: *Language Census*
Note: The author has no data on the Roussillon. However, it is possible to stake that knowledge of Catalan on the French side of the border is significantly low.

of the inhabitants of these territories are fully competent in the corresponding dominant language, Spanish or French, only a minority, especially in the case of Basque, are competent in their own language.

The second reason is that, whereas Spanish and French may be used in all registers, with all types of interlocutors and in all environments in their respective countries, the social scope of use of Catalan and Basque is much more restricted. Hence, not only are the levels of competence of many of the inhabitants of these territories insufficient (Tables 2.1 and 2.2), but speakers who are competent in the languages cannot make widespread use of them.

At the same time, the linguistic and cultural aggression undergone over time has given rise to an acute awareness and powerful social reaction, especially in Spain. Throughout the present century large-scale social movements have arisen, notably during the 1960s and 1970s, in response to the severe repression perpetrated by the Franco dictatorship. Despite ruthless persecution, these movements established a solid political background from which it was possible, after the death of General

TABLE 2.2 *Knowledge of Basque (in %)*

	Understand 1981	Understand 1986	Speak 1981	Speak 1986	Read 1981	Read 1986	Write 1981	Write 1986
Basq. Aut. Com.	22.6	26.7	21.0	24.6	13.3	18.7	10.1	16.2
Navarra				10.1				
Iparralde				33.2				

Source: *Linguistic Census* (Iparralde: SIADECO)

Franco, to launch a widespread process aimed at the recovery of Catalan and Basque signs of identity.

The first legal manifestation of this recovery, reflecting the democratic changes that took place in post-Franco Spain, was the adoption of the present Statutes of Autonomy of the Basque Autonomous Community (1979), Catalonia (1979), the region of Valencia (1982) and the Balearic Islands (1982), all of which proclaimed Catalan or Basque to be their respective regions' 'own' language and granted them co-official status with Spanish within their own territory. The second legal manifestation, of capital importance with reference to this paper, was the promulgation of 'Laws of Linguistic Normalization' in the Basque Autonomous Community (1982), Catalonia (1983), the region of Valencia (1983), the Balearic Islands (1986) and the Community of Navarre (1986). These laws stipulated, among other things, the legal limits which were to govern the various forms of instruction 'in' and 'of' the Catalan and Basque languages.

It is important to point out how this whole complex historical evolution constantly affects education. Just as in the nineteenth century, and even more so during the twentieth century, schooling was a powerful tool of Castilianisation and Gallicisation in the hands of the central governments in Madrid and Paris, education was likewise a key element in the resistance movements between 1960 and 1975, and later became one of the basic goals of the process of linguistic 'normalisation' undertaken by the respective autonomous governments during the 1980s. In this respect, the role played by the so-called 'active schools' in the Catalan Countries, and by the 'ikastolas' in the Basque Countries was crucial. These schools, which were the fruit of the spontaneous initiative of groups of parents and teachers during the 1960s, constitute a movement of linguistic, cultural and pedagogic renewal which, though it initially affected only a minority, was to provide the indispensable foundations for the construction of high quality Catalan and Basque schools.

Some of the models of teaching which appeared in the Catalan and Basque countries during the 1980s to redress earlier distortions in language usage are outlined below. These models which fulfil certain prerequisites, will be referred to as immersion programmes, though of a specific type.

Requisites for a Successful Home–School Language Switch: Immersion Versus Submersion

The first school experiment amounting to what would later be called an immersion programme began in 1965 at the Saint Lambert School in

Montreal, Quebec. This programme was born as a reaction to the inefficiency of learning a second language in school by treating it exclusively as an academic subject and basically proposed that the new language be acquired through its habitual use as a medium of instruction and of social relations in the school. In the words of Swain & Lapkin (1983: 9):

> as a general statement, the immersion approach to second language education involves emphasizing the communication of meaningful content material through the L2, rather than focusing on teaching of the second language itself.

Thus, in accordance with the idea that the L2 is learned by being used, which has been stressed in recent years by various specialists in second language acquisition (Hatch, 1978; Long, 1983; Artigal *et al.*, 1984; Fillmore, 1985; Swain, 1985; Di Pietro, 1987), the basic goal of immersion programmes is to make the school into a 'large and natural L2 use/acquisition context' (Artigal, 1991b: 31).

Though the most obvious characteristic of immersion programmes is this widespread school use of the target language 'at least 50 per cent of instruction must be provided through a second language' (Genesee, 1987: 1), it is also true that teaching through a language other than the home language is not always beneficial to the children.

For this reason, and in accordance with authors such as Lambert & Tucker (1972), Cummins (1979), Swain & Lapkin (1982) or Genesee (1987), we will be using the term immersion exclusively to refer to types of education involving a change of language in which certain specific requisites are fulfilled. We will be particularly concerned with five main requisites.

The first concerns the social status of the home language. Studies show that situations involving a home–school language switch are beneficial when the mother tongue has high status because this guarantees widespread presence of the mother tongue outside the school and ensures that pupils have a positive image and assessment of themselves. As Genesee writes (1987: vii):

> immersion programmes are a form of bilingual education designed for majority language students, that is, students who speak the dominant language of society upon entry to school.

The second requirement is that the pupils should have a positive attitude and motivation towards the new school language and that access to the programme should be voluntary. Studies indicate that the pupils' attitude towards the new school language and the set of motivational factors which encourage them to acquire it have as much to do with the success or failure of programmes involving a change of language as their academic abilities.

The third requisite is that the teachers who introduce the L2 be bilingual themselves, that is, they must have a thorough knowledge of the language in which they are to teach, and also be sufficiently proficient in the home language of the pupils to be able to understand them when they use it. Thus, though the teachers will only offer input in the new language, respecting the principle of 'one language, one person', they will at least during the initial period enable the pupils to express themselves in their L1.

The fourth requirement is that the teachers should have a thorough pedagogical training and be capable above all of establishing effective communication with the pupils, despite the use of a language which, at the beginning of the programme, will be new to them. Hence the teachers must be proficient in certain specific techniques which guarantee at all times the meaningfulness and effectiveness of the interactions conveyed through a language which their pupils initially do not share.

The fifth requirement is that the treatment of the home language must not be overlooked. As Cummins (1984) and Genesee (1987) recall, immersion programmes are a specific form of bi- or plurilingual education in which the home language is always studied, so that pupils may achieve the same level of competence in it as they do in the non-home language to which priority is given at the outset.

If all these requisites are fulfilled, an immersion programme will ensure that the new school language is correctly learned, as well as guaranteeing the full development of the home language and constituting a point of departure second to none from which to learn third and fourth languages, all this without any type of academic or psychological loss for the children. If, on the contrary, these conditions are not met, then the result will be 'submersion', in which case it can truly be said that:

> second language acquisition might pose a threat to the students' home language and culture and thereby impede both their linguistic and academic development (Genesee, Holobow, Lambert & Char-trand, 1989: 251).

According to the above criteria, the Catalan and Basque immersion programmes are a form of bilingual education designed for Spanish-speaking pupils, that is, for pupils who speak the dominant language of society and who choose of their own free will to attend a school where Catalan or Basque, the minority languages, receive priority (as will be explained later, there are no immersion programmes in the Basque and Catalan regions of France). In other words, in all the cases considered under the heading of Catalan and Basque immersion programmes in this article, the family language and culture of the children attending the programmes are the dominant ones; their attitudes and motivation towards the school language and the optional character of the programme are guaranteed; the teachers are bilingual, since they necessarily have to be competent in the new school target language, Catalan or Basque, and in addition, in view of the status of the languages in question, they are also all competent in Spanish; the pedagogic quality of the teaching in immersion classes is generally acknowledged; and finally the treatment of Spanish, the dominant language and the home language of the children who follow these programmes, is always introduced into the curriculum, from Grade 4 at the latest.

Immersion Programmes

The immersion programme in Catalonia

In accordance with the Statute of Autonomy of Catalonia and the Law of Linguistic Normalization, all children in Catalonia must know Catalan and Spanish by the end of Basic General Education (BGE), that is, by age 14. The action of the Catalan Department of Education in the pursuit of this objective from 1978 to the present day can be divided into two major phases. During the first phase, which lasted from 1978 to 1983, the main goal was the enforcement of the compulsory minimum number of hours of Catalan Language Arts for all children, regardless of the type of school attended. By the end of this first period, in 1983, over 90% of the pupils in Kindergarten and BGE classes in Catalonia were being taught Catalan Language Arts at least four hours per week (Arenas, 1986: 88). However, on account of the social dominance of Castilian, these hours of Catalan as a subject alone proved totally insufficient. The study published by the 'Servei d'Ensenyament del Català' (SEDEC) in 1983, *Quatre anys de català a l'escola*, showed that the learning of Catalan, the weaker language, could not be guaranteed by this minimum number of hours of Catalan as a subject. The study accordingly concluded that 'the language which is ill-treated in the environment . . . is the one that must acquire most importance in school' (cf.: SEDEC, 1983: 133).

From 1983 onwards a decisive reversal in educational policy took place in Catalonia. Since then the aim has been to give priority to the educational level of the socially weaker language by making it a predominant instrument of communication and instruction within the school.

Though the decision as to the language to be used as the main medium of instruction depends, in accordance with the Law of Linguistic Normalization, on the choice made by the parents the first time they register their children in school, and though over 50% of the parents, and 65% in the case of public schools, have Spanish as their mother tongue, the last decade has seen a sweeping change in Catalan schools.

In order to understand the extent of this change, we must bear in mind the three types of school currently in existence in Catalonia in terms of the treatment they give to languages. In the first type, which we will refer to as schools with 'predominantly Catalan-medium instruction', 100% of the teaching is in Catalan from Kindergarten, which starts at 3–4 years, to Grade 2 of BGE (age 7). In these schools, therefore, the children also learn to read and write through Catalan, and later on, from Grades 3 to 8 (between the ages of 8 to 14), Spanish is introduced as a subject and as the language for teaching one other subject. In the second type, which we will call 'schools with bilingual instruction', basic learning, including learning to read and write, is done in Spanish, and four hours per week of Catalan Language Arts are

TABLE 2.3 *Evolution of the number of schools in Catalonia providing predominantly Catalan-medium instruction in Kindergarten and BGE (in %)*

Type of school	1978–79	1989–90
Public		85%
Private		60%
Total	3%	76%

Source: Bel, A. (1991) *Deu anys de normalització lingüística a l'ensenyament.*

introduced in Kindergarten and Grades 1 and 2, followed by four hours of Catalan language arts and one subject taught through Catalan in Grades 3, 4 and 5, and four hours of Catalan language arts and two subjects taught through Catalan in Grades 6, 7 and 8. The third type of school we will refer to as schools with 'Spanish-medium instruction'. These use Spanish as the sole language of instruction throughout the school and treat Catalan merely as a subject. To these three basic types, a transitional fourth type must be added, which we will refer to as schools 'evolving towards predominantly Catalan-medium instruction'. This comprises schools which have begun to introduce predominantly Catalan-medium instruction from Kindergarten upwards but still have bilingual or Spanish-medium instruction in certain higher grades.

If we now take the variable 'schools 1989–90' from Table 2.3 and apply to it the typology of schools just described, the result is Table 2.4.

Table 2.4 shows clearly that the decision of the authorities from 1983 onwards to offer schools which give priority to the weaker language, together with the decision of the majority of parents to send their children to such schools, have brought about a vast and decisive change which would have been virtually unthinkable a few years ago under the repressive Franco dictatorship.

It can of course be argued that many of the schools providing predominantly Catalan-medium instruction are in rural areas and have few pupils. Or that many of the schools where Catalan is gradually being introduced as the main language of instruction have only just begun the change-over from Kindergarten upwards and are not yet using Catalan at all levels of BGE. All this is true. But even so, if we add together the categories 'predominantly Catalan-medium instruction' and 'evolving towards predominantly Catalan-medium instruction' in Table 2.4, the total is an impressively high 76% of all schools—85% in the case of public schools—which already use Catalan as the main medium of instruction or will soon be using it from Kindergarten to the end of BGE.

At the same time it is also true that in many of these schools, all or the majority of the pupils are Catalan speaking and that, since Catalan is the weaker language, what they are receiving is a 'home language maintenance programme'. However, Table 2.5 will reveal that this cannot be the case for all the children.

Since, according to Table 2.5, 53% of the families are Spanish-speaking, it follows that the 76% in Table 2.4 must include children

TABLE 2.4 *Distribution of schools in Catalonia according to the main language of instruction in Kindergarten and BGE (1989–90 school year)*

Main language of instruction	Schools		%
Predominantly			
Catalan-medium instruction	Public	619	37
	Private	357	33
	Total	976	36
Evolving towards predominantly			
Catalan-medium instruction	Public	793	48
	Private	285	27
	Total	1.078	40
Bilingual instruction	Public	235	14
	Private	410	38
	Total	645	24
Spanish-medium instruction (Catalan only taught as a subject)	Public	9	1
	Private	22	2
	Total	31	1

Source: Vial, S. (1991a) *Dades de la llengua a l'escola Primària de Catalunya.*
Note: In Table 2.4 the different categories are mutually exclusive. Thus, while the category 'Predominantly Catalan-medium instruction' includes only those schools where this model has reached all levels of Kindergarten and BGE, the category 'Evolving towards predominantly Catalan-medium instruction' comprises those schools with at least one level, but not all, where instruction is primarily in Catalan. Similarly the category 'Spanish-medium instruction' includes only schools where none of the levels corresponds to any of the other categories.

from the socially stronger language who have opted for schools in which the other language receives priority. This is especially true in the case of the public schools where, though 65% of the families are Spanish-speaking, 85% of the schools are offering predominantly Catalan-medium instruction or are in the process of converting to it. Among the 53% of Spanish speaking families, it is precisely these who have opted for a home–school language switch and make up the bulk of the pupils in immersion programmes.

In this context, in Catalonia the school situations classified as immersion are those which, besides fulfilling the criteria already laid out

TABLE 2.5 *Distribution of pupils in Kindergarten and BGE in Catalonia according to their home language*

Academic year	Type of school	Catalan speaking families	Bilingual families
1981–82	Public	24,84	9,81
	Private	42,95	15,57
	Total	33,71	12,64

Source: Bel, A. (1991) *Deu anys de normalització lingüística a l'ensenyament.*

(the optional character of the programme, the bilingual competence and appropriate pedagogic training of the teachers), also meet two more requirements. The first is that the pupils must be attending a school with predominantly Catalan-medium instruction, or a class in a school evolving towards Catalan-medium instruction which has already begun schooling in the predominantly Catalan model. The second is that between 70% and 100% of the pupils in the class must have Spanish, the socially dominant language, as their home language. All other situations involving a home–school language switch, including those in which the home language is Spanish but the class contains over 30% of pupils from the weaker language group, are not considered, or treated pedagogically, as immersion. Therefore, the immersion programmes in Catalonia may be considered as a case of early total immersion, that is[1], as models including an initial period during which all instruction, including learning to read and write, is conveyed exclusively in the weaker language and in which the treatment of the majority language is not introduced until a later stage (in the case of Catalonia, from Grade 3 of BGE).

Table 2.6 shows the number of schools and pupils which, in accordance with the above criteria, were doing immersion during the 1989–90 school year in Catalonia.

Finally, though not much research has yet been carried out to assess the linguistic and academic results of the immersion programmes in Catalonia, the few studies which have been conducted indicate that the Spanish-speaking children who follow an immersion programme attain significantly higher levels of Catalan (L2) than those reached by other Spanish-speaking children attending schools classified above as offering 'bilingual instruction' or 'Spanish-medium instruction'. At the same time, with respect to Spanish and other subjects on the curriculum, the research shows that the children who follow an immersion programme perform

TABLE 2.6 *Number of schools and pupils following an Early Total Immersion Programme in Catalonia (1989–90 school year)*

Grades	Schools	Total	Pupils	Total
K1	46	46	13.457	13.457
K2	48	94	13.432	26.889
BGE 1	75	169	13.126	40.015
BGE 2	173	342	11.618	51.633
BGE 3	55	397	7.226	58.859
BGE 4	51	448	5.991	64.850
BGE 5	36	484	4.858	69.708
BGE 6	23	507	4.737	74.445
BGE 7	11	518	3.936	78.381
BGE 8	168	686	1.989	80.370

Source: Vial, S. (1991b) *Enquesta sobre l'ús del català a l'ensenyament primari.*

Note: 'K1' and 'K2' refers to Kindergarten (4–5 years old); 'BGE 1, ..., BGE 8' refer to the grades from 1 to 8 of the 'Basic General Education', i.e. from 6 to 14 years old.

as well and sometimes better than their Hispanophone peers who do not (Serra, 1990; Arnau & Serra, in press; Boixadera, Canal & Fernández, in press). The results of the last study, the authors of which compare two groups of pupils in the 3rd Grade of BGE, i.e. 8 year olds with comparable IQs and home sociocultural backgrounds, may serve as an example. The first group is made up of Spanish-speaking pupils following immersion programmes. The second comprises Spanish-speaking pupils who have begun their schooling in their home language and during Kindergarten and Grades 1 and 2 of BGE have done only four hours per week of Catalan as a subject. Among other results, the levels of oral expression achieved by the two groups in the Catalan and Castilian languages are as in Table 2.7.

When examining Table 2.7 we must note the difference between the two groups with respect to oral expression in Catalan, the socially weaker language. But, above all, we must highlight the fact that, as already observed in other immersion programmes, the immersion group also obtains slightly better results in Spanish, the socially stronger language, even though for this group the school treatment of Spanish language did not commence until Grade 3 of BGE.

TABLE 2.7 *Mean scores on Catalan and Spanish Language tests obtained by Spanish students in third year BGE in immersion and non-immersion programmes*

Mean score	Non-Immersion 0/100%	Immersion 0/100%
Catalan Oral Expression	39,2	74,6
Spanish Oral Expression	87,4	86,7

Source: Boixaderas, Canal & Fernández (in press) *Avaluació dels nivells de llengua Catalana, Castellana i Matemàtiques en alumnes que han seguit el programa d'immersió lingüística i en alumnes que no l'han seguit.*

The immersion programme in the Basque autonomous community

Except in the very small number of 'ikastolas' already referred to at the beginning of this article, 'in the year 1978–79 the Basque language was still absent from schools in the Basque Country, which were totally Spanish monolingual' (Gabiña *et al.*, 1986: 7).

In order to overcome this clearly diglossic situation and ensure that all children acquired a sound knowledge of both Basque and Spanish, during the 1980s three models of education, referred to respectively as A, B and D, were proposed to the Basque Autonomous Government. In model A, which is mostly aimed at Hispanophone pupils, the language of instruction is Spanish and Basque is treated only as a subject. In model B, also addressed primarily to Hispanophone pupils, teaching is provided simultaneously in Basque and Spanish (normally 50–50%) from the very beginning of Kindergarten, though the children learn to read and write through Spanish. In Model D, which appeared at the beginning of the 1960s for Basque-speaking pupils, but was also applied to Hispanophones from 1970 onwards, the language of instruction is Basque, and Spanish does not become a subject until Grades 3 or 4 of BGE. Mention must also be made of the so-called model X, at present extinct, in which only Spanish was used and Basque was not even treated as a subject. Tables 2.8 and 2.9 describe the evolution of these models during recent years.

In Table 2.8, Model X, which before was virtually the second most widespread, has almost disappeared while Option A, though declining, remains ·the commonest model with twice as many pupils as any of the others. Table 2.9 on the other hand shows that the present trend among parents not only eliminates Model X altogether but points to the eclipse

TABLE 2.8 *Evolution of pupils in Kindergarten and BGE enrolled in the different educational models in the Basque Autonomous Community*

| | 1983–84 | | 1990–91 | |
	pupils	%	pupils	%
Model X	60.048	15,24	3.501	1,17
Model A	227.041	57,63	148.178	49,47
Model B	41.518	10,54	74.603	24,91
Model D	65.353	16,59	73.247	24,45
Total pupils	393.960		299.529	

Source: Central publications of the Basque Government (1990) *10 años de Enseñanza Bilingüe*.

TABLE 2.9 *Distribution of pupils in Kindergarten 1, 2 and 3 (3–5 years) enrolled in the different educational models in the Basque Autonomous Community in the 1989–90 school year, and of pupils in Kindergarten 1 only in the 1991–92 year (in %)*

	1989–90 K1, K2 and K3[1]	1991–92 K1[2]
Model X	0 %	0
Model A	32,5%	22%
Model B	36,0%	37%
Model D	31,5%	40%

Sources: 1. *10 años de Enseñanza Bilingüe*.

2. *EGIN*, 7 September 1991, according to official data of the Department of Education of the Basque Autonomous Community.

Note: The data referring to K1 in the 1991–92 year comprise 100% of the children in that age group enrolled in school.

of Model A and to a preference for those models which lay greatest stress on the socially weaker language.

In order to understand this marked trend among parents in their choice of educational models, it is important to bear in mind the findings of studies which have compared the various programmes. Below are some of the results obtained by the 'EIFE 2' study which measured the levels of oral expression and comprehension attained by pupils in the 5th grade of BGE (age 10) in Models A, B and D during the 1986–87 year.

The prime conclusion to emerge from the above tables is that, in a situation of diglossia such as that existing in the Basque Autonomous Community, the levels of knowledge of the weaker language are closely dependent on the educational programme followed, whereas, by virtue of its status, the dominant language is assured of obtaining almost

TABLE 2.10 *Mean scores on Language tests obtained by pupils in fifth year BGE in models A, B and D*

	Model A	Model B	Model D
Basque			
Oral Comprehension 1	6.88	9.66	9.97
Oral Comprehension 2	3.00	7.95	9.38
Oral Comprehension 3	2.31	6.65	8.49
Oral Expression 1	2.94	7.44	9.62
Oral Expression 2	1.89	5.34	7.41
Overall scores[2]	23.17	59.96	79.04
Spanish			
Oral Comprehension 1	9.91	9.79	9.85
Oral Comprehension 2	9.62	9.48	9.01
Oral Comprehension 3	7.92	7.63	7.65
Oral Expression 1	9.82	9.77	9.31
Oral Expression 2	7.95	7.81	7.57
Overall scores[2]	79.81	77.48	73.77

Source: Olaziregi & Sierra (1989) *EIFE 2. La enseñanza del euskera: influencia de los factores. Estudio de 5º de EGB en los modelos A, B y D.*

Notes: 1. The subtests are marked out of 10.

2. The overall scores come from the mean scores of the sub-test for every pupil. The formula used to integrate all the scores of the different subtests is based on their coefficient of variability.

homogeneous levels, regardless of the school treatment it receives. In the words of Cummins (1989: 16):

> the EIFE studies in the Basque Country show essentially (that) students in Model D and Model B perform considerably better in Basque than those in Model A. Yet there are minimal differences in the proficiency that students in Models, D, B, and A develop in Spanish, despite the fact that students in Models D and B have had much less instruction in Spanish than those in Model A. This pattern of transfer of academic skills from the minority to the majority language has also been reported in virtually all the bilingual programs implemented in North America (e.g. French immersion programs in Canada) and is thus a well-established result.

It is on the basis of the above description of Models A, B and D that we will now proceed to discuss the presence in the Basque Autonomous Community of situations involving a home-school language switch which fulfil the requirements of immersion as defined earlier. In accordance with the findings of Olaziregi & Sierra (1987), Sierra (1991), and Olaziregi & Sierra (1990), we can distinguish between three types of immersion programme.

The first type, which has the structure of so-called 'Early Partial Immersion', includes the majority of Model B programmes. Essentially this is a model which, by taking the mother tongue as the point of departure, endeavours to construct an outline curriculum comprising 50% of each language. The second type is made up of certain Model B programmes referred to as 'Intensive' (Olaziregi & Sierra, 1990; Olaziregi & Sierra, in press) which differ from the preceding 'Official' Model B in two ways: it includes an initial period of instruction exclusively in Basque during which the pupils learn to read and write through the medium of Basque; and Basque is present as a language of instruction and communication throughout BGE to an extent which exceeds the 50% mentioned above. Hence this model belongs to the category of Early Total Immersion already considered in this article with reference to Catalonia. Finally the third type of programme consists of those D models which are applied to groups with a majority of Hispanophone pupils. Since in this model all the teaching is done in Basque, the pupils' L2, and Spanish is only introduced as a subject from Grade 3 or 4 of BGE, it can be considered a 'Super Immersion Programme' (Genesee, Holobow, Lambert & Chartrand, 1989: 251). In all three models described the requirements of an immersion programme are fulfilled: the pupils belong to the majority language group, the programme is optional, the teachers are bilingual and have received appropriate training, and the school treatment of the family language is as stipulated.

Although no data exist on the precise number of pupils following these three types of immersion, some specialists indicate that of the 74,603 pupils in Model B in the 1990–91 school year, between 50% and 60% may correspond to the 'Official' Model B with the structure of Early Partial Immersion, while between 15% and 20% may be enrolled in 'Intensive' Model B which is comparable to Early Total Immersion. At the same time, of the 73,247 children in Model D during the same year (1990–91), between 20% and 25% may well be Hispanophones following a 'Super Immersion Programme'.

Certainly, one of the most interesting aspects of the immersion experiments in the Basque Autonomous Community is that they afford the opportunity to compare three different types of programme within the same context. That is precisely what Olaziregi & Sierra (in press) have done. Their study compares levels of reading comprehension and written expression in Basque and Spanish among Hispanophone pupils in Grade 8 of BGE, 14 year olds, who are following 'Official' Model B, 'Intensive' Model B, and Model D programmes respectively. The results indicate that children in 'Intensive' Model B classes (Early Total Immersion) reach similar levels to their companions and in some tests significantly outperform the pupils in 'Official' Model B classes. These results make it possible for the authors to make two claims. The first is that increasing the time of exposure to the L2 to above 50% or so bears fruit and enables pupils in 'Intensive' group B classes to attain higher levels in Basque than pupils in 'Official' group B classes. The second is that, with respect to the Super Immersion models, 'longer exposure does not necessarily and automatically mean better results, especially beyond certain limits' (Olaziregi & Sierra, in press).

The immersion programme in the region of Valencia

The approval of the Statute of Autonomy of the region of Valencia in 1982 and of the Law on the Use and Teaching of Valencian[2] in 1983 regulated the teaching of Catalan as a compulsory subject and recognised the possibility of setting up educational models in which Catalan is the main medium of instruction.

However, as in Catalonia and the Basque Autonomous Community, the treatment of Catalan as a subject produced very poor results. At the same time, in this region the models giving priority to the weaker language were initially confined to Catalan-speaking children and operated exclusively as 'home language maintenance programmes'.

Consequently in the 1986–87 school year, some parents, teachers and pedagogic co-ordinators who were aware of the Catalan experience in immersion, set up immersion programmes precisely in areas where the social presence of Catalan is very slight. These programmes, which were originally the result of popular initiative, finally obtained specific legislation and explicit official recognition in 1990.

In most ways, the immersion programme in the region of Valencia is similar to the model used in Catalonia and to the intensive B model in the Basque Country: from Kindergarten to the second grade of BGE 100% of the instruction is provided in the minority language; reading and writing are learned first in the minority language; and from Grade 3 to Grade 8 of BGE, Spanish is treated as both a language arts subject and as a medium of instruction. At the same time, as always, access is optional, and the teachers are bilingual and have the required training.

However, the type of immersion which is applied in the region of Valencia corresponds to what some specialists in the USA have termed 'Two-way Early Total Immersion' (Snow, 1987; Lindholm, 1987) since it consists of putting in the same classroom similar percentages of children from dominant and minority language backgrounds. On account of the fact that the presence of the minority language outside school in the context where the immersion programme is applied is slight, and precisely

TABLE 2.11 *Evolution of the number of schools and pupils in Kindergarten and BGE following immersion programmes in the region of Valencia*

Academic year	Schools	Pupils
1986–87	10	227
1987–88	18	577
1988–89	32	1.190
1989–90	48	2.213
1990–91	55	3.350

Source: Torró & Brotons (1991) *El Programa d'Immersió al País Valencià*.

in order to offset this lack of extra-school situations in which it can be used, pupils of both languages are mixed. In this way, at the same time as the home language maintenance programme is guaranteed for pupils who have the socially weak language as their first language, those who come from majority language homes are assured of an Early Total Immersion programme in which the use of the new language will go beyond the strict pupil–teacher relationship.

Finally, though no studies have been conducted specifically to evaluate the immersion programmes in the region of Valencia, according to all specialists (Torró, 1990; Torró & Brotons, 1991; Pascual & Sala, 1991; Peiró, in press) the results obtained so far are comparable to other similar experiments in immersion. This procedure is thus the best available in the context discussed in order to enable children from the majority language group to successfully learn the weaker language as well as their own.

Immersion programmes in the Balearic Islands and the community of Navarre

In the Balearic Islands and the Community of Navarre various home language maintenance programmes in Catalan and Basque respectively appeared during the 1980s. Moreover the present autonomous governments of both regions have passed laws making Catalan and Basque compulsory subjects—though in Navarre these laws affect only the so-called Basque-speaking zone.

Despite this, only very small-scale experiments in immersion have been conducted in these communities. Though no data are available, it seems that some 15 schools in the Balearic Islands (A. Moll, private communication) which follow the model of 'Early Total Immersion' fulfil the requirements for immersion laid out in the present article, as do some 30 Model D schools in Navarre (A. Biain, private communication) which are comparable with those Super Immersion Programmes already mentioned with reference to the Basque Autonomous Community.

The situation in the Roussillon and Iparralde

The present situation of the Catalan and Basque languages in the schools belonging respectively to the Roussillon and Iparralde is one of neglect on the part of the corresponding French authorities. Only 4 'Bressoles' in the Roussillon (Le Bihan, 1990), and 18 'ikastolas' in Iparralde (Federation of Ikastolas, private communication) ensure the existence of home language maintenance programmes built exclusively on the private initiative of groups of parents and teachers. In these regions, however, it is not possible to talk of immersion.

Final Remarks

We would like to end by highlighting three points based on the Catalan and Basque experience in immersion which may be relevant to other immersion programmes in Europe.

The first is the extremely important role played by the parents in the development of Catalan and Basque immersion programmes. In the first place it is the parents who, by choosing immersion from among the various models of education available to them, have definitively consolidated the programmes. And in the second place because their wholehearted support, which is partly the fruit of the non-obligatory character of the programmes themselves, has contributed decisively, as most specialists acknowledge, to the pedagogical success of the experiment.

The second point is related to the pedagogic training of the teachers. As was pointed out earlier, the so-called 'active schools' and 'ikastolas' of the 1960s and 1970s were part of an important movement of theoretical and methodological renewal which, when later supported and expanded by the respective autonomous governments during the 1980s, led to widespread reflection on the type of teacher–pupil and peer interactions which should be proposed in school. All this work on the best way of building and structuring classroom interaction, and on the crucial role of language as a tool for such interaction, also became a highly important variable providing pedagogical support to the Catalan and Basque immersion programmes at present in operation (Arnau, 1985, 1989, in press; Arnau & Boada, 1986; Artigal 1987, 1991a, 1991b; Vila, 1985, in press; Olaziregi & Sierra, in press).

The third point concerns the notion that languages are learned as they are used and therefore that the languages which can be most easily and rapidly acquired are those which offer learners most contexts for use. If we assume this to be so, then present-day minority languages may be the best 'second languages' for children from dominant language homes to learn in the context of languages in contact. Thus, it would seem more advisable, pedagogically speaking, to apply immersion in an internationally lesser used language which is present in the environment than to implement programmes which give priority to a foreign language that is 'universally useful', like English, German or French. By proposing as a second language one which is likely to be widely used during the learning process, we make this whole process easier and at the same time greatly facilitate later access to English, German, French or others as third or fourth languages.

In short, for a Europe which is interested in conserving its present linguistic and cultural diversity as a unique heritage, and indeed a sign of identity, immersion is an extremely useful tool. A community which wishes to safeguard its own pluralism must of necessity be built upon the ability of its members to recognise one another and this ability is based, not exclusively, but to a large extent, on language. To this extent at the very least, the experience in immersion acquired by the Catalan and Basque Countries may be of use.

Notes to Chapter 2

1. According to the criteria established by the main scholars on the subject, there is no single model of immersion. The different models can be classified in terms of three variables: (1) By taking into account the moment at which the new school language begins to be used as a medium of instruction, we distinguish between early, delayed and late immersion. (2) By considering the amount of time devoted to the new school language during a given school year, we distinguish between total and partial immersion. (3) When the factor considered is the family language of the pupils, then the term 'immersion', unqualified by any adjective, is applied to those classes in which 70–100% of the pupils are from the dominant language group, and are thus in a situation of home–school language switch. On the other hand, according to Snow (1987) and Lindholm (1987), the term 'Two-way Immersion' is applied to those situations in which pupils from the majority language group are mingled with 30–50% of pupils who have the minority language as their first language.
2. Translator's note: the variant of the Catalan language spoken in the region of Valencia is commonly known in that region as Valencian.

References

ARENAS, J. 1986, *Catalunya, escola i llengua*. Barcelona: Ed. La Llar del Llibre.
ARNAU, J. 1985, Educación en la segunda lengua y rendimiento escolar: Una revisión de la problemàtica general. In M. SIGUAN (ed.) *Enseñanza en dos lenguas y resultados escolares*, 7–20. Barcelona: ICE-Universitat de Barcelona.

— 1989, Conversational interaction strategies of teachers in Catalan immersion classes. Paper presented at the Annual Meeting of the American Educational Research Association, San Francisco. (unpublished).

ARNAU, J. AND BOADA, H. 1986, Languages and school in Catalonia. *Journal of Multilingual and Multicultural Development*, Vol. 7, Nos 2 & 3, 107–22.

ARNAU, J. and SERRA, J.M. in press, Un model d'anàlisi per a l'avaluació de la competència oral dels alumnes castellanoparlants que assisteixen a un programa d'immersió, *Comunicacions. Segon simposi sobre l'ensenyament del català a no-catalanoparlants*. Vic: EUMO.

ARTIGAL, J.M. *et al.* 1984, *Comfer descobrir una nova Ilenfua*. Vic.: EUMO.

— 1987, Le programme de 'bain de langue' pour l'enseignement de la langue à des enfants d'immigrés dans les écoles maternelles de Catalogne. *Revue de Phonétique Appliquée* 82-83-84 (1987), 134–42.

— 1991a, *The Catalan Immersion Program: A European Point of View*. Norwood, N.J.: Ablex.

— 1991b, The Catalan immersion program: The joint creation of shared indexical territory. *Journal of Multilingual and Multicultural Development* Vol. 12, Nos 1 & 2, 21–33.

BEL, A. 1991, *Deu anys de normalització lingüística a l'ensenyament, 1978–1988*. Barcelona: SEDEC, Departament d'Ensenyament, Generalitat de Catalunya.

BOIXADERA, R. CANAL, I. and FERNÁNDEZ, E. in press, 'Avaluació dels nivells de llengua Catalana, Castellana i Matemàtiques en alumnes que han seguit el programa d'immersió lingüística i en alumnes que no l'han seguit', *Comunicacions. Segon simposi sobre l'ensenyament del català a no-catalanoparlants*. Vic: EUMO.

CENTRAL PUBLICATIONS SERVICE OF THE BASQUE GOVERNMENT, 1990, *10 años de Enseñanza Bilingüe*. Vitoria-Gasteiz: Servicio Central de Publicaciones del Gobierno Vasco.

CUMMINS, J. 1979, Linguistic interdependence and educational development of bilingual children. *Review of Educational Research*, 49, 2, 222–51.

— 1984, *Bilingualism and Special Education Issues in Assessment and Pedagogy*. Clevedon: Multilingual Matters.

— 1989, Foreword. In I. OLAZIREGI, J. SIERRA, *EIFE 2. La enseñanza del euskera: influencia de los factores. Estudio de 5º de EGB en los modelos A, B y D*, Vitoria-Gasteiz: Servicio Central de Publicaciones del Gobierno Vasco.

DI PIETRO, R. 1987, *Strategic Interaction. Learning Languages Through Scenarios*. London: Cambridge University Press.

FERGUSON, C.A. 1959, Diglossia. *Word*, 15, 325–40.

FILLMORE, L.W. 1985, When does teachers' talk work as input. In M. GASS and C. MADDEN (eds) *Input in Second Language Acquisition*. Cambridge, Mass.: Newbury House, 17–50.

GABIÑA, J.J., GOROSTIDI, R., IRURETAGOIENA, R., OLAZIREGI, I. and SIERRA, J. 1986, *EIFE. La enseñanza del euskera: influencia de factores*. Vitoria-Gasteiz: Servicio Central de Publicaciones del Gobierno Vasco.

GENESEE, F. 1987, *Learning Through Two Languages: Studies of Immersion and Bilingual Education*. Cambridge, Mass.: Newbury House Publishers.

GENESEE, F., HOLOBOW, N., LAMBERT, W., and CHARTRAND, L. 1989, Three elementary school alternatives for learning through a second language. *The Modern Language Journal* 73, iii, 250–63.

HATCH, E. 1978, Discourse analysis and second language acquisition. In E. HATCH (ed.) *Second Language Acquisition* pp. 401–35. Rowley, Mass.: Newbury House.

LAMBERT, W.E. and TUCKER, G. 1972, *Bilingual Education of Children* Rowley, Mass.: Newbury House.

LE BIHAN, J.P. 1990, Una provocació: La immersió a Catalunya Nord, *Escola Catalana* 274, 16–17.

LINDHOLM, K. 1987, *Directory of Bilingual Immersion Programs: Two-way Bilingual Educational for Language Minority and Majority Students.* Center for Language Education and Research. Los Angeles: UCLA.

LONG, M. 1983, Native speaker/non-native speaker conversation in the second language classroom. In M. CLARKE and J. HANDSCOMBE (eds), *Tesol '82: Pacific Perspectives on Language Learning and Teaching* 207–23. Washington, D.C.: TESOL.

OLAZIREGI, I. and SIERRA, J. 1987, *PIR-5 Hizkuntz testa. B eta D ereduetako 5–6 uteko haurrentzat.* Vitoria-Gasteiz: Servicio Central de Publicaciones del Gobierno Vasco.

— 1989, *EIFE 2. La enseñanza del euskera: influencia de los factores. Estudio de 5º de EGB en los modelos A, B y D.* Vitoria-Gasteiz: Servicio Central de Publicaciones del Gobierno Vasco.

— 1990, *EIFE 3. La enseñanza del euskera: influencia de los factores. Estudio de 2º de EGB en los modelos A, B y D.* Vitoria-Gasteiz: Servicio Central de Publicaciones del Gobierno Vasco.

— in press, Diversas alternativas de enseñanza bilingüe. Evaluación y comparación. In M. SIGUAN (ed.) *Modelos de enseñanza en dos lenguas.* Barcelona: Horsori/ICE-Universitat de Barcelona.

PASCUAL V. and SALA, V. 1991, *Un model educatiu per a un sistema escolar amb tres llengües.* València: Conselleria de Cultura, Educació i Ciència.

PEIRO, J. in press, Las lenguas en el sistema educativo de Valencia. In M. SIGUAN (ed.) *Modelos de enseñanza en dos lenguas.* Barcelona: Horsori/ICE-Universitat de Barcelona.

SEDEC 1983, *Quatre anys de català a l'escola.* Barcelona: Departament d'Ensenyament, Generalitat de Catalunya.

SERRA, J.M. 1990, Resultados académicos y desarrollo cognitivo en un programa de inmersión dirigido a escolares de nivel sociocultural bajo. *Infancia y Aprendizaje,* 47, 55–65.

SIERRA, J. 1991, La inmersión y la enseñanza bilingüe en el Pais Vasco. *Comunicación, Lenguaje y Educación* 10: 41–55.

SNOW, A. 1987, *Innovative Second Language Education: Bilingual Immersion Programs.* Center for Language Education and Research. Los Angeles: UCLA.

SWAIN, M. 1985, Communicative competence: Some roles of comprehensible input and comprehensible output in its development. In M. GASS and C. MADDEN (eds) *Input in Second Language Acquisition* (pp. 235–53). Newbury House Publishers.

SWAIN, M. and LAPKIN, S. 1983, *Evaluating Bilingual Education: A Canadian Case Study.* Clevedon: Multilingual Matters.

TORRÓ, T. 1990, La immersió lingüística a Elx. *Escola Catalana* 274, 12–13.

TORRÓ, T. and BROTONS, V. 1991, El programa d'immersió al País Valencià.

Comunicacions: segon simposi sobre l'ensenyament del català a no-catalanoparlants. Vic: EUMO, 323–32.

VIAL, S. 1991a, *Dades de la llengua a l'escola Primària de Catalunya.* SEDEC, Departament d'Ensenyament, Generalitat de Catalunya. Barcelona.

— 1991b, *Enquesta sobre l'ús del català a l'ensenyament Primari.* SEDEC, Departament d'Ensenyament, Generalitat de Catalunya. Barcelona (unpublished).

VILA, I. 1985, *Reflexions sobre l'educació bilingüe: llengua de la llar i llengua d'instrucció.* Barcelona: Direcció General d'Ensenyament Primari. Generalitat de Catalunya.

— in press, La immersió lingüística, *Comunicacions: segon simposi sobre l'ensenyament del català a no-catalanoparlants.* Vic: EUMO.

3 Bilingual or Bicultural Education and the Case of the German Minority in Denmark

MICHAEL BYRAM

Introduction

In the course of this article describing the model of schooling for the German minority in Southern Jutland, Denmark, I propose to raise the question of the appropriateness of the term 'bilingual' education. My doubts about the term are based on theoretical considerations of the nature of language learning—to what extent is language learning culture learning?—but this is not just an academic quibble. Labels are important, and parents who send their children to a bilingual school ought to be aware that this does not just enable their offspring to acquire another way of encoding their messages, expressing 'what they want to say' in another language. For to learn another language is to enter into another way of life, i.e. another culture, from which viewpoint the learner's own culture appears relative and even problematic. This experience may be positive and desirable, creating an increased understanding of others and 'otherness' and a greater flexibility in relationships across linguistic and cultural boundaries. It can also be a threat to learners' security and identity and a destabilising factor in the sensitive period of transition from childhood to adulthood.

The Context—*die deutsche Volksgruppe in Nordschleswig*

The term *Volksgruppe* to describe the minority which lives just north of the German–Danish border indicates something of the origins and contemporary identity of the minority. It was created by the establishment in 1920 of the existing frontier, as a consequence of a postwar referendum.

The region has long been the home of a number of ethnic groups, whose history could be traced back to the *Völkerwanderungen* (migration of peoples), more recently to the rise of nationalism in the nineteenth century, or to the Treaty of Versailles and the re-alignment of frontiers in Western and Central Europe. In 1920 the former Duchy of Schleswig was divided by the new frontier and a substantial minority of German-oriented inhabitants decided to remain in Nordschleswig, which became part of the Kingdom of Denmark.

In the inter-war period, children of German origin could attend a private German school or a German branch of a public Danish school. After the 1939–45 war and the animosity created by the German invasion of Denmark—during which some members of the minority supported the invading army—all German schools were closed. They were gradually re-opened as private schools under Danish private school law in the following decade. Eventually, in 1955, a joint declaration by governments in Bonn and Copenhagen gave a firmer basis to the schools in the German minority and to those in the Danish minority south of the border (see Søndergaard in this volume). In particular, the German schools were accorded the right to hold the public examinations of the Danish state, and this gave them a higher status and the possibility of becoming independent in most aspects of their philosophy, structure and administration.

The schools today are still operating under private school law and, in principle, each is a separate, self-governing institution financed partly from state subsidies and partly from independent sources, including subsidies from Germany (see Byram, 1986: 21–28 for details). In practice the 18 schools and 24 kindergartens work together under an umbrella organisation, the *Deutscher Schul- und Sprachverein für Nordschleswig* which issues curriculum guidelines and statements of the aims and philosophy of the German schools. Table 3.1 gives an overview of the numbers of schools and pupils.

The schools are distributed in an area up to approximately 30 kilometres north of the border. They educate children from kindergarten age to university entrance age but there is no provision for higher education in the minority and pupils have a choice of going to university in Germany or Denmark since their qualification is recognised in both countries. There is however a *Nachschule* which offers a range of vocational and general education for young people who do not go to the academic *Gymnasium*. The largest group of schools are those which cater for children of obligatory school age, 7–16 years in Denmark, and which also offer a pre-school class and an optional tenth year of schooling. Not

TABLE 3.1 *German schools in Denmark*

School-type	Number of schools	Number of pupils	
Kindergarten	24	599	(1.7.90)
School (6–16 years)	16	1018	(1990/91)
Gymnasium (17–20)	1	110	(1990/91)
'Nachschule' (17 upwards)	1	59	(1990/91)

(From *Jahresbericht of the Deutscher Schul- und Sprachverein*, 1991)

all the schools have the full range of classes and most offer years 1–6 or 7, after which pupils transfer to one of the 5 schools with classes 1–10. In the following pages, I shall discuss above all the organisation and philosophy of the schools offering education to pupils of compulsory school age, one of which is described in detail elsewhere (Byram, 1986).

A German School or a Danish School?

The nature and educational philosophy and practice of the schools cannot be separated from the professions of belief of the minority as a whole. And it is because of this that the discussion of the schools as a model of bilingual education inevitably raises the question of biculturalism mentioned above.

It was becoming evident to the leaders of the minority in the early 1980s, that changes in the relationship of individuals to the minority were taking place, particularly amongst the younger generations. In a review of the minority and its future, they published a statement which describes the philosophical and cultural basis on which the minority is founded. The first two paragraphs contain the tension of biculturalism:

(1) The spiritual basis of the German minority is the profession of Germanness. It is, in this spirit, necessary to nourish and maintain the values of German tradition and of German language and culture which have grown up historically in the Nordschleswig homeland and in Nordschleswig families. This profession must be clearly and self-confidently made visible *vis-à-vis* surrounding society.

(2) German Nordschleswigers attach importance to playing their part,

loyally and equally as citizens of the state of Denmark, in socio-political tasks. (*BdN*, 1982, 5, author's translation.)

On the one hand, members of the minority should be true to and proud of their German origins and ethnicity, on the other they have to be loyal citizens of the Danish state. As long as state and nation are considered to be synonymous—as they are in the ideology of nationalism still prevalent in the late twentieth century—and as long as a nation is defined in terms of its language and its cultural values, the tension between German ethnicity and Danish citizenship remains. This is not to say that being German requires some political allegiance to the German state, for it is evident that 'German' when used in the minority refers to the fact of being a member of a group whose historical and social identity is firmly anchored in Nordschleswig as an integral part of Denmark; there is, today, no suggestion that the region should be part of a German state. It does mean, however, that 'German' cultural values and 'Danish' values can be—and often are—at odds. The individual has therefore to live with the tension that this may create.

The same tension is to be found in the statement of the educational aims of the schools, but with one significant addition. In the philosophy of the schools the cultural focus shifts from the minority itself to a wider cultural world:

(1) Our school is a German school. It intends to introduce its pupils in the German language to the German cultural world and reinforce the German sense of community.
(2) Our school is a German school in the Danish state. It intends therefore to introduce its pupils to the Danish cultural and language world and to prepare them for life as citizens of this state. (Author's translation.)

Although here too the word 'German' might be taken to refer to Nordschleswig, curriculum documents state quite clearly that they have been drawn up with reference to curricular reforms in Germany (i.e. Schleswig-Holstein) as well as in Denmark. The reference point for 'the German cultural world' is thus south of the border; the minority itself cannot be culturally self-sufficient. There is a clear sense of cultural values, artefacts and traditions being imported from Germany past and present. This is reinforced by the recruitment of the teaching force, most of whom are seconded from the Schleswig-Holstein education system where they were trained and achieved civil servant status. Thus, even though approximately half of them were born and raised in the minority, they are nearly all imbued with German educational and cultural values and practices.

A closer analysis of the curriculum and its hidden and explicit values shows that the schools have an educational character which is neither entirely imported from Germany nor transferred from the traditions and values of mainstream Danish education (Byram, 1986: 52–63). Furthermore, such analysis also demonstrates that the 'purist' intentions that the schools should be entirely 'German', with the exception of lessons where Danish is the subject, are not maintained. Pupils speak their dialect of Danish to each other, and sometimes to their teachers (Byram, 1985); the teaching of German language and literature has some characteristics of second-language teaching rather than the mother-tongue approach which is official policy; the role of Danish varies for different pupils according to their home language and their career intentions. These contextual factors are thus fundamental to a full understanding of the functioning of the minority school as a bilingual or bicultural school, to which we turn in more detail in the next section.

A Bilingual School?

The question of whether the minority school is a bilingual school has been much debated within the minority itself. On the one hand there are those who deny this and stress the German character of the school, fearing that bilingualism is a threat to the minority but accepting that the pupils are bilingual as a matter of course rather than as a consequence of the aims and practices of the school. On the other hand, the falling birthrate and threat to viability of schools has led some to open their doors to children from the majority and actively advertise as bilingual schools (Byram, 1986: 24 and Søndergaard, 1983).

There is no doubt that, at the end of their school career, pupils are bilingual in German and Danish, or more accurately trilingual in German, Standard Danish (*Rigsdansk*) and dialect (*Sønderjysk*). There is also no doubt that the minority school promotes their bilingualism by teaching German as a subject and as a medium of instruction and Danish as a subject. Before considering how successfully this is done, let us establish how the schools are organised linguistically.

The official language of the schools is German. All subjects but Danish are taught in German; all official documents are written in German, including documents for parents; pupils and teachers are expected to speak

German whenever possible. Teaching materials are, however, drawn from both German and Danish sources and Danish materials are deliberately used in some subjects, such as mathematics, in order to ensure familiarity with technical terms in both languages. Pupils' reports for parents in the first seven years are given using the German system of marks from 1–6; thereafter the Danish system is used. When pupils reach school-leaving age, they take Danish examinations provided by the state, although they also take an additional German language examination which ensures recognition of their qualifications in Germany. The distribution of lessons for German and Danish as subjects is evident from Table 3.2.

The emphasis on German in the first two years is a consequence of the need to induct all pupils—but especially those who do not speak German at home—into the use of German as the language of learning. Although precise statistics are difficult to obtain, it is evident that about 20% of pupils speak German at home, 50% speak the dialect (*Sønderjysk*) and the rest speak combinations of these two and Standard Danish (Byram, 1986: 41; Søndergaard, 1990a: 107).

During these first two years, the lesson of Danish is an informal 'play lesson' (Søndergaard, 1981) which gives Danish a status in the school. There is, however, no attempt to teach the written language. This begins in the third year when the acquisition of reading and writing has, in principle, been largely completed in German.

Teachers in the minority's schools are, as already mentioned, usually trained in the German system, especially in Schleswig-Holstein. Indeed many of them will have completed their training just south of the border in Flensburg and then opted to serve in the minority schools. Many of them stay in Nordschleswig throughout their professional life and, though they may have had little or no specialist training for working in minority schools, they have opportunities for further training within the Danish

TABLE 3.2 *Distribution of German and Danish lessons in compulsory schooling*

	Year									
	1	2	3	4	5	6	7	8	9	10
German	7	5	5	5	5	5	5	4	4	5
Danish	1	1	5	5	6	6	5	5	5	6

system. They thus become familiar with Danish educational philosophy and traditions, and the blend of German and Danish educational philosophy gives the minority schools their particular character.

Parents are closely involved in the administration of the schools because of their status under Danish private school law. Each school has a committee which is responsible for the school in the eyes of the state and which administers its finances. Control by the state itself consists of the appointment of one person, who is not a parent of a child in the school, to establish that standards are 'equal to what is normally required in the (public) *folkeskole*'. This responsibility, as far as the minority schools are concerned, is vested in the *Schulrat* (Education Officer) who is the executive officer of the *Schul- und Sprachverein für Nordschleswig*, the umbrella organisation which issues curriculum guidelines and provides a general co-ordination of the schools.

At the end of compulsory schooling pupils take the standard examinations provided by the Danish state education system. They are not treated differently from pupils from other schools and must take the examinations in Danish. Some subjects are examined both orally and in written papers, others are examined orally only. There has never been any rigorous comparison with the examination results of pupils from mainstream Danish schools, nor is there likely to be. It is clear that minority pupils will have an advantage in German, which is examined as a foreign language, whereas for them it is much more than a foreign language. On the other hand a comparison with the timetable of a mainstream Danish school shows that minority pupils have fewer lessons of English and Danish. The Education Officer of the minority is, however, satisfied that the results are not affected; smaller teaching groups, he claims, compensate for the reduction in hours (Christiansen, 1990: 102).

Whatever the linguistic attainments of pupils, it remains significant that they not only acquire a minority language but also a minority culture. After an initial phase of primary socialisation in the family, children experience the world above all through the process of secondary socialisation which begins at school (Berger & Luckmann, 1966: 166). It is through the German language and the (Nordschleswig) German culture of the school that pupils are socialised into the values and meanings of the minority. This takes place in the detail and the process of the open and hidden curriculum mentioned above. It is the particular and unique combination of German and Danish values and traditions which give the schools their specific character and their pupils their specific cultural identity. In the final analysis, it is because one goes to a minority school that one is a member of a minority, rather than the more visible characteristic that one speaks German. In this sense the schools are not 'bicultural', for they do not socialise into two separate cultures, German and Danish. They help their pupils to adopt and assimilate the values and meanings of the minority culture.

A Successful School?

The success of a school system with respect to its pupils' bilingualism cannot be judged in absolute terms. It is necessary to consider the societal context in which pupils live and will seek to earn a living after leaving full-time education. Essentially, an evaluation needs to establish whether the linguistic—and cultural—demands of the society in which members of the minority will live can be met by them as a result of their education in a minority school.

The minority itself has seldom asked these questions in public, although they are frequently discussed by teachers and educational administrators. One public statement by an Education Officer indicates the anxiety that proposals for change arouse:

> We are aware that our work in the language of the country is of the greatest significance for the future lives of our pupils. This teaching cannot be too good. We must however also see that a change in our language of instruction (e.g. increased Danish in other subjects: Geography, History, Mathematics . . .) would limit the time given to German. All the declarations of our decision-making bodies have pointed in the direction that we, as German schools in Nordschleswig with German as the language of instruction, have our particular task—not to be 'language schools' (Sønnichsen, *Der Nordschleswiger*, March 1983, author's translation.)

Behind this rejection of 'language schools' lies a further issue: the question of whether the minority's schools and kindergartens should be open to children from the majority. Although this may at first sight appear unlikely, the opportunity for their children to become bilingual through attending the minority school could appeal to some parents. And it is clear that schools which have seen enrolment fall in the last decade—for many reasons, including a fall in birth-rate—have been tempted to maintain viability by attracting parents to 'bilingual' schools.

Parents may also be attracted by the different education tradition of German schools, perceived as more 'traditional' than mainstream Danish education. This has certainly been evident in enrolments to kindergartens where, as Søndergaard (1990b) demonstrates, the appeal of higher 'standards' has induced many parents from the majority to send their children to German kindergarten. That it is not, in fact, an attempt to make them bilingual is evident from the strong tendency to withdraw children from the minority education system after kindergarten and send them to Danish schools. Their incipient bilingualism is therefore quickly lost (Søndergaard, 1990b: 425).

This would suggest therefore that the schools have little to fear from a 'watering-down' of their principal purpose and character by pupils and parents seeking only a bilingual education. The anxiety nonetheless remains and is frequently expressed.

Despite this anxiety, the minority has encouraged academic research in its schools. Much of this work has been carried out by local researchers and occasionally by teachers themselves (see Pedersen, 1990 for a recent collection of research). The author of this article was also allowed to work for a period as participant observer in one school and to offer an evaluation of linguistic issues in the minority.

Among researchers there is a clear consensus that the current distribution of time and methods of teaching for Danish and German are unsatisfactory. Byram (1986: 73ff) argues that despite official policy German is in fact taught as a second language, not as a first language or *Muttersprache*. Furthermore, the teaching of Danish, though apparently satisfactory in examination results, cannot prepare pupils for their linguistic needs in Standard Danish in the majority society where they must earn their living. In the recommendations, made at the request of the Education Officer, Byram suggests that more emphasis should be given to Danish, that a conscious policy of bilingual teaching should be developed and that pupils and teachers should be encouraged to acquire a better understanding of the nature and significance of their bilingualism.

Similar proposals have been made by Søndergaard, who has argued, from comparisons with other bilingual models, for a much more rigorous approach to developing pupils' linguistic repertoire. He has suggested in some detail that different levels of teaching should be offered to pupils, corresponding to their existing competences consequent on their use of German, Standard Danish and dialect in their home environment (Søndergaard, 1984, 1990a).

As part of a longitudinal study of the language repertoire of children throughout the region—from minority and majority—Pedersen (1990) too has proposed changes. She suggests that the 'play lessons' should be replaced by an earlier introduction of reading in standard Danish. The spoken language would continue to be dialect where children felt the need to use it, until spoken standard Danish is gradually introduced and pupils are made aware of its function within the majority and the minority (Pedersen, 1990: 10).

Whatever the merits of these various proposals, they are unlikely to be accepted; Søndergaard's model was rejected quite explicitly (Søndergaard, 1990: 108). The fears that a reduction in German will mean a weakening of German identity are not so far allayed by arguments that it is the philosophy and character of the school as a whole, rather than the use of German, which creates a minority identity (Byram, 1986: 129–30). It can therefore be argued that the minority and its policy-makers put the interests of the group above those of its members, especially those of school age (Byram, 1991). Parents who choose the minority school for their children are thus making a very important decision.

That decision is not one which can be taken by weighing advantages and disadvantages in a cold objective way. Parents' own ethnic identity sways their decision and the sense of belonging to a group and the security this gives should not be underestimated (Byram, 1986: 132–38). On the other hand, the schools should attempt to ensure that pupils will not be disadvantaged in their contacts with the majority; their competence in the language and culture should be adequate in those domains of activity on which their economic survival and welfare depend.

They must be able to adapt and be accepted by those who hold economic power in the majority society: on leaving school they have to find a job by competing linguistically and culturally with members of the majority. Yet it appears to the teachers and leaders of the minority that too much exposure to majority culture will encourage its members to pass over into the majority. A view of the minority culture from the majority perspective can relativise it and undermine its self-evident significance for its members.

This process of relativisation is the effect of any acquisition of anotherlanguage, be it in a minority school, a bilingual school for majority pupils or simply in the foreign language classroom. It has indeed long been the aim of foreign language teaching to encourage rational acceptance of other cultures and, consequently, relativisation of the learners' own (Byram, 1989). The success of foreign language teaching in this respect is still in doubt (Byram, Esarte-Sarries & Taylor, 1991). With respect to bilingual immersion programmes, evaluators have paid little attention to this issue.

Where bilingual education has been successful, however, there is some evidence of a shift in sociocultural perceptions which might indicate a relativisation of learners' own language and culture (Swain & Lapkin, 1982: 77).

A Question of Transfer?

The purpose of comparative studies is not to resolve one set of problems by seeking solutions in other contexts and situations, and I do not propose to deal directly with the question of whether this model of bilingual and bicultural education is suitable for use elsewhere. It is more interesting and fruitful to conclude by reflecting upon the model in its own context and the general principles it exemplifies.

I have suggested above that a major function of the school is to create and maintain children's ethnic identity, even if this means running the risk of reducing their capacity to function in the socio-economic world of the majority. Minority schooling is not only a question of language but, more significantly, a question of enculturation and socialisation. Thus, when parents choose a school for their children—in any situation, monolingual or bilingual—they are choosing the character of the next step of socialisation to follow from the primary socialisation of the family.

In the case of the German minority in Denmark, parents who send their children to the German kindergarten and then onwards to the German school are choosing a German minority identity for them. Similarly, parents who choose immersion schooling in Canada are choosing an identity for their children which, if not bilingual, nonetheless causes them to reflect on and perhaps challenge the values of the society in which they live. The long-term effects of such choices are difficult to discern. Some children resent their minority education and pass over into the majority as soon as possible, but the effects will be mitigated by imponderables beyond the foresight of even the wisest parents.

The value of considering models of minority or bilingual education is not, therefore, to predict effects but to make us aware that to choose 'bilingual' education whatever the model, is in fact to choose 'bicultural' education. The effects cannot be predicted and the significance of a specific content will be crucial. Research on additive and subtractive bilingualism (Lambert, 1978) reminds us that social class and ethnic origins and statuses are determining factors in the nature of bilingual development. The relationship with bicultural and ethnic identity development is an issue for further research. In the meantime let us be clear that to label programmes as 'bilingual' is misleading when they are in fact 'bicultural'. Teachers and parents working in such programmes, for minority or majority children, need as much clarity as possible to guide their day-to-day decisions and actions.

References

BdN 1982, Grenzland 92 Apenrade: Bund deutscher Nordschleswiger.

BERGER, P.L. and LUCKMANN, T. 1966, *The Social Construction of Reality*. Harmondsworth: Penguin.

BYRAM, M. 1985, Language choice in a minority school. *International Review of Education* 31, 3, 323–33.

— 1986, *Minority Education and Ethnic Survival: Case-study of a German School in Denmark*. Clevedon: Multilingual Matters.

— 1989, *Cultural Studies in Foreign Language Education*. Clevedon: Multilingual Matters.

— 1991, Bilingualism in minority education: the conflict of interest between minorities and their members. In K. JASPAERT and S. KROON (eds), *Ethnic Minority Languages and Education*. Amsterdam: Swets and Zeitlinger, 15–23.

BYRAM, M., ESARTE-SARRIES, V. and TAYLOR, S. 1991, *Cultural Studies and Language Learning*. Clevedon: Multilingual Matters.

CHRISTIANSEN, F. 1990, Sprachenfolge an den deutschen Minderheitenschulen. In K.M. PEDERSEN *Sprache und Unterricht in der deutschen, dänischen und friesischen Minderheit*. pp. 97–102. Aabenraa: Institut for Graenseregionsforskning.

LAMBERT, W.E. 1978, Some cognitive and socio-cultural consequences of being bilingual. *The Canadian Modern Language Review* 34, 3, 537–47.

PEDERSEN, K.M. 1988, Second language learners in the German minority in Denmark. In *Bilingualism and the Individual, Copenhagen Studies in Bilingualism 4*, Clevedon: Multilingual Matters, 1–12.

— (ed.) 1990, *Sprache und Unterricht in der deutschen, dänischen und friesischen Minderheit*. Aabenraa: Institut for Graenseregionsforskning.

SØNDERGAARD, B. 1981, Et sprogpädägogisk eksperiment—tidlig indføring af andetsproget i en bilingual skole. In E. EJERHED and I. HENNINGSEN (eds), *Tvåspråkighet*. Umeå: Umeå Studies in the Humanities, 36, 302–308.

— 1983, Öffnung ja—Identitätsverlust nein? Zur Problematik der deutsch–dänischen Minderheitenschulen, *Grenzfriedenshefte* 84–89.

— 1984, *Sprogfordelingen: det bilinguale curriculum*. Aabenraa: Amtscentralen for undervisningsmidler.

— 1990a, Die deutsche Schulpraxis in Nordschleswig aus der Sicht des Zweisprachigkeitsforschers. In K.M. PEDERSEN (1990) *Sprache und Unterricht in der deutschen, dänischen und friesischen Minderheit*. pp. 103–12.

— 1990b, Problems of pedagogical continuity within a minority, *Journal of Multilingual and Multicultural Development*, 11, 5, 421–33.

SONNICHSEN, P. J. 1983 *Der Nordschleswiger*. Aabenraa: Amtscentralen for undervisnigsmidler.

SWAIN, M. and LAPKIN, S. 1982, *Evaluating Bilingual Education: A Canadian Case Study*. Clevedon: Multilingual Matters.

4 The Problem of Pedagogy versus Ideology: The Case of a Danish–German Bilingual School-Type

BENT SØNDERGAARD

The Approach

It is a much debated question how much transfer there is between research results and actual experience in bilingual pedagogy. The two extremes are contained in the following views:

(1) There is significant transfer because all bilingual teaching, despite external differences, attempts to resolve the same basic pedagogical problems.
(2) There can only be minimal transfer, or even none at all, because the conditions for this type of pedagogy are so fundamentally different from place to place, that each bilingual teaching situation is unique.

I shall return to this issue after I have described the nature of the pedagogic problem in a Danish–German school-type.

The Framework

It is necessary to begin with a few facts about this particular type of school.

The most northern part of the German Federal State of Schleswig-Holstein, which is called *Sydslesvig* in Danish and *Landesteil Schleswig* in German, has a particular pedagogical character because, beside the public German schools, there exists a group of Danish minority schools (see Figure 4.1).

On 1 September 1990 these special Danish minority schools in

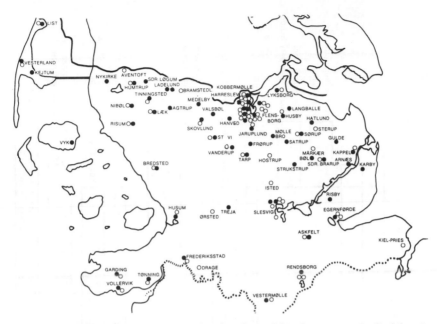

FIGURE 4.1 *Map of private Danish schools and kindergartens in Sydslesvig.*

Germany consisted of 53 schools, including 4 *Realskoler* and 1 *Gymnasium*, servicing a total of 5,246 pupils. In addition there were 62 kindergartens/nurseries with a total of 1,896 children (*Årsberetning*, 1989–90: 32ff.). Thus the Danish minority in northern Germany has at its disposal a fully developed alternative to the public German education system, where pupils can remain within this specific educational framework for 16 years.

Structurally these schools are caught between the large differences that exist between the Danish and the Schleswig-Holstein education systems, as is evident from Figure 4.2.

On the one hand these schools wish for ideological reasons to be as Danish as possible, and follow Denmark's undifferentiated nine-year unitary school model. On the other hand they are obliged to adapt themselves to the school structure in the 'host state' in order to be able to function as *staatlich anerkannte Ersatzschulen* (state recognised alternative schools) so that their examinations are recognised by the German authorities. Schleswig-Holstein has a school-system with tripartite external differentiation after the first four years (= *Grundschule*). (It must be noted, however, that in recent years there has been a growth

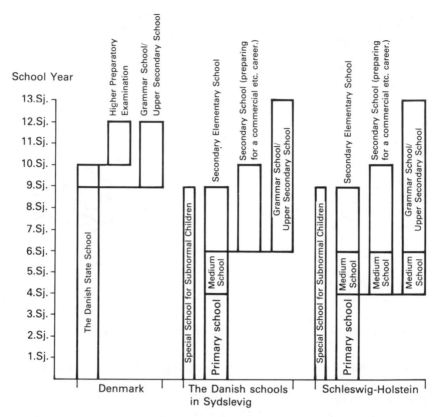

FIGURE 4.2 *Overview of the Danish, the Sydslesvig–Danish and the Schleswig-Holstein school systems* (from Hoop, 1991: 57).

in the number of *Gesamtschulen* (comprehensive schools) as an alternative to the tripartite system.)

The Danish minority schools have chosen a compromise between the two systems by delaying the streaming of pupils until after the 6th grade, which, moreover, produces problems for the small *Hauptschulen* (secondary elementary schools) because they have fewer pupils (Hoop, 1991).

Parents can send their children to the Danish minority schools without paying fees. They are financially supported by both the state of Schleswig-Holstein and Denmark. In the most recent change in Schleswig-Holstein's education act of 13 March 1990 there is, for the first time ever, a precise reference to the amount of this public subsidy:

For schools of the Danish minority there will be paid a subsidy, independent of need, of 100% of the sum agreed as the average in the state for a pupil of a comparable public school in the preceding year. (*Årsberetning*, 1989–90: 17).

Money which is required above and beyond this for the running of the schools is paid by the state of Denmark.

Historical Background

In order to understand some of the pedagogical problems these schools contend with it is necessary to delve into their history. Their existence is closely linked to the establishment in 1920 of the present frontier between Germany and Denmark. Since Danish-oriented and German-oriented citizens lived side by side in the region, following upon the establishment of the border, a pro-German minority was left north of the frontier (in Nordslesvig) and a pro-Danish minority to the south (in Sydslesvig), with the old duchy of Slesvig being divided in two.

As a central feature of their linguistic and cultural autonomy the two minorities were granted their own schools. At that point in time the climate in frontier politics was different from that which prevails today. Amongst other things, both countries were dissatisfied with the position of the border and both hoped for a re-alignment; the Germans wanted it moved further north while the Danes wanted it further south. These aspirations were resilient and did not officially die until the mid-1950s.

In order to understand the context of these schools, it is therefore important to bear in mind that they originally had a historical, national–political and ideological foundation, which still leaves its traces today.

Bilingual schools which were created in a border area at a period of great national tension between minority and majority are predestined to reflect a lack of balance in the curriculum between the two languages and cultures. The schools in Sydslesvig were to be, according to their own view of themselves, as Danish as possible, i.e. as little German as possible. The attitude to the German language was an instrumental one and German culture was to play a very secondary role. What might appear anomalous today is that changes in the climate of frontier politics over recent decades, from struggle to co-existence, have not brought with them more radical changes in the schools under discussion, as will be seen below.

As is evident from Figure 4.3 the number of pupils in the Danish private schools has been very unstable. Three phases of development can be extracted from the data in Figure 4.3:

(a) after 1920 numbers joining the minority schools were very small and declined even more under Nazi persecution;
(b) following on the Second World War, there was a rapid rise and then a sudden fall (accounted for in Biehl, 1960, and Søndergaard, 1981a);
(c) recent decades have been marked by a degree of stability.

In the years following the Second World War there were explicit criteria according to which parents had the right to send their children to Danish schools (Biehl, 1960: 37ff.). But in the *Erklärung der Landesregierung Schleswig-Holstein über die Stellung der dänischen Minderheit* of 26 Sep-

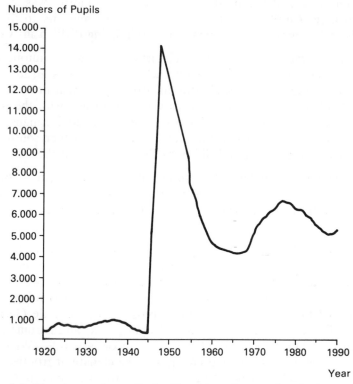

FIGURE 4.3 *Numbers of pupils in Danish private schools from 1920 to 1990* (from Hoop, 1991: 55).

tember 1949 (Declaration of the Schleswig-Holstein Government concerning the position of the Danish Minority) the following was stated:

> Parents and guardians may decide freely whether their children shall attend schools with Danish as the language of instruction. (Biehl, 1960: 54)

This opened the way for all parents, not just for minority parents, to choose a Danish school for their children. In fact many parents with no connection with the minority use this opportunity: '[The majority population] is using the Danish kindergartens and schools to an increasing degree as neutral bilingual institutions' (Hoop, 1991: 11). This is a paradox, because the *Dansk Skoleforening for Sydslesvig* (Danish School Union for Sydslesvig) has emphasised again and again, in complete accord with the Union's statements of intention, that it is *not* a neutral bilingual and bicultural school. A few quotations will demonstrate this:

> our Danish school is not in all respects a neutral school, but is in fact a school with an attitude, with a clear Danish viewpoint. (*Årsberetning*, 1983–84: 10).

> Perhaps the falling numbers of pupils might tempt some people to diverge from this view [of being a Danish school for the Danish population] in the hope thereby of getting a few more pupils. This would undermine both the school's work and Danish activity in the region as a whole. (*Årsberetning*, 1983–84: 19).

> There shall thus be no doubt that the Danish school is the school for those who join the Danish population [. . .]. It is not merely an alternative to the public German school. [. . .]. On the contrary those [Germans without allegiance to the minority] do not belong in the Danish school. (*Årsberetning*, 1986–87: 8f.).

> We must do all we can to explain to parents who are interested in the Danish school that we are not running neutral language schools. Our schools are for those who believe in the Danish language and culture. (*Årsberetning*, 1988–89: 18).

> Parents who have only a limited interest in Danish language, culture and life-style and who only use our schools in order to find some alternative to the public German school, ought not to send their children to a Danish school. (*Årsberetning*, 1989–90: 9).

The above evidence has been selected in order to illustrate the paradox that, even if these schools are old-fashioned in relation to modern bilingual pedagogy, and even if they emphasise their specific minority perspective with a Danish national ideology, they nonetheless appear attractive to some parents outside the circle to which they address themselves—in spite of the fact that the schools tell them that they don't belong there at all!

The problem is complex. We do not know how large this group is, but it cannot be very small, since the *Dansk Skoleforening* is often occupied with the question. Neither do we know for certain anything about the motives for these parents' choice of school. A few years ago I suggested carrying out a scientific investigation of the issue, but this was rejected by the *Dansk Skoleforening*.

In this connection suffice it to point out one significant factor. Private primary schools are a rare phenomenon in Schleswig-Holstein and thus the Danish school will in many parts of Sydslesvig be the only alternative to the public schools for those parents who, presumably for widely differing reasons, do not wish to send their children to the latter. By opting out of the public schools, they automatically come to opt into the Danish schools, i.e. not for language-specific reasons, but for general pedagogical reasons, which makes the pupil clientele very heterogeneous. A contributing cause for the choice of school may be certain stereotyped values which are in the environment. In some, but certainly not all, German circles the concept of Danish schooling is linked with associations such as 'warm', 'humane', 'progressive', 'more democratic', 'without pressure for results'. Whether these ideas are valid or not is immaterial here, but their mere existence can help explain the paradox that language and culture are not the primary reason for some parents' choice of a specific minority school. This does not, of course, exclude the fact that there are also other parents for whom language and culture are precisely the decisive element in their choice of school.

Language Distribution in the Curriculum

The internationally recognised definition of a bilingual school presupposes that L1 and L2 are used both as subjects and as medium of instruction (cf. definitions in Søndergaard, 1984a). In relation to this definition, it can be established that the Danish schools in Sydslesvig are not really bilingual, since they do not fulfil the requirement of the use of L2 as a medium of instruction. For there are no obligatory requirements that German shall be used instrumentally, but only that pupils shall know the German terms in the natural sciences. The usual practice is that German is only taught as a subject throughout the whole period of schooling, whereas Danish is both subject and medium of instruction in all other subjects.

This distribution of languages cannot be understood on pedagogic but rather on ideological grounds. As it stands it is more in keeping with the pedagogy in the past than the present—and it has scarcely anything to do with the pedagogical future. From a modern scientific viewpoint, it has to be described as anachronistic. This is both remarkable and ironic in light of the fact that in Flensburg, Sydslesvig's main city, there was a 13 year advanced bilingual and bicultural teaching experiment carried out in the nineteenth century, with parity of use of Danish and German as subjects and as media of instruction, described in Søndergaard, 1984b.

> The paradoxical conclusion to be drawn from this is therefore that the bilingual pedagogy of the bilingual schools of Flensburg [in the middle of the last century] was methodologically modern and that the corresponding pedagogy [today] is methodologically dated— which in both cases is no matter of chance, seen ideologically. The question then arises: Would it be possible to transfer the methodologically good bilingual pedagogy of the last century to the contemporary minority schools? The answer is yes. This would however mean a redefinition of the ideological basis of the schools, for such schools would have necessarily to be depoliticised and de- ideologised, as true bilingual and bicultural schools with both quantitative and qualitative equality of both languages and cultures. (Søndergaard, 1981b: 374f.)

It is immediately evident that a language distribution model in a bilingual school which isolates one language as a subject only cannot optimally cover the different language needs which pupils have in their further education. The correct distribution of instrumental languages is of fundamental importance, not least for the balance of vocabulary between the two languages. In general terms it can be asserted that the Sydslesvig schools qualify their pupils to cope better in further education in Denmark than in Germany (as a consequence of the absence of German as instrumental language). There are also criticisms made of pupils' German skills by people in German commerce and industry (*Årsberetning*, 1989–90: 10), but if this skewed language distribution does not have more fateful consequences it can doubtless be attributed to the fact that the majority of pupils have German as their mother tongue.

A special problem arises with those pupils who have maximal bilingual school attendance, i.e. right through to the school-leaving, matriculation examination (*studentereksamen*) in the form of a German–Danish *Abitur* which gives them formal right to study at institutions of higher education in both Germany and Denmark. Unless certain linguistic pre-conditions are fulfilled, the perspectives in the German–Danish *Abitur* are in fact of more theoretical than practical interest. For in many forms of study the linguistic medium plays a central role, which means that the student's language competence is decisive. With respect to the vocabulary, not only the core vocabulary, but also specific-purpose vocabulary is important. One substantial methodological question in bilingual pedagogy is therefore: how can one ensure that pupils acquire the largest possible vocabulary in both languages— also in subject-specific areas? It is precisely the language distribution in the curriculum which is the key to the solution of this problem. The model used by the Sydslesvig schools is, from this perspective, quite inadequate. Søndergaard (1984a: 61ff.) develops a model for an adequately integrated use of instrumental languages for Danish and German. The schools have however not taken this up.

One consequence of the present language distribution is that students from the Danish minority schools do not have a good subject-specific linguistic base for studying at institutions of higher education in Germany. In conversation with the present author, one student who began a course in Germany but abandoned it after a few years and completed his education in Denmark, expressed the following view:

> We are not educated for living and functioning in German society. I, for example, did not master the subject-specific language of mathematics or biology. We are thus obliged to complete our education in Denmark. We are betrayed by the fact that the school does not give us subject-specific German.

The view expressed here is doubtless representative for a group of young people. The consequence is that the majority of young academically educated people study in Denmark and thereafter not many of them return to Sydslesvig, which is not without problems for the minority, in terms of a 'brain-drain'.

It is important to set the language distribution in the Danish schools' curriculum in the context of the pupils' languages in the home, since the majority of children attending Danish kindergartens and schools have German as their home language. This shows clearly that the Danish minority is not primarily a linguistic and cultural minority, but rather an ideological one, often characterised by the term 'conviction minority'.

As discussed in more detail in Søndergaard, 1980b, Standard Danish has, for historical reasons, never been a widespread language of the home among indigenous minority people and the region's original Danish dialect, which is now disappearing, has never been a linguistic symbol for a pro-Danish attitude, since language and national identity have never been identical concepts. The position of Standard Danish has been described as follows:

> Since the Second World War the knowledge of Standard Danish in Schleswig-Holstein has certainly increased considerably, because during this period many children have had their education in Danish private schools. However, this has not had any effect on the extension of Danish as a living minority language [. . .]. It only means that many people are able to understand Danish, and are also able, to a varying degree, to speak it [. . . but not that they] use Danish as their daily spoken language. [. . .] Danish has come into Southern Schleswig first and foremost through institutions, such as the kindergartens, the schools and the church. [. . .] Because Standard Danish [. . .] has never been the natural spoken language of many natives in Southern Schleswig, it could have been predicted that the introduction of Standard Danish as an 'institutional language' would not noticeably influence the home language, even if the leaders of the minority have sometimes had the idea that it might do so and have agitated for it. [. . .] It is impossible to change this situation, but it is likely to be fatal to Danish as a living minority language. The language distribution in Southern Schleswig thus shows a pronounced degree of linguistic bifurcation [. . .]: German is the home language [. . .] and Danish remains the 'institutional language'. (Søndergaard, 1981a: 140f.)

It would be most reasonable to accept that such a distribution of languages in the home creates clear limitations for the development of Danish language and culture, but this is clearly difficult for some. As shown in Søndergaard, 1987, there exists language pressure in informal situations where the choice of language code ought to be free. It is also clear that there are limitations to running bilingual schools in a situation where the schools' first language does not exist as a living language in many homes—the situation tends to be one of 'school bilingualism'. I have had among my students in the last twenty years or so a number of bilingual Sydslesvig people. A consistent characteristic of the linguistic and cultural competence in Danish of individuals without Danish as home language has been:

(a) acceptable mastery of spoken Danish,

(b) often insufficient mastery of written Danish,

(c) severely limited cultural competence.

One has to recognise that in situations where the linguistic and cultural influences are not double-sided (from both the home and the educational institution), even a pedagogical influence over many years will often only give superficial results.

Analysis of Syllabuses for Danish and German

An analysis of the syllabuses for German and Danish will reveal how the schools give priority to the two subjects. In the *Erklärung der Landesregierung Schleswig-Holstein über die Stellung der dänischen Minderheit* of 26 September 1949 there is the following assertion:

> In schools with Danish as medium of instruction, there shall be adequate instruction in the German language. (Biehl, 1960: 54)

This must still be the case since it is a precondition for the schools being *staatlich anerkannte Ersatzschulen*, but the concept of adequate can be interpreted in different ways.

Let us begin with the quantitative relationship between the two language subjects in the present curriculum (cf. Figure 4.4). As is clear from the 3rd grade onwards there is approximate quantitative equality. But is this sufficient? The answer to this question depends on the point of view. In judging, we must take into consideration that the aims for German as a subject are set so high, 'that pupils of Danish schools shall have reached by the end of their school career the same level of

Form	:	1	2	3	4	5	6	7	8	9	10
Danish	:	9	8	7	6	5	5	4	5	5	5
German	:		6	6	6	5	5	5	5	5	5

Form	:	R7	R8	R9	R10
Danish	:	4	4	4	4
German	:	4	4	4	5

FIGURE 4.4 *No. of lessons in the subjects Danish and German in* Grund- und Hauptschul-*classes and in classes of Orientierungsstufe and* Realschule (From Terkelsen, 1990: 72).

achievement as comparable pupils of the public schools' (Terkelsen, 1990: 66).

The full competence in German of the latter group is however dependent on the linguistic input in lessons of German as a subject, together with the use of German as instrumental language in other subjects. The *Dansk Skoleforening* is aware of this:

> The special position of the subject German in Danish schools makes special demands on German teaching. In contrast to the public schools, German in Danish schools is only used as language as a subject not as a teaching language. Thus, in other subjects the pupil does not have the possibility of using and developing his knowledge of German in areas of written language accuracy. Therefore it is necessary to give adequate attention to the written dimension of the subject. (*Læseplan: Tysk, realskolen*: 3).

In the syllabus there are however no detailed pedagogic suggestions as to how the absence of German as an instrumental language shall be compensated for in the subject German.

In bilingual schools with well-grounded language teaching it is, moreover, still necessary to have detailed methodological indications as to how the teaching in L1 and L2 shall be co-ordinated, but these syllabuses contain surprisingly little of a concrete nature on this issue. Only exceptionally can be found, for example, the beginnings of a true contrast, such as:

> As soon as possible, and when it occurs naturally in teaching, attention should be drawn to differences and similarities between ways of writing Danish and German, (*Læseplan: Dansk*: 10)

which is then illustrated by the diagram in Figure 4.5.

At significant points in bilingual pedagogy the syllabuses provide all too little concrete guidance, whereas in other aspects they are very complete. This is the case for the methodology of teaching beginners in Danish:

> [This] shall be organised with regard to the special language conditions in Sydslesvig. The majority of children attending Danish kindergarten and school come from families with German as the home language. The first meeting with Danish thus usually takes place when the 3-year-old child starts kindergarten. The teaching of Danish is thus a central task in kindergartens and schools. (*Læseplan: Dansk*: 4).

Eksempler på ortografiske fejltyper, der er betinget af dansk hhv. tysk skrive-måde:

Hyppige fejltyper	da / ty	Eksempel
1. Vokalforveks-linger.	e / ä i / ie, ih, ieh y / ü æ / e æ / ä ø / ö å / o	nemlig/nämlich si/sie, ihn, sieh fylde/füllen tænke/denken æbler/Äpfel høre/hören båd/Boot, åben/oben
2. Konsonantfor-vekslinger.	c / z d / l f / v v / w	medicin/Medizin det "bløde" d (kun dansk) fire/vier vand/Wasser
3. Forvekslinger af lydforbind-elser.	eg, ig, ej, aj / ai, ei ov / au øg, øj / äu, eu	jeg, dig, arbejde, maj/Arbeit, Mai tov/Tau løg, tøj/Leute, läuten
4. Forvekslinger af konsonant-ophobninger.	ks / chs, cks, gs, x k-kk / ck kv / qu	fiks/fix, Fuchs, Klecks, unterwegs buk/Bock, klokke/Glocke kvik/quick, bekvem/bequem
5. Konsonant/dob-beltkonsonant som udlyd.	nd / nn ld / ll n / nn m / mm	mand/Mann fald/Fall kan/kann dum/dumm
6. Stort/lille begyndelses-bogstav.		/alle substantiver

FIGURE 4.5 *Examples of contrastively arranged orthographic error-types in Danish and German* (from Læseplan: Dansk: 55).

This is the background to the large number of Danish lessons in the first two years of schooling.

With respect to language as a subject, one can thus speak of a quantitative balance between Danish and German in the majority of the period of schooling. This is however not the case in qualitative terms. Thus it is stated that 'this language [Danish] has, of course, in the context of school, a higher status [than German]' (Terkelsen, 1990: 67). One can also come to the same conclusion by comparing the statement of primary aims for the two subjects. First, Danish:

> The aim of teaching is that pupils should develop their capacities to enter into linguistic fellowship with other Danish people and to use Danish as their natural means of communication, and that they become familiar with essential aspects of Danish culture. (*Læseplan: Dansk*: 3.)

(One linguistic detail is striking—but scarcely ideologically coincidental—that is the use of the adjective 'Danish' instead of 'Danish speaking' in connection with 'a linguistic fellowship with other Danish people', given the fact that the majority of 'indigenous' children in Danish schools are German citizens.)

The corresponding paragraph in the syllabus for the subject of German is as follows:

> The aim of the teaching is that pupils should develop their linguistic skills, so that they can live and work in German society and so that they acquire knowledge of essential aspects of German culture. (*Læseplan: Tysk*: 3.)

At first glance the differences may not appear to be large, but it is noticeable that the formulation in Danish is more comprehensive (and more emotionally laden). In reality they can however be larger than is explicitly expressed here. I have heard the leader of the Danish minority school system interpret the difference in the following way: pupils shall learn to *love* Danish, i.e. something emotional, and they shall *have knowledge of* German, i.e. something intellectual.

In summary, we can say that the analysis in this and in the previous sections lead to the same main conclusion: in these schools the main requirement in many modern bilingual–bicultural schools is not fulfilled, namely that both languages/cultures must have the same status.

Research

There has been very little research in this Danish–German bilingual pedagogy. Independent, critical research is, moreover, difficult. The schools are, as a consequence of their own understanding of themselves, not interested in a scientific evaluation of the pedagogy used. For this reason any judgement must necessarily rest on an uncertain basis, since hypotheses and disparate observations have to play a disproportionate role. The degree of subjectivity in the judgement of pedagogic practice remains noticeable.

The only area where there is coherent linguistic and language-pedagogic research, of modest dimensions, is in the issue of vocabulary acquisition by bilingual Sydslesvig children in relation to monolingual children. This research was begun by Wieczerkowski but, insofar as it must be considered to be fully professional research, contains serious linguistic flaws (cf. Søndergaard, 1980a: 26). The subjects in the investigation consisted of 4 groups of pupils in 4th and 5th grades, each with 38 informants, bilingual speakers from Nordslesvig (cf. Byram this volume) and from Sydslesvig. They are compared with monolingual German and Danish children with the same socio-economic background, intelligence and sex, and measured using a comprehensive battery of tests. The results of the verbal test can be seen in Figure 4.6. The main results can be summarised as follows:

> On the whole there was evidence of differences of achievement in verbal tasks to the disadvantage of the bilingual samples: deficits in achievement were to be found in both languages in tests of *vocabulary*, in *spelling* and in *tasks of association*. (Wieczerkowski, 1973: 69.)

In the vocabulary tests the bilinguals from Sydslesvig attained 79% in German and 85% in Danish in relation to monolinguals. The author comments on these main results in the following way:

> There were thus different values in fields of linguistic behaviour for both groups. Presumably the 'normal' (*incidental*) stimulation of the bilingual environment, in which the range of use of both languages is not evenly balanced, is not sufficient to create a vocabulary which can fully compete with that of children growing up unilingually. (Wieczerkowski, 1973: 72.)

The same tendency can be found in Linde's (1976) later investigation. Here, 24 bilingual 5 and 6-year-old kindergarten children were given a test which measures passive vocabulary in Danish and German. A control group consisted of monolingual children of the same sex, age, social status and length of kindergarten attendance. On the other hand there was no comparison of intelligence measures.

The main result of the investigation is as follows:

> In Sydslesvig the monolingual subjects had an average score of 2.58 raw score points above that of bilingual subjects. This means that

		Test Language: German			Test Language: Danish		
		Mono-lingual German Pupils	Bilin-gual Danish Pupils	Bilin-gual German Pupils	Mono-lingual Danish Pupils	Bilin-gual Danish Pupils	Bilin-gual German Pupils
Reading Test – Le	x̄	31,2	27,5	26,8	29,0	27,9	24,0
HI 19	s	7,49	10,63	10,21	8,82	12,18	10,72
Vocabulary Test – Wo	x̄	29,3	23,2	24,8	30,2	25,6	22,3
HI 19	s	6,96	9,22	10,00	7,33	9,26	9,68
Letter Guessing – Br	x̄	12,6	12,7	12,6	15,8	15,3	10,9
BTS	s	3,48	2,25	4,50	5,12	7,25	4,94
Striking out what is wrong – Us	x̄	9,2	8,9	9,1	10,1	9,0	8,6
BTS	s	2,45	1,99	2,28	2,57	3,41	2,38
Spelling – RS	x̄	42,4	38,0	39,6	46,8	39,4	35,2
BTS	s	8,41	9,34	9,92	11,09	15,44	10,96

Maximale Punktwerte: Le 50; Wo 50; Br 30; Us 16; Rs 60.

FIGURE 4.6 *Test results for the two monolingual and two bilingual test groups in five language tests in German and Danish* (from Wieczerkowski, 1973: 44).

on average they scored 7.37% better than their bilingual peers. (Linde, 1976: 83.)

There is also vocabulary deficit in Danish, compared with monolinguals. Horn (1972) already demonstrated a deficit in the active German vocabulary of bilingual 5-year-old kindergarten children, compared with the vocabulary of monolinguals of the same age, together with a rather smaller vocabulary in Danish than in German. The latter tendency was further supported in Dethlefsen (1979) where the active vocabulary in both languages was measured in a small group of 8-year-old bilingual Sydslesvig pupils.

The demonstrated vocabulary deficit in bilingual Sydslesvig children can hardly be characterised as significantly large, the more so because with increasing age there appears to develop a partial levelling out between bilinguals and monolinguals with respect to size of vocabulary. There is nonetheless a deficit of such an order that it is real, which means that it cannot be neglected and one ought to work towards reducing it within the educational context. It remains a major question which method ought to be used. The following suggestion has been made:

> There is presumably a need for intensive language programmes *in both languages* which are developed in accordance with the particular linguistic learning situation and which make use of *contrastive* procedures in order to level out the disadvantages which can be established in comparison with pupils growing up monolingually, or indeed to avoid them completely. (Wieczerkowski, 1973: 74.)

The significance of such pedagogical initiatives should not be underestimated. On the other hand it has to be asserted that simple methods cannot completely solve such a comprehensive problem.

In particular, with regard to the issue of contrast in language teaching, the following needs to be noted. It is clear to someone who has observed a lot of Danish and German teaching in the border region, that there are very few teachers who have a good command of contrastive methods, which means that the amount of interference is unacceptably high (cf. Søndergaard, 1985: 364ff.).

The teachers' maintenance of a methodologically obsolete one-language principle in both Danish and German teaching is scarcely founded, in many cases, on pedagogical beliefs, but rather can be attributed to the fact that their training is inadequate for teaching in bilingual schools. Between 80 and 90% of the over 600 teachers in the Danish minority schools have had Danish teacher training, which means that they are trained to teach Danish as a mother tongue; but Sydslesvig Danish teaching is not mother tongue teaching. Only a limited number of teachers have also studied German with the intention of teaching German as a foreign language in Denmark. But the teaching of German in Sydslesvig is not foreign language teaching, since it aims to give pupils mother tongue competence, as pointed out above. Some of the teachers trained in Germany have studied German for mother tongue teaching. A few of them also have qualifications in teaching Danish as a foreign language.

The basic pedagogic assumption that a teacher who shall teach in a bilingual school shall him/herself be bilingual and also have some methodological training in bilingual pedagogy seems to exist only in a few cases. Indeed there is not even an understanding of the necessity for this; there is no systematic in-service training in bilingual pedagogy— which is again an indication that the basis for the schools is in ideology not pedagogy.

I shall now return to the main problem in Danish–German bilingualism, i.e. the question of vocabulary deficit. It is also known from other bilingual combinations that it is the mastery of vocabulary, and not for example, phonetics, morphology or syntax, which is the bilingual's vulnerable point. There can, however, be no doubt that here the problem is increased because of the 'bilingual bifurcation' between home and school. One experience from the Danish–German border region, which is presumably highly transferable, is that the absence of one language (here: Danish) in the individual's environment cannot be fully compensated, even with the most effective linguistic stimulus in kindergarten and school. Thus the problem cannot be completely solved through improvements in teaching. Fundamentally, the problem is unsolvable, but it could be much reduced by a more conscious bilingual pedagogy. Søndergaard (1980a) suggests various possibilities. For example, higher priority given to vocabulary learning in relation to grammar teaching. Additionally, the importance of the restructuring of the use of instrumental language should be emphasised. Finally, emphasis must be given to the value of an earlier introduction of the school's second language in an alternative based on the pedagogy of 'play'. This latter idea has been tried out at a later stage in some schools, with good results, partly in order to strengthen mother-tongue development in German-speaking pupils and partly to give Danish-speakers an early and gentle introduction to German in the first grade (see Terkelsen, 1990).

Transfer Versus Lack of Transfer

I have attempted above to give an introduction to the pedagogical problems of a particular bilingual school-type, as it appears to me after almost two decades of trying to interpret it. Let us now return to the problem mentioned in the introduction to this paper on transfer or lack of transfer by putting the following question: Can other bilingual schools in quite different situations learn something from these special Danish schools, and if so, what?

The answer must probably be negative, above all for the following reasons:

—these schools fall outside the usual definition of a truly bilingual school;
—they do not consider bilingual pedagogy to be a central issue, since they are not based on a pedagogical philosophy but on a national ideology;
—the schools arose in a specific historical situation in an area of national-political tension between two countries—as such they form part of the European past, but scarcely of the future;
—even if the original conditions for the schools have changed, they themselves have shown remarkably little interest in changing the pedagogical structure in the direction of a modern bilingual and bicultural school. From the researcher's viewpoint, there is pedagogical fossilisation.

There is for me no doubt that an integrated Europe will need bilingual schools to a degree which we can scarcely imagine today. They will also be needed as a part of the public education system in countries hitherto rather homogeneously monolingual, such as Denmark. They must, however, be based on quite different pedagogical concepts. There are scarcely any roads leading to this from the Danish minority schools in Sydslesvig.

References

Årsberetning for Dansk Skoleforening for Sydslesvig: 1981–82ff., Flensborg.
BIEHL, Hans-Hinrich 1960, *Minderheitenschulrecht in Nord- und Südschleswig.* Hamburg: Hansischer Gildenverlag.
DETHLEFSEN, Anke 1979, *Forholdet mellem ordforrådet på dansk og på tysk hos tosprogede børn.* Semesteropgave. Pädagogische Hochschule Flensburg (unpublished).
HOOP, Siine 1991, *Argumente für und wider eine Schulkonzentration—veranschaulicht an Beispielen des dänischen Schulwesens in Südschleswig.* Examensarbeit. Pädagogische Hochschule Flensburg (unpublished).
HORN, ANNE S. 1972, *Tosprogethed.* Årsopgave. Abenraa Børnehaveseminarium (unpublished).
Læseplan for: Dansk (for førskolegruppen, 1. klassetrin, 2. klassetrin) 1990 Dansk Skoleforening for Sydslesvig (unpublished).

Læseplan for: Tysk (for 1. klassetrin, for grundskolen og mellemtrinnet, for hovedskolen, for realskolen, for gymnasiet) 1983–91 Dansk Skoleforening for Sydslesvig (unpublished).

LINDE, Antje 1976, *Zum Wortschatz ein- und zweisprachiger Kinder im deutsch–dänischen Grenzgebiet. Südschleswig.* Examensarbeit. Pädagogische Hochschule Flensburg (unpublished).

SØNDERGAARD, Bent 1980a, *Sprogligt deficit. Sprogpædagogiske betragtninger over den dansk-tyske bilingualisme.* Mit deutscher Zusammenfassung. Aabenraa: Amtscentralen for Undervisningsmidler.

— 1980b, Vom Sprachenkampf zur sprachlichen Koexistenz im deutsch–dänischen Grenzraum. In P. NELDE (ed.), *Sprachkontakt und Sprachkonflikt.* Wiesbaden: Franz Steiner, 297–305.

— 1981a, The fight for survival: Danish as a living minority language south of the German border. In E. HAUGEN *et al.* (eds), *Minority Languages Today.* Edinburgh: Edinburgh University Press (paperback edition 1990).

— 1981b, Zweisprachige Schulen im deutsch–dänischen Grenzgebiet in Vergangenheit, Gegenwart und Zukunft, *Die Heimat* 88, 12, 373–7.

— 1984a, *Sprogfordelingen i det bilinguale curriculum.* Aabenraa: Amtscentralen for Undervisningsmidler.

— 1984b, Dansk og tysk som undervisningssprog i Flensborg mellem de to slesvigske krige, *Uddannelseshistorie*, 31–86.

— 1985, Interferenz und Kontrastierung im Spracherwerb. In H. BECK (ed.), *Arbeiten zur Skandinavistik.* Frankfurt a.M.: Peter Lang, 359–66.

— 1987, Om sprogtvang i en bilingual kontekst—et psykologisk problem (with an English summary). In E. WANDE *et al.* (eds), *Aspects of Multilingualism.* Uppsala: Acta Universitatis Upsaliensis.

TERKELSEN, Helga 1990, Deutsch in der ersten Klasse. Ein Unterrichtsversuch an Schulen von Dansk Skoleforening for Sydslesvig. In K. M. PEDERSEN (ed.), *Sprache und Unterricht in der deutschen, dänischen und friesischen Minderheit.* Aabenraa: Institut for Grænseregionsforskning.

WIECZERKOWSKI, Wilhelm 1973, Verbale Fertigkeiten bilingualer Schüler im deutsch–dänischen Grenzgebiet. Hamburg (published as manuscript).

5 Bicultural Programmes in the Dutch-Language School System in Brussels

JOHAN LEMAN

The European and Brussels Contexts

Large-scale sociocultural changes taking place on a European level (Roosens, 1991) are reflected on a smaller, more condensed scale in Brussels. Whereas the United States has hitherto tended to present itself as a monocultural model to very different ethnicommunities, the European model appears to be becoming fundamentally multicultural, not because of Europe's immigrant minorities but because of the indigenous composition of Europe itself.

Commenting on the differences between Europe and the United States with reference to the consequences of their immigrant profiles, Glazer stressed two points:

> In Europe, it is possible, in spite of historical centralization and the creation of a unique national language that is taught compulsorily in all schools, also to leave room for a particular language and culture that can be preserved through the school;

also,

> one must note that the amount of immigration to the USA and the size of the resulting minorities are so enormous in comparison to the case in Europe that the preservation of linguistic and cultural differences could damage national unity (Glazer, 1987: 212; translated from the French).

More so than is the case in Europe, the United States appears to need a simple 'myth' which is borne by one single language and which is not excessively subtle, so that everyone can identify with it. In Europe, it would seem that the unification process, perceived from a cultural perspective, will be more complex and will have to make room for multiculturalism and multilingualism, together with certain pragmatic agreements on the evolution towards a 'lingua franca' for specific gatherings. This process is, at present, in full momentum.

The Brussels situation is essentially a precursor of this evolution, albeit one that is biased somewhat by a specifically Belgian multilingual point of departure. The absence of a 'myth' about the nature of Europe, however, may complicate the unification process for some time to come.

The specifics of the Brussels linguistic situation will not be gone into here (for more details, cf. Leman, 1990: 7–10; Witte & Baetens Beardsmore, 1987). Suffice it to say that Brussels has a predominantly French-language image, though in some districts and in particular places English, and to a lesser extent, German, also have a strong presence. Most of the geographic and economic links of Brussels are with the Dutch-language north of the county, however, a minority in Brussels. Moreover, there are two major non-indigenous European groups present in the Belgian capital, namely Italians and Spaniards, because of earlier immigration, while two major non-European groups have arrived since the 1960s, Moroccans and Turks.

The employment market in Brussels imposes multilingualism (primarily in French and Dutch) as the norm, and it is also an advantage socially, even though sociological pressures cause much interaction to take place in French, and certainly in immigrant circles. Turkish families which remain strongly attached to their language of origin may be a possible exception to this rule. Within immigrant families in general, there often remains a particular openness to their language variant of origin.

European and Non-European Communities in Brussels

The perception of Southern European communities by North-West Europeans is in full evolution, in Brussels as elsewhere. Increasingly, clichés about what used to be considered as somewhat 'retarded' Mediterranean European areas are being dismantled. The unification of Europe is playing a role in this, as well as the settlement of elites from these countries in the Brussels area. Also, the awareness is gradually beginning to dawn on the public at large that countries like Spain and Italy have been making impressive economic, social, and cultural progress. Although Southern Italy has not yet been able to divest itself of its Mafia structures, a region like Sicily has been doing so since the end of the

1970s, presenting a different picture than that formerly described by anthropologists, novelists, and movie makers (Leman, 1987a and 1988). In the northern countries to which they emigrated many second- and third-generation Italians and Spaniards have since achieved significant upward social mobility through education, in the role of entrepreneurs, and even at times in politics.

The indigenous Brussels population is becoming accustomed to the notion that Italians and Spaniards are Europeans (there being fewer Greeks and Portuguese, their presence is less noticed), who are to be recognised as having social status equal to that of the British, the French, and people from other neighbouring countries. That official TV channels from Spain, Italy, Great Britain, Germany, France, and The Netherlands can easily be received in Brussels via cable TV is further promoting this sentiment of equality among Europeans (cf. Baetens Beardsmore & Van Beeck, 1983).

Although evolution in perception proceeds slowly, it is nevertheless irreversible, creating a new situation in cities like Brussels.

Developments among the non-European minorities may not be following the same path. In Belgium these are predominantly Moroccans and Turks. A new law on the acquisition of Belgian nationality came into effect on 1 January 1992 making third-generation children automatically Belgian, while the granting of Belgian nationality to the second generation has been considerably simplified. Dual nationality, formerly forbidden, is also now possible. As yet it is too early to predict what the repercussions of this new law will be on the linguistic and cultural allegiance of the people involved. Nevertheless, the question remains as to what place to reserve in a city like Brussels, which already has an official bilingual French–Dutch status, for Turkish and Arabic in education. It also raises the issue as to what is to be understood by, and accepted as, biculturalism within the school curriculum.

With reference to the teaching of minority languages, Paulston has pointed out that,

> . . . the uncertainty in language planning could be reduced if account were taken of the social context in which the language problem occurs and particularly of the social, economic, and cultural forces that contribute to the preservation of, and shifts in, language use. Even the most carefully designed school policies intended to benefit minority groups are doomed to failure if one opposes social forces, particularly when no account is taken of the economic situation (Paulston, 1987: 301–302, translated from the French).

Paulston here touches upon a crucial point for the inception of specific linguistic and cultural programmes in the education of immigrant children. In starting bicultural and multilingual programmes in the Dutch-language school system in Brussels it was crucial to appraise whether it would be advantageous to Italian children, for example, to be able to continue to speak and write Italian in Brussels, both from the parental perspective and from a socio-economic point of view. The same applies for Spanish children. But should this be the case, does it also apply to non-European children, particularly now that they can, in the second generation, or will, in the third generation, be Belgians? Is it sufficient for the parents to consider it important?

Paulston points out:

> [. . .] It seems to me that the planners for the preservation and shifting of languages have to recognize and accept that other than strictly pragmatic considerations are involved . . . Thus, religious groups take the preservation of their language particularly seriously . . . and the same applies for some ethnic groups (Paulston, 1987: 302; translated from the French).

Communities that attach great importance to their specific religion in Brussels are those with Arabic as the language of the Koran (e.g. Moroccans), or those with Aramaic like the Aramaean or Christian Turks. Communities strongly attached to their ethnicity are the Turks as just one example.

Such considerations played an important role in the setting up of bicultural educational projects in the Dutch-language school system in Brussels. These are generally known as 'Foyer Projects' in Belgium, after the socio-pedagogic centre from which they arose. The minority languages that were included in the curriculum had to enjoy sufficient social prestige (economically, religiously, or ethnically), at least within the particular community and if possible outside it. Other important considerations taken into account have been discussed elsewhere (Leman, 1990: 10–13).

Dutch-language Education in Brussels

In greater Brussels there are two official educational networks, a French-language system and a Dutch-language system. The present paper limits itself to the Dutch-language educational system, the only one where bicultural education programmes are offered.

In recent years the proportion of new enrolments in Dutch-language kindergartens in Brussels were divided as follows; about 35% of new enrolments came from homogeneous Dutch-language families, about 30% from mixed-language families, about 20% from homogeneous French-language families, and about 15% from foreign families. Mixed-language families are those in which one of the parents is of Dutch-speaking origin, although French is the predominant language at home. These figures represent an increase in the mixed-language families and in the foreign families and a decrease in the homogeneous Dutch-language and French-language families. Given demographic developments in Brussels it can be assumed that this trend will continue for some time to come. If one considers the problem from the standpoint of the Dutch-language educational system, the question arises of the best strategy to adopt, given that children from homogeneous Dutch-speaking families (that is, those whose children hear Dutch spoken at home as L1) constitute only about 35% of the newly registered school population. One specific problem is that some ethnic minority children have to learn Dutch as a third language. For some time in the early years at school the immigrant child will receive Dutch as a 'foreign language', i.e. a language that is taught only in the classroom, without this learning process being supplemented by spontaneous language acquisition outside school. This challenge deserves special attention, not because such a learning process would be impossible, but because it obviously requires an adaptation of the way language is offered in school together with special other techniques.

Given that there are also French-speaking Belgian children in the Dutch-language schools, this means that subtle mechanisms have to be worked out for the dosage of language input to be spread out over time and place; this is necessary if languages on offer are to be formulated in a way that takes into account the reality of the children, the societal context, as well as the educational institution itself. Also, the school authorities must see to it that the Dutch-language school does not lose its Dutch character.

The 'Foyer Model' in the Dutch-Language School System

Bicultural education according to the Foyer Model is given in ten Dutch-language primary schools in Brussels. Three projects are oriented to Italian children, three to Turkish children, two to Moroccan children, one to Spanish children, and one to Aramean Turkish (or Christian

Turkish) children. This means that in each of the ten schools, there is a dominant group of other-ethnic children alongside the children from Dutch-speaking, French-speaking, and mixed-language families. What is important here is that an implicit numerus clausus is postulated to avoid the formation of schools of high concentrations of foreigners.

In two schools with Turkish children, however, due to the changing composition of the neighbourhood, Moroccan children are more and more taking the place of Belgian children, so that these schools, in fact, are becoming Turkish–Moroccan schools where only the Turks and not the Moroccans are supported in their mother tongue, the Moroccans being nevertheless supported in their second language learning, with parental participation, and with a Moroccan minority language teacher at their disposal.

The norm is that children will be taught the complete curriculum from kindergarten on, and that an effort must be made to have the number of immigrant children from the target group vary around 30% per year. The first project was started in 1981, a new project having been added each year for the following ten years.

At present the ten projects can be viewed as a specific component of the educational policy of the Flemish Community in Belgium (Leman, 1991c). Extensive evaluations of these Foyer projects have been published (Byram & Leman, 1990; Leman, 1991a, b).

The model the Foyer advocates for immigrant children in Dutch-language basic education (kindergarten and elementary school) in Brussels is that of gradual integration, whereby as much importance as possible is attached to the preservation and reinforcement of the children's own cultural identity and, implicitly, the mother tongue, particularly in the early years of kindergarten and the first two years of elementary school.

Gradually, Dutch (L2) is built onto what is learned through the mother tongue (L1), and with time occupying an ever greater place in the timetable. At the same time the child maintains an elementary knowledge of French as the 'language of the street' (Spoelders, 1985; Danesi, 1988a, b; Leman, 1985, 1990).

This leads to the following profile for the Italian, Spanish, and Turkish projects:

—*Kindergarten (3 years)*: 30% separately as an ethnic-cultural group in L1; 70% together with the Flemish children in Dutch.
—*Elementary education, 1st year*: 30% separately in L1 for the basic

courses; 25% separately in L2 'as specific L2 education'; 45% constructive integration activities 2nd mathematics together with the Flemish children in Dutch.

—*2nd year*: 25% separately in L1; 20% separately in L2 'as specific L2 education'; 55% integration activities and mathematics in Dutch.

—*From the 3rd through the 6th year*: 90% of the time all children together in Dutch; 5 to 3 hours per week in L1 separately and a combined intercultural course; a few hours of French per week.

In the project in which Moroccan children are integrated, an adjustment is made:

—*Kindergarten (3 years)*: 20% Arabic, 40% Dutch 'specifically as L2' and 40% Dutch together with all the other children.

—*Elementary education, 1st year*: mathematics in Dutch, with repetition of the most important concepts in Arabic; learning to read and write in Dutch as L2; 20% in Arabic, i.e. in the courses of world orientation and Islamic culture and religion.

—*2nd year*: continuation in the same way as the 1st year.

—*From the 3rd through the 6th year*: 5 hours of Arabic spread over the courses of world orientation and Islamic culture and religion; a few hours of French per week; basic courses in Dutch.

The adjustment to the Moroccan children is due primarily to the much slower rhythm with which Arabic writing is learned. It also has to do with the relationship between standard and dialect (or Moroccan) Arabic, although to a much lesser extent. For an outsider, the difference is real, but one should not underestimate the degree to which dialect and standard Arabic are related to each other for the Moroccans themselves.

In the Aramaic project, which is at present only in its second year and hence is still only at the kindergarten level, the programme is based on the language dosage that is used for Arabic in the projects with Moroccan children.

What is involved in the ten schools is a bicultural model with an intercultural perspective in which trilingualism is the goal for the project children. Inherent to the model is the encouragement of the participation of immigrant parents in the events at school.

In all the projects, while the immigrant children develop in their mother tongue (L1), the Flemish children are developing on their own level in Dutch.

Mother Tongue

In the Foyer educational projects, the mother tongue occupies an important place, particularly in the early years of basic education. More than once the question has been asked whether this mother tongue is still really the 'mother tongue'. Indeed, at home many of these children hear an impoverished dialect, mixed to a greater or lesser degree with elements from the sociologically dominant language of the surrounding environment, which functions as the primary socialisation language, again to a greater or lesser degree.

While not wanting to go into the problem of the desirability or not of, say, Italian as mother tongue in the sense of a first conceptualisation language for these children, I would argue that the following is the case for the Brussels situation:

—the mother tongue is closer to the life of the immigrant child than Dutch;
—the mother tongues, moreover, appear to be the languages that have the greatest personal and emotional overtones for the child (Leman, 1987b);
—within the projects, the mother tongues taught have a special social relevance in the life of the child.

The last point deserves some clarification. In the Foyer Project so far the mother tongues have been Italian, Spanish, Turkish, Arabic and Aramaic (i.e. for Aramaic or Chaldean Christian Turks), and not for example, Berber for some Moroccans. What do we mean by this? Italian and Spanish are languages that, at least in Brussels, have, of themselves, a certain social importance, and their importance will probably increase in the future as prestigious European languages. In the case of Turkish, this language has a strong role in determining cultural identity for Turks, both in Turkey and abroad, apart from whether or not Turkey ever enters the EEC (which is not to be excluded in the long run). Arabic and Aramaic, finally, have great religious (and for the Chaldeans also ethnic) importance. Thus, for each case the mother tongue is supported by social significance, and this is of importance for its survival.

An investment in mother-tongue education at school, however, seems less justified for languages that do not immediately have a prestigious social role, do not have a strong identity-determining role, or do not exercise an important religious function (Paulston, 1987), as seems the case for Berber.

External evaluations by Danesi for Italian and by Fernández de

Rota and Pilar Irimia Fernández for Spanish were favourable about the level of mother-tongue education achieved in the Foyer projects (Danesi, 1990; Fernández de Rota y Monter & Pilar Irimia Fernández, 1990). Of course, levels attained were lower than those achieved by comparable native speakers in the region of origin, but they were very high in comparison with those generally achieved in intercultural projects.

In his concluding remarks Danesi, studying the Italian projects, noted that the Foyer Project 'constitutes a solid case in favour of additive models of education' (Danesi, 1990). The evaluation of the level of acquisition of linguistic skills in Spanish, based on a series of tests of 'Evaluation of Minimal Education' developed by the Service for Evaluation and Renewal in Education of the Spanish Ministry of National Education, and comparing the Spanish pupils of the Foyer Project with their contemporaries in Spain, concluded that 'in many cases, [they] have achieved good mastery of Spanish' (Fernández de Rota y Monter & Pilar Irimia Fernández, 1990).

Dutch and French

The major criterion for an evaluation of the success of the specific curriculum in the bicultural projects for the target-group children, however, is not the degree of mastery of the mother tongue but the extent to which, at the end of primary school, they are able to succeed in secondary education.

The projects are considered successful if the distribution of children in secondary schools over general, technical, and vocational programmes is the same, and certainly not less favourable, than for Belgian children. In view of the nature of primary education, this means that the knowledge of Dutch must be clearly acceptable.

Annual tests at the end of the sixth or last year of primary school show that the knowledge of Dutch among the other-language target-group children in the bicultural programme is somewhat lower than the knowledge of Dutch of children from Dutch-speaking families but just as good as other-language Belgian children in the same schools who have not participated in a bicultural programme but who were educated completely in an assimilation curriculum.

Additional criteria for rating the success of the bicultural programme are the social and mental maturity achieved by the target-group children and their degree of feeling at ease at school. The target-group children score very positively in these respects.

The additional language that the children have to master well in the Brussels context is French. For most of them, this is the language of the street and also the language from which very many elements are taken up in their language of primary socialisation.

For the school, this comes down to allowing the children to evolve here, too, on their own level so that they are taught French in a more advanced manner than are the children from Dutch-speaking families, and in a way adapted to their particular situation.

A separate discussion should be devoted to questions of harmonisation of methodological and didactic approaches by the teachers who come in contact with the children in the different languages. Important here, too, is that there be unity of school management for all the teachers alike.

The Intercultural Dimension

It would, of course, be fascinating in itself to investigate what being bicultural means for the children involved (Byram, 1991: 131–71). Although the Foyer projects contain elements of bicultural education, one could not call them strictly bicultural. They are more complex and also clearly have elements of intercultural education.

For the development of an intercultural dimension, the place occupied by the peer group (Fernández de Rota y Monter & Pilar Irimia Fernández, 1991), by the teachers, and by the parents (Marchi, 1991) is very important. The content of the textbooks is also not a mere detail to be ignored. At all times, attention must be given to the 'hidden' and the 'planned' curriculum that the minority and the indigenous children both have to go through.

For the development of an intercultural perspective, Foyer has divided the curriculum into five categories: language use, the strictly academic courses (mathematics and sciences), the world orientation courses (history, geography, religion, and ethics), physical education and the more artistic courses.

As regards languages, Foyer takes the position of Camilleri, who has observed that,

'language segments and interprets reality in accordance with a group's conceptual profile, needs and interests, according to the cultural models which govern them. Also, as the privileged medium of communication, it distributes these models in space from group member to group member. Finally, it is the main support of cultural reproduction through time' (Camilleri, 1986: 132).

For the conservation of minority languages, however, it is assumed that the societal context outside the school, i.e. language homogeneity and social status of the minority language, will be largely determinant over the long term.

The more strictly academic courses seem to lend themselves less to an intercultural orientation on the level of the planned curriculum, but the world-orientation courses do this in a more obvious way. Artistic and other courses that imply a more emotional impact offer a special opportunity of emotional growth in an intercultural perspective.

In the Foyer project, in practice the trend has developed to achieve the intercultural orientation by means of an adequate allocation of elements from the five areas (Leman, 1991a): the programming of languages; a restricted link between the strictly academic courses and mother-tongue education, because of the hidden curriculum (in the first grade); an opening of the world-orientation course in an intercultural perspective, but not limited to the cultures of the children present in the class, and with care that no confusion is created in the children; and, finally, a certain attention to emotional and artistic enrichment via elements of several cultures.

As already noted, it is enormously important to involve all the parents in the school events as much as possible. It is also essential for the minority-group teachers to be seen as full-fledged colleagues of the teaching team, with the same rights and obligations as their indigenous colleagues. On this last point Foyer projects are strong from the organisational perspective. As for parent involvement, Flemish-Brussels education is at present rather weak, and, in practice, most of the collaboration is done with the parents of the immigrant children, and then under the auspices of the Foyer and with the assistance of some immigrant organisations (Cittadinanza Migrante and Dar al Amal).

What those involved in the Foyer Projects have learned above all is that intercultural education, for it to be successful, must not be seen essentially as remedial education or as education that is given in lower-quality schools. It is important in a situation like that of Brussels, and presumably elsewhere, that the monocultural perspective must actually be understood as demonstrably less adequate than the intercultural one and that it be experienced as such by both parents and teachers. As long as this is not the case and as long as the mainstream of the people involved in the school are satisfied with the monocultural perspective for moving efficiently in society, intercultural education will, *de facto*, be predominantly associated with education in more difficult circumstances because of the sociological composition of the school community. This does not contribute to the promotion of the concept of interculturalism.

If education must assist individuals to develop personally, to prepare for a trade, and to prepare to integrate into society, then the intercultural perspective must see to it that demonstrable added value is offered in these three areas. In Brussels, and certainly elsewhere in Europe, this is becoming increasingly the case. Indeed, some European Schools, although they target a higher class, have already completely adopted this perspective (Baetens Beardsmore, this volume).

If Belgium intends to test conceptual and action programmes for the cultural and political future of a Europe that respects cultural identities (Leman, 1989: 163–68), then the educational systems of Brussels in particular will have to make this challenge their own.

Some General Conclusions

There are undoubtedly a number of facets that make the projects in the ten Brussels schools successful on very specific grounds and that prevent us from drawing generalised conclusions. Nevertheless, the route the projects have travelled does permit us to derive a number of orientations that can be generalised.

It seems clear that a multilingual societal context, within which bicultural and multilingual programmes are situated, is an important factor for the amount of time assigned to the various languages in a curriculum. It is also important how the elites of certain communities— and not in the least the socially advancing groups—position themselves socially, culturally, and linguistically.

If bilingualism and biculturalism are solidly built into the global curriculum, if the teachers who teach in the programmes are not inferior as regards quality and legal status to their colleagues, and if they are well integrated into the team, then there is no reason why bilingualism and biculturalism should turn out to the disadvantage of pupils. On the contrary, indications point rather in the direction of equivalent linguistic skills in the dominant educational language and greater self-acceptance and more group related (and thus more general) motivation among the minority children (Jaspaert & Lemmens, 1990; Danesi, 1990 and 1991). Competent bilingualism even increases the social resources one can draw upon.

The languages and cultures involved in the programmes, however, must enjoy a sufficiently high social status, at least in the eyes of the minority group itself but, in time, also in the eyes of society as a whole.

Working with the parents has been an important factor for success in each of the ten schools (Marchi, 1991).

Finally, in each of the ten schools it has appeared that the concrete starting up and implementation of a project requires time and effort. One even has the impression that the same programmes, had they been started up immediately in the ten schools on a large scale and without the necessary preparation, would have had far less chance of success. It can probably be concluded from this that excessively large scale schemes, without preliminary concern for very careful start up and implementation, would lose half of their efficiency from the very outset.

References

BAETENS BEARDSMORE, H. and VAN BEECK, H. 1984, Multilingual television supply and language shift in Brussels. *International Journal of the Sociology of Language* 48, 65–79.

BYRAM, M. 1991, Biculturalisme: l'enfant et l'école. In J. LEMAN (ed.) *Intégrité, intégration. Innovation pédagogique et pluralité culturelle*. Brussels: De Boeck Wesmael, 131–71.

BYRAM, M. and LEMAN, J. (eds) 1990, *Bicultural and Trilingual Education. The Foyer Model in Brussels*. Clevedon–Philadelphia: Multilingual Matters.

CAMILLERI, C. 1986, *Cultural Anthropology and Education*. Paris: Kogan Page— Unesco.

DANESI, M. 1988a, *A Report on a Trilingual Education Project in Belgium*. Toronto: Heritage Language Bulletin.

— 1988b, *Bilingual and Trilingual Educational Programs in Canada and Belgium Involving Italian as the Mother Tongue*. Rome: Studi Emigrazione, 25, 83–96.

— 1990, Mother-tongue literacy and the 'shaping' of knowledge: The experience of Italian children. In M. BYRAM & J. LEMAN (eds) *Bicultural and Trilingual Education. The Foyer Model in Brussels*. Clevedon: Multilingual Matters, 64–76.

— 1991, Préservation de la langue maternelle par l'école et cohésion interculturelle: Étude d'un cas canadien et d'un cas belge. In J. LEMAN (ed.) *Intégrité, intégration. Innovation pédagogique et pluralité culturelle*. Brussels: De Boeck Wesmael, 173–86.

FERNÁNDEZ DE ROTA, J.A. and M. DEL PILAR IRMIA FERNÁNDEZ 1990, Linguistic correction and semantic skills in Spanish children. In M. BYRAM and J. LEMAN (eds), *Bicultural and Trilingual Education. The Foyer Model in Brussels*. Clevedon: Multilingual Matters, 95–114.
— 1991, Identités et culture dans l'expérience 'Foyer' pour élèves espagnols. In J. LEMAN (ed.), *Intégrité, intégration. Innovation pédagogique et pluralité culturelle*. Brussels: De Boeck-Wesmael, 65–109.
GLAZER, N. 1987, Les différences culturelles et l'égalité des résultats scolaires. In X.X. (CERI), *L'éducation multiculturelle*. Paris: OCDE.
JASPAERT, K. and G. LEMMENS 1990, Linguistic evaluation of Dutch as a third language. In M. BYRAM and J. LEMAN (eds), *Bicultural and Trilingual Education. The Foyer Model in Brussels*. Clevedon: Multilingual Matters, 30–56.
LEMAN, J. 1985, The Foyer project: A Brussels model of bicultural education in a trilingual situation. *Studi Emigrazione* Rome, 22, 78, 254–66.
— 1987a, *From Challenging Culture to Challenged Culture*. Leuven: University Press.
— 1987b, Hijos de emigrantes italianos en el proyecto bicultural de una escuela neerlandófona en Bruselas: Tres lenguajes, dos culturas y sus interrelaciones. In J.A. FERNÁNDEZ DE ROTA Y MONTER (ed.) *Lengua y cultura. Aproximacion desde una semantica antropologica*. Sada—A. Coruña, do Castro, 199–215.
— 1988, *La fine di un mito antropologico*. San Caltaldo, Argomenti, 11, 7–13.
— 1989, Quelques réflexions anthropologiques au sujet de la belgitude et de la crise de l'Etat belge. In H. DUMONT *et al. Belgitude et crise de l'Etat belge*. Brussels: Fac. univ. St.-Louis, 163–68.
— 1990, Multilingualism as norm, monolingualism as exception: The Foyer Model in Brussels. In M. BYRAM and J. LEMAN (eds) *Bicultural and Trilingual Education. The Foyer Model in Brussels*. Clevedon: Multilingual Matters, 7–29.
— (ed.) 1991a, Intégrité, intégration. *Innovation pédagogique et pluralité culturelle*. Brussels: De Boeck Wesmael.
— 1991b, Between bi- and intercultural education: Projects in Dutch-language kindergartens and primary schools in Brussels. In K. JASPAERT and S. KROON (eds) *Ethnic Minority Languages and Education*. Amsterdam: Swets & Zeitlinger, 123–34.
— 1991c, The education of immigrant children in Belgium. *Anthropology and Education Quarterly* American Anthropological Association, 22, 2, 140–53.
MARCHI, L. 1991, Faisons aussi jouer l'interculturel aux parents! In J. LEMAN (ed.) *Intégrité, intégration. Innovation pédagogique et pluralité culturelle*. Brussels: De Boeck Wesmael, 199–207.
PAULSTON, C.B. 1987, Conséquences linguistiques de l'ethnicité et du nationalisme dans des contextes plurilingues. In X.X. (CERI) *L'éducation multiculturelle*. Paris: OCDE.
ROOSENS, E. 1991, Migration et interculturalisme. In J. LEMAN (ed.) *Intégrité, intégration. Innovation pédagogique et pluralité culturelle*. Brussels: De Boeck Wesmael, 17–46.
SPOELDERS, M. 1985, Psycho-educational language assessment in the Brussels bicultural education project. *Review of Applied Linguistics*. Leuven, ITL, 67–8, 201–16.

WITTE, E. and BAETENS BEARDSMORE, H. (eds) 1987, *The Interdisciplinary Study of Urban Bilingualism in Brussels*. Clevedon–Philadelphia: Multilingual Matters.

6 Trilingual Education in the Grand Duchy of Luxembourg[1]

NATHALIE LEBRUN & HUGO BAETENS
BEARDSMORE

Introduction

The Grand Duchy of Luxembourg, a country of 1000 square kilometres in size, with a population of 364,602 inhabitants (1981 census) represents a unique example of a western nation where the entire school population is put through a trilingual education system. This situation constitutes a prime counter example to certain assumptions relating multilingualism to notions of under-development, inadequate educational achievement, compensatory or remedial educational strategies, problematic relationships between majority and minority languages and delicate language planning issues.

Luxembourg has had a GNP increase of 3% per annum since 1980, inflation at 1.4% and unemployment at a record low (for Europe) 1.6% in 1989 (*Newsweek*, 10 April, 1989). The country has been independent since 1839 but has undergone considerable influence from its powerful neighbours, primarily Germany and France, and forms a monetary union with Belgium, though it has an independent fiscal and economic policy within the EEC.

Linguistic Background

The Grand Duchy has an indigenous population that is almost 100% trilingual. The languages spoken by its inhabitants are Luxemburger (Letzeburgesch), German and French. Approximately 26% of the population consists of non-native immigrants who have little or no knowledge of Luxemburger and in the capital foreigners form 38% of the inhabitants, with high concentrations of Italian and Portuguese immigrants.

The Luxemburger is by birth monolingual in Luxemburger and becomes trilingual through education. Knowledge of three languages is determined by several factors, primarily the small size of the country. Luxemburger is the symbol of national identity and in 1938 naturalisation was made dependent on its knowledge. It was made a compulsory subject in elementary schools in 1912, with an official spelling and textbook, and was declared the national language in 1983, although its use remains optional. The Constitution states that citizens may address the authorities in Luxemburger, French or German and should receive responses in the language of the citizen's choice, where possible.

French and German are developed as languages of wider impact, due to the need to develop close ties with the neighbouring countries of France, Germany and Belgium, and because of the country's cosmopolitan aspect, particularly the capital, Luxembourg City, which is the seat of several European institutions and a major banking and finance centre rivalling Switzerland.

The celebration of the Grand Duchy's 150 years of independence in 1989 clearly revealed that the indigenous language represents what Smolicz (1979) has termed a 'core value' of culture and national identity. This was stressed in speeches by the Prime Minister to celebrate the event (*L'Avenir du Luxembourg*), as the language is the only symbol to distinguish the citizens from its neighbours, and it has served particularly as a defence from repeated invasion and threats of absorption by Germany. The national motto also reflects the desire to maintain a distinct national identity, in spite of trilingual speech modes; 'Mir welle bleiwe wat mir sin' (We wish to remain what we are).

Luxemburger is a Germanic language related to Low German. To some people it is a dialect, given its lack of standardisation and codification, with regional variants and only a limited written tradition. It comprises many loanwords from German and French and lacks standardised vocabulary for technologically modern concepts, since it is primarily a rural form of speech. The scope of the language is limited, its syntax elementary, with few subordinate clauses, restricted tense, mood and case variations.

Given the nature of the language it is difficult to define clearly the status of Luxemburger. According to Siguan & Mackey (1987) it could be classified as a 'partially standardised language', while according to

Spolsky (1977: 6) it fits the description of a 'local vernacular' in that it 'tends to be unstandardised and to lack vocabulary and possible styles to handle significant areas of technology in modern life'. Fishman (1976: 75) refers to Luxemburger as a 'neglected minority mother tongue', partially because it fits into a group of countries characterised by 'very faint if present at all rumblings of recognition for minority mother tongues (in bilingual education)'.

The problem here lies with what is meant by 'recognition'. Although the language is only taught for 125 hours of the school curriculum it nevertheless represents the vehicular language for communication by all social categories and is used at all levels of the educational process when speakers find themselves at a loss in the other two languages in the curriculum. The reason why the language is not promoted further is determined by the language community's small size, together with the lack of tension between the three languages in contact, since there is general consensus on the advantages of possessing three languages.

A 1983 survey (published in 1986 *Enquête sur les habitudes et besoins langagiers au Grand-Duché de Luxembourg*) showed that Luxemburger is the language most frequently used for oral exchanges in private life, as claimed by 71% of the sample, but only 53% of respondents claimed to use Luxemburger exclusively when talking to close relatives or friends. The survey also revealed how all three languages, Luxemburger, French and German, are used by the inhabitants in their private lives in different ways. In oral communication the order of preference was Luxemburger, French, German, while in written private communications the order of frequency of use was German, French and Luxemburger. In official and public life the order of languages is somewhat different. Parliamentary debates, for example, may be conducted in any of the three languages, though occur predominantly in French or Luxemburger, but are printed in German and distributed free of charge to every householder in the country. On the other hand, government texts are published in French.

More than 50% of the population always use French when writing to administrations or businesses, but in oral communications with such bodies 62% use Luxemburger, 20% prefer French, while 18% use German.

The two national newspapers publish predominantly in German but are in fact bilingual with French material and occasional texts in Luxemburger. Television is available in French or German on the national channels (with 2 hours on a Sunday afternoon in Luxemburger), and from across the borders in French from Belgium and France, and in German from Germany.

The use of Luxemburger is not restricted to lower-level social groups but is used by all classes, though the higher the social level the more French may occur, due to the education process. Hence Luxemburger cuts across all social groups for usage, whereas the class division or rural/urban division is more likely to be reflected in quantity of use of German versus French.

Languages in the Education System

Trilingualism is achieved via the education system, which is a complex, long-term process, showing similarities with the Canadian immersion phenomenon, which it pre-dated, but with specific characteristics which involve the three languages across the entire curriculum.

Compulsory education consists of nursery school at the age of 5, primary education from 6 to 11 and secondary education from 12 to the age of 15, with voluntary further education subsequently. Secondary education is of three types, general, technical and complementary, the latter for pupils with little desire to pursue studies beyond the legal minimum number of years.

In nursery schools and the first years of primary education Luxemburger is used as the medium of instruction. In primary school Luxemburger is progressively replaced by German and by the end of grade 6 the transition to the almost exclusive use of German must be completed. German is taught as a subject in grade 1 of primary school, while in the second semester of grade 2 French is introduced as a subject.

The process of language switch operates on the principle of introducing the child to schooling in the home L1, followed by a related, but distinct L2 as a subject, but not a medium of instruction in grade 1, prior to a rapid elimination of the L1 in favour of the related L2 as a medium of instruction. Note that the Luxembourg system differs from Canadian early total immersion by laying the foundations of education in the child's L1. It also differs from Canadian early partial immersion, where the L1 likewise forms the language of the introduction to schooling, in that in Luxembourg the L2 is introduced as a subject prior to being used as a medium, whereas in Canadian early partial immersion the L2 is used as a medium when it is introduced, without any focus on the language as a subject. Moreover, in the Luxembourg system all three languages involved will be the focus of attention as a subject in parallel to their being used as a medium of instruction, which may well have implications for the quality of the outcome in terms of productive accuracy. A further difference with the Canadian programmes is that the L3, French, is introduced as a subject from the second grade of primary school in an extended preparation for the transition to its being used as the medium of instruction in secondary education.

In secondary education most classes are taught through the medium of German in the first three grades, except for French as a subject, and mathematics, which are now taught through the medium of French. Pupils who follow the less demanding 'complementary education' programme, which ends after the first three grades, have a less well-developed knowledge of French than those in the normal and technical secondary programmes. (In 1985–86 almost 53% of children in 'complementary education' were foreigners). In the other secondary programmes French replaces German as the medium of instruction from the fourth grade, while German remains taught as a subject in language and literature classes.

This complex system results in a working knowledge of three languages for the entire population. Proficiency in French depends on the length of time pupils stay on in school, those progressing into the higher classes having a better knowledge of French than those who leave younger.

Moreover, the level of proficiency in French may also be influenced by other factors, the most important being geographical location, since in the areas nearest to the German border German is used with greater prevalence than in the capital, Luxemburg City, or the southern areas bordering on France, where French knowledge and use appear to be higher.

The large concentration of foreign immigrants in certain regions of the country poses particular problems to the trilingual education system. In the canton of Luxemburg City, almost 59% of children in nursery schools are foreign immigrants who do not have Luxemburger as the home background language, while in some nursery schools the percentage may reach 87% of all children enrolled (1985, *Bildung und Migration in Luxembourg*). To cater for the heterogeneous population of immigrants nursery school teachers find themselves teaching Luxemburger to aid integration into the primary school network, with mitigated results. Special reception classes have been created for foreign children of school age who cannot follow the normal school programme because of lack of knowledge of Luxemburger. Foreign children may not stay in these special classes for more than one year, at the end of which they should be inserted in the normal school programme. In these reception classes efforts concentrate on learning either German or French sufficiently well for children to express themselves in the language.

If we attempt to classify Luxembourg's education system along the frame of reference developed by Fishman (1976) we must take into account the unique trilingual nature of the programme, together with the special status of Luxemburger, as a partially standardised national language. Fishman talks of 'monoliterate bilingualism' where literacy is only developed in the L2, but oral skills are developed in both languages involved. The school programme in the Grand Duchy develops biliterate trilingualism but even so does not clearly fit into Fishman's categorisation. In the monoliterate bilingual case literacy is developed in the majority language of the outside environment while oral skills are used in the minority language as well as the wider out-of-school language. Such programmes represent an intermediate between language maintenance and language shift policies. In Luxembourg, however, the L1 is a majority language since it is the common language used by the entire population. Moreover, although literacy skills are developed in German and French, there is a transfer of literacy from German to Luxemburger, facilitated by the genetic relationship between the two languages. Hence the programme subsumes Cummins' (1984) interdependence hypothesis as well as his common underlying proficiency hypothesis which accounts for successful transfer from one language to another in literacy skills, as happens in Canadian immersion programmes (Swain & Lapkin, 1982). Again, the peculiar status of Luxemburger accounts for this possibility. It is the dearth of printed matter in the L1 and the genetic relationship between Luxemburger and German which makes it unnecessary to develop literacy in Luxemburger, yet easy to transfer German literacy skills as the need arises.

According to Fishman most bilingual education programmes are said to promote one of three options; language maintenance (in the case of small and threatened languages), transition to a different language (in the case of temporary bilingual provision till proficiency in the second language is considered adequate) or of the enrichment type (when a second language is added to the curriculum but at no cost to development of the first language). In Luxembourg the education system is a combination of all three. Although Luxemburger is rapidly eliminated from the curriculum the system does not lead to language shift. On the other hand it clearly operates on a transitional basis by the stepwise nature of the introduction and replacement of each language as pupils get older. Further, the programme represents an enrichment type in that both oral and literacy skills in the L2 and L3 are pushed to their maximum capacity so as to become complete vehicles for further education if necessary, and for full usage in all aspects of professional life. Hence the programme in Luxembourg is an enrichment programme, though of an unusual type in that it involves three languages.

The Trilingual Programme

A more detailed breakdown of the education system and the role which different languages play will reveal how the transition from the L1 home language, through a distinct but related L2 (German), to a non-related, distinct L3 (French) operates (ignoring the immigrant population).

In nursery school Luxemburger is the sole medium of instruction. The same is true for the early years of primary education, though by the age of 12 the transition to German as a medium of instruction must be completed, in preparation for entry to secondary education. In primary school approximately one third of the time-table (11–12 lessons out of 27) are devoted to the study of languages as a subject, Luxemburger, German and French, though it is impossible to calculate accurately the percentage of time taken up by each language as a medium of instruction, due to individual variations within the classroom according to each teacher's perceptions of comprehension, use of code-switching and personal preferences. All that can be stated is that Luxemburger is the sole language used in the first two grades, but that by the final grade German will predominate in its role as official medium, while French figures only as a subject and is not used as a medium. Introduction to reading and writing takes place in German, given the non-codified nature of Luxemburger. In this respect there is a similarity with Canadian immersion practice, where literacy also begins in the L2, though in Luxembourg the distance between the L1 and the L2 is not as great as that between French and English in immersion programmes.

In order to appreciate the progressive nature of the switch of languages in the secondary programme it is necessary to examine the proportions of time devoted to each language, both as a subject and as a medium of instruction, according to the grade and the nature of the study cycle, standard or technical.

Whatever options are taken pupils will devote at least one fifth of

TABLE 6.1 *Time per language as a subject in the primary curriculum, expressed in percentages*

	Grade					
	1	*2*	*3*	*4*	*5*	*6*
Luxemburger	—	—	1.7	1.6	1.6	1.6
German	19.2	27.7	13.6	15.1	15.1	14.8
French	—	5	23.9	23.5	25.2	23.1

TABLE 6.2 *Amount of time in the secondary standard curriculum devoted to each language expressed in percentages*

Subject	Grades						
	1	*2*	*3*	*4*	*5*	*6*	*7*
Lux. subject	3%	—	—	—	—	—	—
Lux. medium	—	—	—	—	—	—	—
Fr. subject	20%	20%	15%	13–16%	10–16%	10–16%	0–17%
Fr. medium	13%	10–30%	26%	40–60%	40–66%	43–70%	38–83%
Ger. subject	13%	13%	10%	10–13%	10–13%	10%	0–17%
Ger. medium	50%	36%	36%	0–13%	0–13%	0–20%	0–27%
Other langs.	May use French, German or the target language.						

Note: The variation in percentages depend on the options taken by pupils.

their time in school to the study of languages. Up to the end of the third grade about 50% of the courses use German as a medium, whereas from the fifth grade onwards 80–90% of the courses will be taught through the medium of French.

Of all pupils who completed the standard secondary programme in the school year 1985–1986, 70% succeeded in final examinations leading to higher education (*Statistiques*, 1985–1986).

In the complex linguistic programme found in Luxembourg it is interesting to note that the textbooks and manuals are not generally specifically designed for the system but tend to be imported from neighbouring countries. Manuals used are in the language which serves as

TABLE 6.3 *Number of contact hours per language for the entire curriculum*

Subject	Primary	Secondary	Total
Luxemburger subject	72	54	126
Luxemburger medium	?	—	?
French subject	1080	954–1350	2034–2430
French medium	—	2106–3744	2106–3744
German subject	1224	720–990	1944–2214
German medium	?	1331–2159	?

Note: ? indicates it has not been possible to calculate the amount of time German and Luxemburger have been used as a medium of instruction.

the medium of instruction; for example in grade 2 of the secondary programme, where biology is taught through German, the manual is *Biologie Heute* (Hannover), whereas in grade 6, where the medium is French the same course is based on the manual *Hygiène et biologie humaines* (Paris). Some schools may use books specially designed in Luxembourg for teaching French as a subject in the early grades, but not necessarily all.

Since Luxembourg does not have any universities of its own (though there is a university centre providing certain higher education facilities), all degrees are obtained abroad. Most students select a university in Belgium, France or Germany. All teachers of languages as a subject must obtain their qualifications in a country where the language is used by native speakers, so that a teacher of English must obtain the degree in Britain, a teacher of German in Germany. This has significance for the quality of the language teachers' competence in their subject.

The above description has tried to outline, in simplified form, the major characteristics of the trilingual education system prevailing in the Grand Duchy of Luxembourg. Details of the differences between technical and classical education have not been gone into since they are not significant for an understanding of the system. What is more important at this stage is an appreciation of the outcome, the results produced by the programme. These will be gone into below, based on an investigation carried out in 1988–1989 to appraise the knowledge of French attained.

The Investigation

A series of tests were carried out in four schools, located in different parts of the country, where tests were given to 13+ year olds, in order to discover proficiency in French. Several factors determined the nature of this investigation.

For any valid statements to be made it was necessary to make some comparison. On the assumption that bilingualism should not be compared with unilingualism (Baetens Beardsmore, 1986; Romaine, 1989) but should be looked at in its own right, and along criteria specific to the bilingual nature of the population in question, comparisons were made with other populations undergoing a form of bilingual education, but in a different context and under a different system. In the present context the comparison was made with the Canadian immersion experience on the one hand and multilingual education as provided by the 'European School' network on the other (see Chapter 7 this volume).

Given that the Canadian immersion model is the best documented, and with the most substantive research behind it, it was decided to use tests that had been developed for measuring English speaking pupils' proficiency in French after several years in an immersion programme. The tests had also been previously employed in a comparative analysis between immersion pupils and children in the network of European Schools where again a different bilingual system of education is in operation (cf. Baetens Beardsmore & Swain, 1985).

13+ year olds were selected for two reasons. First, the Canadian tests had been specifically designed for this age group and second, 13 represents a turning point in linguistic development both in the Luxembourg system and the European School network, when French becomes a significant vehicle of instruction and becomes cognitively demanding and context-reduced (Cummins, 1984) whereas previously the language had functioned mainly in cognitively undemanding and context-embedded circumstances.

Before analysing the investigation, however, it is necessary to be aware of the goals set for the teaching of French in Luxembourg. Official documents from the Luxembourg ministry of education stress that oral communication is an end in itself and this must not be considered as a preparation for written expression. From the third grade of primary school onwards, when French gets introduced, about 50% of the time is devoted to the teaching of oral expression and reading. Throughout the programme of both primary and secondary education oral proficiency must be stressed and to achieve this goal the number of pupils per class should not exceed 20, though this ideal is sometimes augmented if numbers are not sufficient to warrant two parallel classes. In the French as a subject lessons after the 3rd grade of secondary school the study of grammar is replaced by the study of literature.

The investigation in Luxembourg covers 14% of the total secondary school population in the second grade, 179 pupils in all. Four locations were chosen for specific reasons. One school in the capital was selected since this was the most prestigious school of all and drew its population from a cosmopolitan environment due to the international status of the city. This probably leads to a greater awareness of the need for several languages and ample opportunity to use French outside school. The second school was in Esch sur Alzette in the south of the country near the French border. This is an industrial town centred on the steel industry with a high percentage of foreigners in the school system. The socio-economic status of the pupils being lower than in Luxemburg City, the presence of many foreigners in the classes tested, and the proximity of France only a few kilometres away, all combined to make this population significantly different from that in the capital. The third school was at Diekirch in the north of the country and has a large agricultural catchment area less strongly influenced by an immediate out-of-school French environment. The fourth school was in Echternach, which is separated from Germany by a river representing the international frontier. This school undergoes the least French influence from the outside environment and is more likely to be strongly influenced by German.

The tests administered had been designed by the Ontario Institute for Studies in Education, the purpose of which was:

> to identify a number of real-life situations in which immersion students might have contact with French speakers, and to measure their understanding of the French used in each situation. (Swain & Lapkin, 1982)

Three tests were used, together with a questionnaire, based on similar questionnaires used both in Canada and in the European Schools, but with modifications to take into account the trilingual nature of the Luxembourg set-up.

The first test was a 22 item multiple-choice test of written comprehension based on authentic extracts such as newspaper and magazine articles and advertisements, horoscopes, television programmes, recipes, poetry and prose fiction.

The second test was a 22 item multiple-choice test of auditory comprehension based on recordings of Canadian broadcasts, including news, sports items, weather forecasts, advertisements, radio drama, chat shows and phone-in shows.

The third test was a cloze test designed to measure global language knowledge.

All tests contained a cultural bias in favour of the Canadians and against the Luxembourg population, in content, which was specifically Canadian, in certain lexical and syntactic structures, and for the auditory comprehension test, in accent. These points should be borne in mind in interpreting the results since it is unlikely that the Luxembourg pupils had ever been confronted with precisely the type of French present in the Canadian materials. On the other hand, since this Canadian cultural bias had not adversely affected results in the previous comparative test with European School children it was not considered a sufficiently disturbing factor in Luxembourg.

The tests were accompanied by a detailed questionnaire aimed at discovering the language background and habits of pupils and their parents, their attitudes towards the different languages, preferences for language of instruction and use of the three languages inside and outside school. The questionnaire was conducted in French.

Results

Results obtained on the three tests were remarkably close to both Canadian and European School results. The remarkable similarity in

TABLE 6.4 *Achievement scores on three standardised tests for Luxembourg (Lux.), European School (ES) and Canadian Pupils*

	Lux. N=179	Stand. dev.	ES N=80	Stand. dev.	Canada N=80	Stand. dev.
Total classroom contact hours	1,450	—	1,325	—	4,450	—
Written comprehension max. = 22	15.26	3.4	15.6	2.9	14.6	4.2
Auditory comprehension max. = 22	14.84	3.5	17.7	3	14.9	3.7
Cloze max. = 41	21.3	4.3	21.95	4.8	19.9	4.3

scores between the three populations (with a non-significant advantage to the Luxemburgers and European School pupils) can only be explained by reference to responses on the questionnaires provided. Both the Luxemburgers and the European School pupils revealed that the multilingual context in which they evolved outside school, and their use of the target language outside the classroom, differed considerably from circumstances in Canada. These differences appeared significant in explaining the similar scores, in spite of considerably fewer classroom contact hours with French and a complex education system for the non-Canadians, involving not two, but three languages.

If we compare the Canadian situation with that in Luxembourg the major points that distinguish the two populations are as follows. In Luxembourg the parents' knowledge of French constitutes an important background feature; since the majority of parents also have recourse to French in some aspects of their lives, unlike the Canadian parents who are primarily Anglophones with little knowledge of French, this might well represent an incentive and add to the naturalness of the process of acquiring the language. According to the responses, 70% of fathers and 68% of mothers were fluent speakers of French in Luxembourg. It should also be borne in mind that learning French is a compulsory part of Luxembourg's trilingual education system, whereas immersion in Canada is on a voluntary basis. A similar factor appeared with the European School where 63% of the fathers and 57% of the mothers were said to be fluent in French.

A second major difference is the self-initiated use of French, both inside and outside school. In Canada relatively few pupils have the opportunity to use French outside school, and apart from inside the classroom, few initiate exchanges in French amongst peers, since all pupils involved are Anglophones. Now in Luxembourg similar conditions prevail, since all pupils are Luxemburgers with Luxemburger as a first language and there is no necessity to use French outside school. Hence there is no absolute external pressure to interact in French outside the Luxembourg classroom, and indeed 65% of pupils claimed they never used French spontaneously at school outside the classroom, 64% never used it with relatives, and 54% claimed never to use it with friends outside school. On the other hand, the trilingual nature of the whole population and the environment where French naturally occurs in interaction probably makes its use less unnatural with peers or others than in Canada. In Luxembourg 93% claimed they use French at least sometimes outside school and only 10% claimed they never used it in shops. Similar trends were found with the European School population (Baetens Beardsmore & Swain, 1985: 12).

Canadian pupils indicated that their use of French media, newspapers, radio and television, was minimal, whereas this was definitely not the case in Luxembourg. This can be accounted for by the fact that there is little media provision in Luxemburger, though there is ample in German as well as in French, whereas in Canada, although there is readily available media provision in French this appears not to be taken up. 53% of the Luxembourg pupils claimed they sometimes read newspapers and magazines in French, while 19% claimed they often did, though scores were lower in the towns located in the more 'German' areas of the country. With the European School pupils 37% claimed to read newspapers and magazines in French and 35% claimed to watch French television for more than six hours per week.

If one examined results for the Grand Duchy according to the location of the schools, significant differences were found on test results and responses to the questionnaire which reflected differences in population make-up, setting, attitudes and self-initiated use of French.

Pupils were asked what their ideal school programme would consist of in terms of languages and in all four towns the majority gave preference to a curriculum in which a third of the time was devoted to the medium of each language equally.

Interpreting the responses to the questionnaires for the four towns leads to the following analysis of positive, neutral and negative effects which may account for the differing results obtained in the pupils' third school language, French. A factor has been called neutral if it does not contrast with responses provided by pupils in a different town and cannot therefore explain any difference in results.

Luxemburg City

Positive factors

Parents' high educational level.
Self-initiated use of French at home and school.

Neutral factors

Attitude towards French.
Use of French media.

TABLE 6.5 *Scores in the Grand Duchy by location*

Factor	Luxemburg N = 48	Esch N = 47	Diekirch N = 41	Echternach N = 43
Written comprehension (0/22)	17.2	15.6	14.5	14.4
Auditory comprehension (0/22)	16.7	15.3	14.2	12.8
Cloze (0/41)	24.6	19.5	19.6	21.5
Father with university degree	50%	17%	12%	19%
French used sometimes at home	25%	19%	12%	34%
French used sometimes at school in breaks	27%	40%	16%	31%
French used sometimes with friends outside school	35%	27%	23%	36%
French used sometimes in shops, etc.	37%	29%	12%	27%
French given too much school time	21%	30%	46%	19%

Negative factors

None.

Esch sur Alzette

Positive factors

Self-initiated use of French at school and outside (probably due to the large number of foreigners who use French as a lingua franca).
Positive attitude towards French.
Use of French media.

Neutral factors

Use of French at home.

Negative factors

Low level of education of parents.

Diekirch

Positive factors

None.

Neutral factors

Self-initiated use of French at home and school.
Use of media.

Negative factors

Little use of French outside school (probably due to the location).
Parents with low educational status.
Slightly negative attitudes towards French.

Echternach

Positive factors

Attitude towards French.

Neutral factors

Use of French media.
Self-initiated use of French at school and home.
Parents' educational level.

Negative factors

Self-initiated use of French out of school (probably due to the location next to the German border).

Discussion

These findings lead one to turn to Fishman's (1977) analysis of the necessary prerequisites for a successful bilingual programme. In the model a distinction is made between four interrelated dichotomies which appear fundamental to the outcome of any bilingual programme. These are:

(a) language of primary emphasis (LPE) as opposed to language of secondary emphasis (LSE) in education;
(b) mother tongue versus other tongue;
(c) minor versus major language;
(d) language support via formal out-of-school institutions or not.

Upon examination, it appears that the Luxembourg case goes counter to the predictions formulated in the model of analysis proposed by Fishman.

(a) If the time devoted in school to one language is more important than that devoted to the other, that language has primary emphasis. In Luxembourg German is given primary emphasis in primary school while French is given primary emphasis in secondary education, while Luxemburger is given tertiary emphasis. Both French and German have primary or secondary status according to the pupils' ages.
(b) Since Luxemburger is the mother tongue both French and German represent other tongues.
(c) Luxemburger represents the minor language by whatever criteria it is assessed while French and German can be considered as equal major languages.
(d) Although all three languages have official recognition French has the highest status in out-of-school formal institutions, German is a near equal, while Luxemburger has the least status, but may oust the other languages even in parliamentary debates.

Fishman's argument is that success in LSE is largely dependent on LPE circumstances which are determined by a set of variables that cluster round the dichotomies presented above. An analysis was made of 60 cases of bilingual education and rated by 20 specialists for success in terms of the goals aimed at with respect to language education. However, the Luxembourg system does not fit into the theoretical framework predicting success, though the test results, university entrance passes and economic prosperity of the country clearly indicate that the programme works.

A variable considered as significant was whether full bilingualism is aimed at or not, with greater success when LPE and LSE goals are high. Since full bilingualism is the ultimate goal this variable can be considered as influencing the positive results, though LPE and LSE fluctuate over time in the curriculum. Moreover, there is no negative effect on Luxemburger, the language of tertiary emphasis.

Admission selectivity was considered as significant in determining success in bilingual education, but since trilingual education is compulsory in the Grand Duchy this criterion cannot affect the positive outcome.

A variable said to influence success is the extent to which the languages involved are dependent on school instruction; success is said to be lower if LPE or LSE are school dependent 'School use of language is just not enough' (Fishman, 1977: 102). Both French and German are partially school-dependent, but also benefit from out-of-school functions. Luxemburger is not dependent on school instruction but on out-of-school social interaction, placing it in a similar position to many vernaculars in Africa which are not codified and absent from schooling.

A nationalist or sociopolitical sentiment with respect to the target languages was also felt to be a criterion for success. Although this may apply to Luxemburger, which plays a minimal role in the curriculum, it cannot be said to apply to German and French.

The variables proposed as predictive of success are useful criteria for analysing the context of a bilingual programme, even though the Luxembourg case goes counter to the ratings supplied by Fishman's judges. They do reveal, however, that the following criteria come to the fore as significant for Luxembourg.

(a) Both French and German are used in the country's formal institutions.
(b) Full bilingualism is the avowed goal of the system as far as French and German are concerned.
(c) The two languages have strong out-of-school support, both in the media and in formal and informal interaction.
(d) Luxemburger fulfils the nationalistic sentiment which leaves it unthreatened by the two other languages (and, unlike Irish which has a similar function in Eire, unaffected by pressures towards language shift).

What the Luxembourg case shows is that a three language policy in education can be successful if certain conditions are met. These appear to be a combination of curricular and extra-curricular elements, similar to those found in the European School system where equal success is present (Housen & Baetens Beardsmore, 1987), together with a long-term commitment in the programme to enhancing both language as a subject and language as a medium of instruction. This last point distinguishes the Luxembourg (and European Schools) from immersion programmes where there is far less emphasis on French as a subject. The Luxembourg case is also instructive for other countries grappling with issues of education through languages other than local vernaculars, as are prevalent in Africa, and societies promoting not two but three languages through education.

Notes to Chapter 6

This article is a modified version of one published under the same title and reprinted here with kind permission from *Bilingual Education, Focusschrift in Honor of Joshua A. Fishman*, edited by Ofelia García. Amsterdam, Philadelphia: John Benjamins Publishers, 1991, pp. 107–20.

References

BAETENS BEARDSMORE, H. 1986, *Bilingualism: Basic Principles*, 2nd edition, Clevedon–Philadelphia: Multilingual Matters.

BAETENS BEARDSMORE, H. and SWAIN, M. 1985, Designing bilingual education: Aspects of immersion and 'European School' models. *Journal of Multilingual and Multicultural Development* 6, 1, 1–15.

Bildung und Migration in Luxemburg (1. Teil: Vorschul- und Primärschulunterricht) 1985, Luxemburg: Ministère de l'Education Nationale et de la Jeunesse.

CUMMINS, J. 1984, *Bilingualism and Special Education: Issues in Assessment and Pedagogy*. Clevedon–Philadelphia: Multilingual Matters.

Enquête sur les habitudes et besoins langagiers au Grand-Duché de Luxembourg, 1986, Luxembourg: Ministère de l'Education Nationale et de la Jeunesse.

FISHMAN, J. 1976, *Bilingual Education: An International Sociological Perspective*. Rowley: Newbury House.

— 1977, The establishment of language education policy in multilingual societies. In B. SPOLSKY and R. COOPER (eds) *Frontiers of Bilingual Education*. Rowley: Newbury House, 94–106.

HOUSEN, A. and BAETENS BEARDSMORE, H. 1987, Curricular and extra-curricular factors in multilingual education. *Studies in Second Language Acquisition* 9, 1, 83–102.

L'Avenir du Luxembourg, 1988, No. 94, 7, '150 ans d'indépendance du Grand Duché du Luxembourg'.

Newsweek, 10/4/1989.

ROMAINE, S. 1989, *Bilingualism*. Oxford: Blackwell.

SIGUAN, M. and MACKEY, W. 1987, *Education and Bilingualism*. Paris: UNESCO.

SMOLICZ, J. 1979, *Culture and Education in a Plural Society*. Canberra: Curriculum Development Centre.

SPOLSKY, B. 1977, The establishment of language education policy in multilingual societies. In B. SPOLSKY and R. COOPER (eds), *Frontiers of Bilingual Education*. Rowley: Newbury House, 1–22.

Statistiques, Année Scolaire 1985–1986, Luxembourg: Ministère de l'Education Nationale et de la Jeunesse.

SWAIN, M. and LAPKIN, S. 1982, *Evaluating Bilingual Education: A Canadian Case Study*. Clevedon: Multilingual Matters.

7 The European School Model[1]

HUGO BAETENS BEARDSMORE

Structure

'European Schools' have been specifically designed as multicultural establishments, i.e. where more than two languages function as medium of instruction. These schools have officially existed since 1958 and have acquired a solid reputation for scholastic achievement, linguistic equity, multilingual proficiency among the pupils and the promotion of multicultural awareness.

European Schools form part of a network of 9 schools situated in 6 different countries (Brussels I and II, Mol, Munich, Culham, Varese, Karlsruhe and Bergen) and are attended by approximately 12,000 children. They were specifically designed to provide education for the children of civil servants working for one of the supra-national European institutions. The schools are collectively controlled by the education authorities of the 12 member states of the European Economic Community. Each school consists of different linguistic sub-sections in which everyone follows the same programme irrespective of the language of instruction. The largest European School (Brussels I) is in the Belgian capital and has about 3000 pupils ranging from kindergarten to the end of secondary education at age 18. At present the Brussels I European School contains 8 sub-sections covering all the official languages of the member states of the European Economic Community except Portuguese, namely, Danish, Dutch, English, French, German, Greek, Italian and Spanish. A Portuguese sub-section exists at the second European School in Brussels where there is no Spanish sub-section.

Priority of access is given to European civil servants' children, ranging from the offspring of cabinet ministers to those of porters and cleaning staff. The schools are under an obligation to admit non-civil servant children if space is available in order to avoid the formation of population ghettoes and to balance out the numbers in each linguistic sub-section where possible. One of the schools has a large number of immigrant steel-workers' children, another a large contingent of ex-miners' children. Education is free, except for the non-civil-servant children whose parents pay a very small, nominal contribution.

European Schools have a distinct philosophy as supra-national institutions which aims to reconcile two apparently contradictory goals. On the one hand they attempt to guarantee the development of the child's first language and cultural identity, while on the other they strive to promote a European identity through instruction for all pupils in at least 2 languages, compulsory learning of a 3rd as a subject and options regarding a 4th language. It is important to bear in mind that within Europe this European identity is not self-evident, and that national differences are keenly felt. The schools need to be constantly aware of the need to eliminate prejudice and nationalistic antagonisms in order for them to function harmoniously and to do so they use multilingualism as a tool for both scholastic achievement and harmonious ethnolinguistic relations.

The following principles determine the nature of the programme in the schools.

(1) The child's distinct national, cultural and linguistic identity must be maintained, underlining the significance of instruction in the first language.

(2) Throughout schooling the child must build up competence in a second language through which he or she will be able to learn content matter and take examinations.

(3) The higher the child progresses in the school the more lessons are taught via the medium of a second or third language.

(4) All children are to be treated equally so that all are obliged to take on a second and third language, the third language becoming a compulsory component of the curriculum from the first year of secondary education. No sub-section is privileged linguistically.

(5) From primary school onwards communal lessons are taught to members of different sub-sections brought together for integration purposes. In the primary section these communal lessons are known as European Hours. The further the children progress in the programme the more lessons are taught to mixed groups from different sub-sections.

(6) In final examinations all pupils are expected to take content-matter examinations, both written and oral, at least in their first and second language; the third language might be examined solely as a subject or for content, depending on the individual's course options.

(7) Examination criteria are theoretically the same whether the pupil is

taking an examination through the medium of the first or the second language. They are also comparable to the criteria used in examinations in the different member states of the European Economic Community.

It should be noted that the nature of the programme in a European School does not fit into any clear-cut model with reference to bilingual education. It is neither an immersion nor a submersion programme. On the other hand it does represent a combination of maintenance, transitional and enrichment programmes. The first language lays the foundations for education, is maintained throughout the programme, but gradually decreases in significance as the pupils get older. Reading and writing are initially taught through the medium of the first language. A second language is introduced as a subject matter from the beginning of the programme and gradually, but not completely, takes over for content matter in secondary education. As the second language gradually increases in significance it represents a type of transitional experience which in theory and in practice will enable the student to pursue higher education through the medium of this language if desired. However, the programme has more in common with the enrichment model since the second language does not take over to the detriment of the first.

A fundamental difference between European Schools and the Canadian immersion model is the place given to formal instruction in the L2. In European Schools the L2 is taught formally as a subject prior to being used as a medium for content. Moreover, once the L2 has become a medium of content instruction it continues to be taught separately as a subject throughout the curriculum. It is probably this factor which accounts for the high level of grammatical accuracy attained by European School pupils by the end of the programme when they are expected to be able to write and speak in a way comparable to native speakers (cf. Swain & Lapkin, 1982).

On the cultural level the European School model shows an attempt to integrate children from different national backgrounds into a broader, communal, new identity which will not threaten that of origin. Thus the school does not exacerbate ethnolinguistic tensions but harmonises modes of thinking while respecting different linguistic backgrounds. The details of how this is achieved will be examined later.

A further significant point is the notion of linguistic equality striven for in the European Schools. All children, whatever their linguistic background, are put through the same constraints where language acquisition is concerned.

Language in the Curriculum

Since there are 8 linguistic sub-sections in the largest European School it is important to evaluate the role of language in the totality of the curriculum. Designers of the programme have had to bear in mind the desire to respect each group's first language together with the need to create a harmonious and integrated school population which does not break up into factions based on linguistic criteria. Thought was also given to the possibility that many of the children might wish to continue their studies through the medium of a different language than their first. Two major strategies help to reconcile these goals. On the one hand there is the promotion of bilingualism for all, and on the other there is a good deal of social engineering, about which more will be said later, which both enhances the language learning process and avoids the dangers of fragmentation on linguistic lines.

In the primary school the majority of instruction is given via the medium of the first language. From the very beginning a second language is taught as a subject to all children. The second language is either English, French or German, which represent the L2s used for inter-group communication. The language of the sub-section in which a child is enrolled may not be selected as an L2 so that an English-speaker has to select French or German as an L2 whereas a Danish speaker may select from any of the three. Often the language of the host community in which the school is located is selected as the preferred L2 of a particular school so that French is the most favoured L2 in the European School of Brussels while English is the most favoured in the school in Britain.

As in all complex linguistic settings the ideal of equal linguistic treatment for all must be reconciled with practical considerations of making the given entity viable. Thus although 8 of the 9 official languages of the member states are on an equal footing in the sub-sections of the Brussels European School they are not all exactly equal. A Danish or a Dutch sub-section, for example, may consist of small groups of one class of pupils per grade whereas there may be 3 parallel classes for each grade of English, French or Italian children; this is unavoidable and reflects European population statistics. Statistics for the 1986/1987 school year reveal that in secondary education there were 738 children in the French sub-section but only 270 in the smallest Danish sub-section. Also, the fact that the compulsory L2 must be selected from either French, English or German, makes these languages more equal than the others. The disparity in numbers and functions of different languages within a given school has consequences on language acquisition since the school represents a multilingual micro-community where social forces affect the acquisition process.

Another factor to be borne in mind is that the schools' policy of admitting non-European civil service children means that there are more languages present than can actually be catered for. The European School of Brussels, for example, has children of 43 nationalities outside the European Economic Community (171 pupils in 1986/1987) on its enrolment and these are distributed among the 8 established sub-sections, with the majority in the English or French sections.

L1 Instruction in European Schools

In primary school teachers pay particular attention to the quality of the L1 since the multilingual environment in which the children evolve is not conducive to optimal input conditions. The majority of children are not in their country of origin, they are all subjected to L2 experience from the beginning of schooling and there are many languages around them. The particular circumstances usually affect the vocabulary so that teachers have to pay more attention than in a monolingual school to extending the range and precision of lexical usage.

Teachers who use the medium of a given language are always native-speakers of that language, a quality considered as essential given the role models they represent and the linguistically mixed population they are confronted with. All teachers are also bilingual to different degrees since they mostly work in a country other than their own and this is considered an asset since it gives them an insight into the nature of bilingualism in the children they teach.

Particular attention is paid to spelling in the L1 and is controlled in all lessons once the children have learned to read and write.

The insistence on a native-speaker requirement in teachers is important in schools where several languages are used as the medium of instruction. In many bilingual programmes teachers often teach through a medium which is not their native language, which at times restricts them as role models. It can also cause problems in cases where there is a significant mismatch between a teacher's non-native patterns of usage and the more native-like patterns children bring with them. This can even be the case if the teacher has specialised in the study of the non-native language. Moreover, the fact that there are native speakers of the L1s among the children implies that the teachers' prestige may be adversely affected if language ability is not at least as fluent as that of the pupils. The European School insist that the native-speaker requirement amongst teachers plays a significant role in the quality of the linguistic outcome of the programme.

The Place of the L2 in Primary Education in the European School

From the very beginning of primary school the different L2s, destined to develop into lingua francas for inter-student communication, are taught by native speakers (not the class teacher, note) as subject matter in the same way that foreign languages are traditionally taught. There is one major difference, however, and that is that the L2s in a European School also figure as the L1 for some pupils within the same buildings, something which brings them to life as observable, genuine tools of natural communication amongst children and adults. Moreover, these same L2s serve as language of instruction for certain subjects in the 3rd, 4th and 5th grades of primary school so that even in the early stages language learning is not totally divorced from language usage. Foreign language instruction is designed to be educationally enriching as well as promoting cross-cultural interaction, and its success is partly due to the fact that it goes on throughout the twelve-years of schooling.

In the primary school the L2 is taught by concentrating on the spoken language, written competence being left to the secondary programme. The focus of attention is on basic grammar and lexis (this process continuing into the secondary programme up to the age of 14, beyond which there is no more structural work on the L2 but the language is used as a medium of instruction for both language and non-language subjects).

Two types of special support are provided for children who arrive in the middle of the school year, perhaps from another country or a monolingual programme. Students with no knowledge of an L2 are sent to 'cours de rattrapage' or 'catching-up classes' during the periods when their classmates are receiving L2 as a subject; they are not separated, however, when the L2 is used for teaching content-matter, where such late arrivals may have difficulty in following in the initial stages. The remedial teachers then try to bring the new arrivals up to class levels by tailor-made intensive teaching which is supplemented by extra lessons outside the normal school timetable, i.e. on Wednesday afternoons which is free for other children. The second type of special provision for late arrivals with inadequate knowledge of the L2 in the secondary programme is known as 'cours de soutien' or 'support classes' where further tailor-made instruction is provided, including help with handling content-matter material taught through the L2. These support classes take place when the late arrivals' classmates follow their optional 'complementary courses' in the secondary programme (cf. p. 130).

From the 3rd grade onwards physical education is taught to mixed groups via the medium of the shared L2, a practice which is continued right through the programme till the end of secondary education. For example, the teacher of physical education might be a native-speaker of French taking a class made up of children from four or five linguistic sub-sections. In theory the teacher will only use French to explain the nature of the game or activity that is to take place. Questioning the children involved reveals that in practice the teacher, in these early stages, will predominantly use his or her native language but may often translate instructions into two or three languages in order to proceed more quickly. This often may go little further than translating a few key words to make sure everyone has understood. Another area where the L2s come into their own is in the set of communal activities known as European Hours which represent an important element behind the philosophy of the schools (cf. below). By the end of primary school the build up of instruction of and through the medium of the L2 means that approximately 25% of the time-table is taken up via the L2 and as children progress through secondary education this proportion increases significantly.

Note the major difference between immersion programmes of L2 instruction and the above model. The L2 is taught as a subject before it becomes used as a medium and when this does occur it takes place in cognitively undemanding and highly contextualised circumstances (cf. Cummins, 1981, 1984) such as physical education or during European Hours. Once the L2 starts to be used as a medium of instruction it continues to be taught separately as a subject.

European Hours

These represent a very important component in the philosophy of the schools. From the 3rd year of primary education 3 lessons per week are devoted to what are called 'European Hours'. These lessons are conducted in the L2 but are not intended as language lessons. Their primary goal is to group children from the various language sections and, by getting them to work and play together, to make them aware of their common European heritage. They form part of the social engineering designed to break down the fragmentation inherent to the presence of 8 sub-sections.

Children are brought together in classes of about 20 to 25, made up of groups of four to five children from each sub-section for one afternoon per week. Nearly 600 children are involved in these European Hours in the European School of Brussels, organised in some 30 groups of roughly 20 children each. Priority is given to co-operative activities based on creative tasks such as sewing, cooking, construction projects, making puppets and often a theme is developed over several weeks, such as preparing for carnival. Teachers are free to carry out any activity they like as long as it mixes children from different sub-sections and encourages them to co-operate with each other. Half way through the school year a different teacher, from a different language background takes over the European Hours, this to reinforce the multicultural aspect of education. All class teachers in the primary school are involved in European Hours.

When a theme is introduced in European Hours the following 5 phases are borne in mind:

(1) creation of an atmosphere where each child will feel comfortable and be encouraged to get actively involved in a group project;
(2) fixing a realisable goal;
(3) forming working groups to attain the goal;
(4) encouraging communication so as to seek to work together;
(5) showing the results to the rest of the school, e.g. through demonstrations, exhibitions, dances, songs.

Observation of a sample lesson during a European Hour revealed the following features. The 22 children in the 5th year class were made up of 5 children from the German section, 6 from the French section, 6 from the Italian section and 5 from the Dutch section. Children from the same group tended to cluster and talk to each other in their own languages. The teacher, a French speaker who used no other language, explained the creative activity which consisted of producing a three dimensional work of art using many different materials. Some children in the class had insufficient command of French to clearly understand what was expected (these were recent arrivals at the school). Other children from the same language background would act as informal interpreters or would show their classmates what to do. Once the activity had been explained the teacher would help individual children to perform the activity. Note that although the 'European Hour' is not a language lesson the L2 assumes great relevance by the very fact that it is the only medium common to the whole group. Of the three lessons per week devoted to 'European Hours' two are classroom activities and one is a games activity conducted outside. No attempts are made to force children to use the L2, though obviously the teacher cannot be expected to know the four languages present in the whole class. By the nature of the circumstances, however, the L2 is perceived as significant as the lingua franca so that children become sensitive to the different roles languages play in their immediate environment and accept the circumstances as natural. Again the activity in the L2 is context embedded and cognitively undemanding.

A second function of the 'European Hours' is that they represent the first instance of the school trying to promote a new European identity, an avowed policy aim. By familiarising the children with representatives of other European countries the schools hope to overcome prejudice and stereotyped reactions before they have had time to develop. Throughout schooling the programme insists on building up a supra-national, European identity and effects this by gradually mixing children from different countries in as many activities as possible.

How successful the programme is in this respect is difficult to assess. It has been noted that whereas in primary school most friendship circles remain within the language sub-section to which the child belongs, by the end of secondary education the majority of friendship patterns are outside the sub-section to which a student belongs. One investigation revealed that among the 17 and 18 year olds studied the majority had their best friends in a sub-section other than their own (Housen & Baetens Beardsmore, 1987).

The above lessons represent the first attempt by the school to manipulate the population so as to interact across the language barriers, and with time such mixings become ever more significant. In a multilingual school it is vital to avoid segregation which might lead to tensions between groups. It is also vital to produce circumstances where an L2 assumes a natural function but where the linguistic demands are not beyond those that can be expected from limited contact with that language. The mixed group sessions provide non-threatening circumstances for interaction across groups.

Primary School Curriculum

The primary school programme consists of a 5 year cycle in which all sub-sections follow the same timetable and same programme, irrespective of the language of the section. Primary education may be preceded by voluntary attendance in the kindergarten which may fulfil a useful function for certain children by consolidating language skills in the language of the sub-section which is later to be attended in school. This may be necessary for children who come from bi- or multilingual home backgrounds, or who have travelled about a lot. Table 7.1 gives the programme for the whole grade for each year, expressed in terms of 30 or 45 minute lesson slots. All subjects are taught through the L1 of the section except those in italics.

Secondary School Programme

The secondary school programme breaks down into 3 phases, the first of which is called the 'observation cycle', and which lasts for 3 years from grades 6–8. During the observation cycle the general programme is followed by everyone, though a limited number of options are introduced. In the 8th grade the L3 is introduced as a compulsory subject and the choice of L3 may be made from any of the official languages in the school which have not yet been studied, except for Irish and Belgian nationals. Irish nationals must take compulsory Irish as an L3 and Belgians their second national language (French or Dutch) if this has not been part of their curriculum lower down in the school; these obligations are made so as to align Irish and Belgian children on the national programmes in their country of origin. The L3 is taught as a subject and not used as a medium of instruction, though later on in secondary education it may figure as a medium of instruction if available on the set of elective courses which pupils may decide to follow.

The L2 takes on a more significant role in the observation cycle. Whereas music and art had been taught in the respective L1s in primary school they are now taught to mixed groups through the medium of the L2. A set of 'complementary activities' are now offered as elective subjects, from which at least two must be selected in the first year of secondary education (grade 6), and these are also taught through the medium of the L2. Complementary activities consist of such subjects as electronics, computer science, photography, painting, typing, needlework, etc. and are aimed at developing other than purely intellectual capacities.

TABLE 7.1 *Primary school curriculum expressed in number of lessons per week and per grade (Lessons using the L2 are in italics)*

Curriculum	No. of lessons per week
1st and 2nd Grades	
L1 as a subject	16 × 30 mins
Mathematics	8 × 30 mins
L2 as a subject	*5 × 30 mins*
Music	3 × 30 mins
Art	4 × 30 mins
Physical education	4 × 30 mins
Environmental studies	2 × 30 mins
Religion or ethics	2 × 45 mins
Recreation	7 × 30 mins
Total	25.5 × 30 or 45 mins per week.
3rd, 4th and 5th Grades	
L1 as a subject	9 × 45 mins
Mathematics	7 × 45 mins
L2 as a subject	*5 × 45 mins*
Environmental studies	4 × 45 mins
Art	1 × 45 mins
Music	1 × 45 mins
Physical education	*1 × 45 mins (mixed langs)*
European Hours	*3 × 45 mins (mixed langs)*
Religion or ethics	2 × 45 mins
Total	33 × 45 mins per week.

Note that in this phase where the role of the L2 is extended the activities in which it is used are still relatively context-embedded and cognitively undemanding.

In grades 6 and 7 the human sciences (i.e. history and geography) are taught via the different L1s of each sub-section in order to familiarise children with their national origins. In grade 8, however, the human sciences are taught to mixed groups through the medium of the L2 and take on a different perspective. The subject matter is now taught in a European light, bringing out the varied perspectives on European history. For example, a French pupil with English as an L2 will be taught the history of the French revolution in English by an English-speaking teacher.

There is one fundamental difference with respect to the L2 when one compares the primary and the secondary school programmes. In primary school communal lessons taught to mixed language groups will include native-speaker peers of the given L2 (for example in European hours). In the secondary programme it is the exception to have native-speaker peers in classes taught through the medium of the L2 since all pupils receive instruction through their non-native language in the same time slot.

In the secondary school programme standard manuals or textbooks play a far less significant role than in monolingual schools. Only for the teaching of languages themselves or for subjects taught through the medium of the L1 are standard text books used, and for the different L1s these obviously differ from sub-section to sub-section. For all other subjects teachers rely far less on standardised textbooks than in monolingual schools and are expected to devise much of their own material in order to meet the requirements of their mixed language populations. Whatever materials are used require slight modifications at this level and teachers may provide multilingual glossaries of the specific subject-matter terminology to ensure that the student has the requisite vocabulary in both the L1 and the L2. Atlases used never provide place names in translation, as would happen in monolingual settings (e.g. Londres = London) but instead give place names in the original language.

Since parents express worries about the capacity of their children to acquire more abstract content-matter through the medium of the L2 when the human sciences switch over to the use of this language briefing sessions are organised where teachers provide reassurance about the nature and outcome of the programme.

At the organisational level the logistics of the secondary school programme are different from those applicable in primary school. Whereas in primary school children had fixed classrooms which represented the 'home-base' of their particular sub-section in secondary school it is not the pupils who have a fixed classroom but the teachers. Thus the 120 teachers in the secondary programme in Brussels each have their fixed classroom in which they can express their personal identity and subject orientation. Pupils are constantly on the move between classrooms during breaks since this more easily allows for the assignment to mixed groups which take into account great flexibility inherent in the number of elective courses available. The movement from classroom to classroom also allows for informal interaction between pupils which also enhances opportunities to use their different languages outside the formal setting.

By the end of the observation cycle (grade 8) the amount of instruction not provided through the L1 has increased to approximately 15 periods a week, or almost half of the curriculum.

Table 7.2 provides the curriculum for the observation cycle in secondary school expressed in lesson slots of 45 minutes per week and per grade.

Two important factors need to be noted with reference to the early grades of secondary education. The first is the increase in time devoted to using the L2 as a medium of instruction and the second is the nature of the transition taking place in the curriculum. Whereas in primary school and the first two grades of secondary school matter dealt with in the L2 is mainly context-embedded and cognitively undemanding, by the 8th grade, when the human sciences are taught via the L2 the task has become more cognitively demanding and context-reduced (cf. Cummins,

TABLE 7.2 *Secondary school programme for the observation cycle (Grades 6–8) (Lessons not using the L1 are in italics)*

Subject	Grade 6	Grade 7	Grade 8
L1 as a subject	5 × 45″	5 × 45″	4 × 45″
Mathematics	4 × 45″	4 × 45″	4 × 45″
Latin (optional)	—	—	4 × 45″
Integrated science	4 × 45″	4 × 45″	4 × 45″
Religion or ethics	2 × 45″	2 × 45″	2 × 45″
Human sciences[a]	3 × 45″	3 × 45″	3 × 45″
L3 as a subject	—	—	*4 × 45″*
L2 as a subject	*5 × 45″*	*4 × 45″*	*4 × 45″*
Graphic & plastic arts	*2 × 45″*	*2 × 45″*	*2 × 45″*
Music	*2 × 45″*	*2 × 45″*	*2 × 45″*
Physical education	*3 × 45″*	*3 × 45″*	*3 × 45″*
Complementary activities	*2 × 45″*	*2 × 45″*	*2 × 45″*
Total	32 × 45″	31 × 45″	31/35 × 45″

(a) Taught through the medium of the L2 in grade 8.
(b) Those who select Latin may drop either music or graphic and plastic arts.
(c) In grade 6 two optional complementary activities must be selected but may be dropped in grades 7 and 8.

1981), and therefore linguistically more challenging. However, it is not as though a completely new subject were being taught through the medium of the weaker language since the same area of study has been dealt with in the L1 in grades 6 and 7. Moreover, the provision of multilingual glossaries serves the function of both helping comprehension in the L2 and ensuring that the pupil can acquire the relevant lexis in the L1.

The Middle Cycle of Secondary Education

The middle cycle of the secondary school programme, covering grades 9 and 10, is known as the 'semi-specialisation cycle' where pupils have a greater selection of options available which enables them to specialise their interests. During this period there is a certain amount of variability in the amount of time taken up by subjects not taught through the L1, depending on the combination of elective courses chosen. A glance at Table 7.3 shows that from a maximum total of 31–35 periods a week, and depending on the choice of elective courses, a pupil can receive 20 periods not taught through the L1, or almost two thirds of the curriculum.

The Final Cycle of Secondary Education

The last two years of secondary education, grades 11 and 12, known as the specialisation cycle, have a limited number of compulsory subjects. In 1986–1987 in the European School in Brussels almost every one of the 400 pupils involved had a tailor-made timetable, leading to complex organisational questions. A new set of elective courses are introduced at this level, known as advanced courses in a particular domain, and consist of a more intellectually abstract approach to the field.

It is impossible to calculate the amount of time devoted to the use of each language at this level, given the great individual variation, though it is clear that the amount of instruction received through the L1 is likely to be about a third of the programme. Religion or ethics, which until now had been taught through the L1, are continued in the L2 as compulsory subjects.

Although there have been no in-depth studies to date on the methodology followed in using the L2 either as a subject or a medium

TABLE 7.3 *Secondary school programme for the semi-specialisation cycle in number of lessons per week and per grade. Lessons not using the L1 are in italics*

Subject	9th & 10th Grades
L1 as a subject	4 × 45 mins
Religion or ethics	1 × 45 mins
Biology	2 × 45 mins
Chemistry	2 × 45 mins
Physics	2 × 45 mins
Mathematics[a]	4 or 6 × 45 mins
L2 as a subject	*3 × 45 mins*
Physical education	*2 × 45 mins*
History	*2 × 45 mins*
Geography	*2 × 45 mins*
L3 as a subject	*3 × 45 mins*
Total	27 or 29 × 45 mins
Elective subjects	
Latin	4 × 45 mins
Greek	4 × 45 mins
Economics & Social Sciences	*4 × 45 mins*
Plastic arts	*2 × 45 mins*
Music	*2 × 45 mins*
L4 as a subject	*4 × 45 mins*

(a) Depending on the student's choice.
(b) Enough elective subjects must be chosen to guarantee a curriculum of minimum 31 and maximum 35 periods per week.

of instruction, observation of a restricted number of sample lessons gives some idea of teaching practice. It has already been noticed that in primary education the L2 is taught as a subject to mixed groups before its introduction as a medium for relatively undemanding cognitive activities. In the L2 language lessons there are no native-speaker peers present (unless children come from mixed marriage bilingual backgrounds as is sometimes the case) since all sub-sections are being taught a different L2. Teachers concentrate on the spoken language and follow standard practice for teaching a second language to young children. In lessons where the L2 functions as a medium of instruction, native-speaker peers may be present in primary school, for example in European Hours discussed earlier.

TABLE 7.4 *Secondary school programme for the specialisation cycle expressed in subjects per grade per week (Subjects not taught through the L1 are in italics)*

Compulsory subjects	Grades 11 & 12
L1 as a subject	4 × 45 mins
Philosophy	2 × 45 mins
Mathematics	3 or 5 × 45 mins
L2 as a subject	*3 × 45 mins*
History	*2 × 45 mins*
Geography	*2 × 45 mins*
Physical education	*2 × 45 mins*
Religion or ethics	*1 × 45 mins*
Elective courses	
Latin	5 × 45 mins
Greek	5 × 45 mins
Physics	4 × 45 mins
Chemistry	4 or 5 × 45 mins
Biology	4 or 5 × 45 mins
L3 as a subject	*3 × 45 mins*
L4 as a subject	*3 × 45 mins*
Advanced course in L1 as a subject	3 × 45 mins
Advanced course in mathematics	3 × 45 mins
Advanced physics and chemistry	2 × 45 mins
Economics	*5 × 45 mins*
Advanced course in L2 as a subject	*3 × 45 mins*
Advanced course in geography	*2 × 45 mins*
Advanced course in history	*2 × 45 mins*
Plastic arts	*2 × 45 mins*
Music	*2 × 45 mins*
Sociology	*2 × 45 mins*
Other subjects	*2 × 45 mins*

Note: A pupil must have a timetable with a minimum of 31 and a maximum of 35 periods per week.

In the secondary programme no lessons using the L2 contain native-speakers of that language except in certain elective courses in the final grades, such as economics or sociology. Teachers all claim that native-speaker peer contacts develop spontaneously the further up the school the pupil moves, and this has been borne out by interviews. Given the size of the Brussels I school and the number of teachers and languages involved it is difficult to describe typical teacher–pupil interaction patterns or instructional style when the L2 is being used. Observations of sample lessons have revealed considerable differences depending on the stage in the programme at which the L2 is being used, the nature of the subject-matter being treated, the particular language involved, and the type of training a teacher has received which reflects that teacher's national background. What does come clearly to the fore, however, is that all teachers are aware of the particular multilingual circumstances of the school so that all share a few basic principles.

For example, when pupils from different sub-sections come together for L2 lessons they automatically tend to group themselves according to language of origin. The majority of teachers try to break up such patternings by encouraging people from different sub-sections to sit together so as to render the use of the L2 necessary and natural. All teachers in L2 classes, whatever their nature, tend to include linguistic features in their teaching, paying particular attention to lexical precision and controlling the accuracy of written production. Teachers observed in L2 medium classes all tended to spontaneously correct minor errors in a naturalistic fashion by merely repeating the correct form before moving on. In the secondary school programme lessons involving the L2 are continued and conducted at a natural pace and the tempo does not appear to be slowed down because of the presence of non-native speakers. Considerable pupil–teacher interaction occurs via rapid and natural question and answer strategies and indeed to the casual observer it is not evident that pupils are receiving instruction through the medium of an L2.

To illustrate the nature of teaching practice four types of L2 lesson will be briefly described.

In grade 8 a combined history and geography lesson was observed being taught via the L2 French by a French teacher. There were 20 students in the class made up of 7 English-speakers, 8 speakers of Greek and 5 speakers of Italian. The lesson was observed during the second week of the new school year, i.e. at the beginning of the phase where the L2 is first used as a medium of instruction for cognitively demanding activities and therefore a new experience for the students. The manual used was a standard text-book published in France for French native-speakers. Content-matter was presented in a highly structured fashion, though with many questions and answers provided fluently with little hesitation. A Greek and a British pupil were first invited to summarise points dealt with in the previous lesson and prepared for homework. The British boy was requested to correctly identify neolithic, paleolithic and bronze-age specimens present in the classroom on a time scale. Population densities were discussed and comparisons made with populations in the different countries represented in the class. Almost all pupils were called upon to provide information at some time. The very few language errors that were made were spontaneously corrected by the teacher repeating the correct forms without dwelling on them. As the lesson progressed the teacher provided a sentence-by-sentence summary of the major points which pupils copied from the blackboard on the right-hand page of their notebooks. On the left-hand page pupils were requested to note down new words, concepts and definitions. For homework pupils were requested to look up the words 'nomade' and 'sédentaire' in any French dictionary and to be prepared to discuss these concepts in the following class.

The above lesson can be compared with a 10th grade economics lesson provided in the L2, English, by a British teacher in the second week of the school year. Again this represented a new experience since economics was a new elective subject. There were 13 pupils, including 2 native-speakers of English as this is an elective course, 6 Danish-speakers, 2 French-speakers and 3 German-speakers. A standard British manual designed for native-speakers was used, supplemented by photocopies of newspaper extracts. In this introductory lesson very basic concepts were defined by means of rapid questions and answers stimulated by cartoon drawings. All pupils were called upon to help make the concepts precise; there was no language correction and the pace of the lesson appeared similar to that of a native-speaker class. The quality of English was fluent and not significantly marked.

In lessons observed where the L2 was the subject of instruction, as opposed to the medium, there was a notable difference in approach according to the language. A 10th grade lesson in L2 French as a subject, taught by a French national, concentrated on a literary analysis at a level of abstraction similar to what is likely to occur in the same type of lesson where French is the L1. Of the 21 pupils present, 9 were English-speakers, 4 Dutch-speakers, 3 Italian-speakers, 2 Greek-speakers, 2 Danish-speakers and 1 German-speaker. The pace of the lesson was extremely lively with rapid question and answer strategies directed towards discovering the structure and theme of the text. The level of abstraction led to problems of lexical availability which were dealt with either by synonym-seeking or by direct reference to grammatical terminology. The liveliness of this lesson might be accounted for by the teacher's personality and the fact that in Brussels French is the out-of-school language which provides it with massive reinforcement. What was more striking was the fact that to the observer it did not come across as significantly different from an L1 lesson and that pupils obviously coped and enjoyed the activity.

An 11th grade lesson where L2 English was the subject of discussion differed significantly from the preceding in that it was far more obviously a language lesson. The class of 24, taught by an Irish teacher, was made up of 8 Italian-speakers, 7 Spanish-speakers, 2 German-speakers, 2 speakers of Greek and 1 speaker of Danish. An advanced English-as-a-foreign language manual was used as a basis for discussion after certain extracts had been read aloud by the teacher. Discussion developed freely after intensive questions and answers. The teacher concentrated specifically on highly idiomatic vocabulary, there was little correction and no writing involved, though pupil intervention was lively. The difference in nature between the English and French L2 lessons could be accounted for in several ways, primarily the fact that English is not the major out-of-school language in Brussels and therefore requires more language-focused treatment. Although pupils were generally fluent accents were more marked than in the similar French lesson as was the occasional grammatical feature. Another explanation for the difference is perhaps that the English teacher was qualified in English-as-a-foreign language whereas a similar qualification is rare in France. A third difference might be explained by different intellectual and teacher-training traditions in the countries from where the teachers came and which were reflected in the lessons, the French lesson reflecting a quest for abstraction and generalisation whereas its English counterpart reflected pragmatic considerations. What was striking, however, was that in spite of these differences, the amount of pupil involvement was equally lively, fluent and spontaneous.

The above descriptions merely serve as illustrations and may in no way represent all L2 lessons in European Schools. Indeed, the difference observed may have been purely coincidental since the English-as-a-subject L2 programme also contains the study of literature and may just have been absent from preoccupations at the point of observation.

Timetables

In order to get a clear understanding of the organisation of a school which contains 8 parallel sub-sections it is interesting to examine the timetables of both teachers and pupils. Irrespective of the language sub-section they are enrolled in all pupils follow the same curriculum and same timetable, except for new arrivals in the middle of the school year or those who join a European School programme from a standard monolingual school and who need special tuition in order to reach their class L2 level. Such new arrivals follow the same programme as their classmates except during language lessons when they may attend special remedial classes (cf. pp. 125–8); they may also be requested to attend special remedial classes on Wednesday afternoons when the rest of the school has a half-day holiday. The school day starts at 8.10 a.m. and classes end at 16.35 p.m. in the secondary school, a little earlier in primary school.

In the primary school timetables are fairly straightforward. Since all children spend most of the time with their class teacher the curriculum consists of 8 parallel timetables side by side as if they were in one monolingual establishment. In the time slots devoted to lessons on the L2 as a subject everyone is involved with different languages so that children move to the class where the L2 chosen by their parents is taught. These L2 as-a-subject lessons do not normally contain native speakers. Teacher timetables fit into this distribution, whereby native-speaker primary school teachers of the L2s (English, French and German) take on mixed groups instead of their normal classes while the others, e.g. Danish or Greek class teachers, may take on physical education to mixed groups. In communal lessons children are split up and directed to a particular class in groups of about 5. All primary school teachers are involved in European Hours which are not considered as language lessons and where any combination of pupil make-up may exist; these lessons are gathered into one half-day per week so that the timetable is straightforward.

In the secondary school timetables must be worked out individually. Each child is given a tailor-made timetable which he or she is expected to have readily available as a means of identification, given the size of the population. Since there are 2000 secondary pupils constantly moving from class to class on the Brussels site this personalised timetable is one of the few means of controlling the legitimacy of free periods. As in the primary school the same timetable applies to a particular grade irrespective of the language sub-section, though elective choices may well mean that a given pupil's timetable is very different from that of a classmate. Individual timetables contain the time-slot, name of the subject, teacher's name and classroom number.

To illustrate how pupils are combined and separated according to their sub-section, their L2 option and their electives Table 7.5 compares two 9th grade pupils and Table 7.6 two 12th grade pupils.

As far as teacher timetables are concerned these are designed in European Schools in terms of language, subject matter and level in the programme. Primary school teacher timetables are similar to those in monolingual schools in that each teacher in a given sub-section is responsible for the class for a particular grade.

In the secondary school programme attempts are made to enable pupils to have the same teacher for each subject for the whole of one of the three cycles so as to provide continuity. Table 7.7 illustrates an English language teacher's timetable. This teacher teaches English as a native language and as an L2 to different grades. Timetables for teachers

TABLE 7.5 *9th grade timetables for pupils from the French and English sub-sections (Communal lessons to mixed groups are in italics)*

Pupil no. 110 9th grade French sub-section

	MON	TUES	WED	THURS	FRI
1	*Phys. Ed.*	Physics	*L4*	Maths	Maths
2	Physics	Maths	*Music*	L2	*Music*
3	Maths	Maths	*Phys. Ed.*	Biology	L2
4	*History*	Geography	*L3*		*L4*
5	*L4*	L1	*History*	Chemistry	L1
6					
7	Maths	*L4*		*Geography*	Religion
8	*L3*	Biology		*L3*	
9	*L2*	L1		L1	Chemistry

Pupil no. 38 9th grade English sub-section

	MON	TUES	WED	THURS	FRI
1	*Economics*	Physics	Computer	*Phys. Ed.*	L1
2	Biology	L1	*Art*	L2	*Art*
3	L1	*Phys. Ed.*		Physics	L2
4	*History*	Geography	*L3*	*Economics*	
5	Computer	Biology	*History*	Chemistry	Ethics
6					
7	Maths	*Economics*		*Geography*	*Maths*
8	*L3*	L1		*L3*	*Economics*
9	*L2*	Maths		Maths	Chemistry

TABLE 7.6 *12th grade timetables for pupils from the French and the English sub-sections (Communal lessons are in italics)*

Pupil no. 91 12th grade French sub-section

	MON	TUES	WED	THURS	FRI
1	Maths	L1	Chemistry		*L2*
2	*Ethics*	Chemistry	Maths		*L3*
3	Chemistry	*History*	Maths	Philosophy	Physics
4					
5	L1	Maths	*L3*	Maths	*Geography*
6	*L3*	*Geography*		*Phys. Ed.*	
7	*L2*	Physics		Physics	Maths
8	*History*	*L2*		Maths	
9					Maths

Pupil no. 62 12th grade English sub-section

	MON	TUES	WED	THURS	FRI
1	*Religion*	L1		L1	*L2*
2	Maths		Chemistry	*Phys. Ed.*	*L3*
3		*Geography*	Chemistry	L1	Biology
4	Maths	Chemistry	Chemistry	Philosophy	Philosophy
5	L1	Maths	*L3*		*Geography*
6	*L3*	*History*		Biology	Biology
7	*L2*			Chemistry	Biology
8	*History*	*L2*		Maths	Biology
9	*Phys. Ed.*	Biology		Maths	

of non-language subjects are similar to those in monolingual schools so that for example, mathematics teachers in a French or Italian section would have similar or even parallel timetables since they do not have to cross over languages or teach to mixed groups.

Teachers and Staff

Teachers and directors of European Schools are seconded from their different national education systems for a period of years which differs from country to country. Hence all teachers using a given language are native-speakers of that language, irrespective of the population make-up

TABLE 7.7 *Secondary school programme: English teacher's timetable*

	MON	TUES	WED	THURS	FRI
1	Grade 11 L1				Grade 12 L2
2	Grade 7 L2	Grade 7 L2	Grade 11 L1	Grade 9 L2	Grade 6 L1
3			Grade 6 L1	Grade 12 L1	Grade 9 L2
4	Grade 6 L1	Grade 11 L2		Grade 7 L2	
5	Grade 12 L1	Grade 6 L1		Grade 6 L1	
6					
7	Grade 12 L2	Grade 11 L1		Grade 11 L2	Grade 7 L2
8		Grade 12 L2			Grade 11 L2
9	Grade 9 L2	Grade 6 L1			Grade 11 L1

Note: This particular teacher teaches English as an L1 subject to native-speakers and as one of the compulsory L2s to pupils from other sections. Each teacher is required to teach 23 periods a week.

of the classes, and all must be bilingual. After a particular director's period of office his or her successor must be of a different nationality.

No special certification is requisite for work in a European School beyond national teacher certification requirements. The European Schools represent an exception in that national teacher certification is not recognised in the different member states of the European Economic Community so that teachers from one country cannot normally work in a different country.

There is no training available in Europe for working in a multilingual school and most teachers learn how to adapt to the special circumstances of the school while on the job. Some of the British teachers have specialist qualifications in EFL but this is an exception. When new teachers are engaged they usually spend two or three weeks in the European School the year preceding their contract so as to become familiar with the system. New teachers are also assigned to the care of an existing teacher who acts as a guide and mentor in the initial stages. Given the complexity of the programme as far as languages and nationalities are concerned new teachers sometimes need time to adapt to the circumstances of a curriculum totally different from any they may be familiar with.

The whole network of European Schools regularly organises in-service re-training sessions or study seminars for different groups of teachers. In 1986/1987, for example, the following courses took place for teachers, a seminar for teachers of Italian as a first or a foreign language, one for teachers of Danish as a first or foreign language, one for music teachers; working group sessions for biology, physics and chemistry teachers.

In order to co-ordinate the activities across grades and across languages non-remunerated co-ordinators are elected among the teachers for a 2 year period whose task it is to unify the treatment of subject-matter. Alongside the teachers are a group of pedagogic advisers who are responsible for the care and control of each grade, the library and the classrooms, while the natural sciences also have a team of laboratory assistants.

In the primary and secondary school there are teams of remedial teachers whose mother tongues are those of the 8 language sub-sections. The functions of these remedial teachers are to provide extra instruction to new arrivals, who may join the school at any time of the year, either in the L1 of the sub-section to which they are assigned, or more usually in the L2. A child who is not up to grade level in the L2 receives special instruction in this language for up to two years, both inside the normal timetable and in the form of extra lessons after class. Lack of proficiency in the L2 during this adaptation period will not hold a child back as the grade moves up since the L2 test results are excluded from the overall grade averages during the adaptation period.

Two types of special support are provided for children who arrive in the middle of the school year, perhaps from another country or a monolingual programme. Pupils with no knowledge of an L2 are sent to 'cours de rattrapage' or 'catching-up classes' during the periods when their classmates are receiving L2 as a subject—they are not separated, however, when the L2 is used for teaching content-matter, where such late arrivals may have great difficulty in following in the initial stages. The remedial teachers then try to bring the new arrivals up to class levels by tailor-made intensive teaching which is supplemented by extra lessons outside the normal school timetable, i.e. on Wednesday afternoon which is free for other children as is standard in many European countries.

The second type of special provision for late arrivals with inadequate knowledge of the L2 is known as 'cours de soutien' or 'support classes' where further tailor-made instruction is provided, including help with handling content-matter material taught through the L2. These support classes take place when the late arrivals' classmates follow their optional 'complementary courses' in the secondary programme.

Secretarial support services are made up of personnel who between them speak all the languages of the different sub-sections.

There is a medical service available made up of part-time and full-time personnel. In the largest school in Brussels this consists of a doctor of Italian nationality who speaks Italian and French and a psychologist of Finnish nationality who speaks French and English, both of whom work on a part-time basis. There is a full-time Belgian nurse who speaks French, German and Dutch and a full-time French nurse-secretary who speaks French. The medical team can also call upon the services of 8 people of different nationalities and languages who work as auxiliary staff to help children who suffer from dyslexia, psycho-motor and graphic problems.

Directors, teachers, pedagogic advisers and secretarial staff are all bi- or multilingual so that a student can always find someone to help him or her in the dominant language. This is highly important given the fluctuation in student turnover as children arrive in the school from a monolingual national system at almost any age.

An important factor on the organisational level is the multilingual nature of the support staff which enables a child to get assistance in his or her strong language. The fact that all personnel are bilingual is also significant since it gives staff an insight into the facts of life with respect to manipulating more than one language and gives them greater sympathy and understanding about the nature of bilingualism.

The presence of remedial teachers to assist new arrivals to the programme is of great significance since such pupils are not left to struggle alone or to depend on the availability of the class teacher to help overcome the hurdles of insertion into the bilingual environment.

Parental Involvement

Although the internal working language of each school tends to be that of the host environment, e.g. French for the school in Brussels, communication from the school to parents occurs in the languages of the sub-sections, i.e. the child's L1. Parent–teacher meetings on the school premises that take place either in the language of the sub-section involved, or if a larger, mixed language meeting, in the working language of the school with interpreting available where necessary.

The parents' associations tend to be quite strong since the schools themselves do not undertake the responsibility for transportation or the provision of meals but delegate this to the parents' association. Hence bussing and catering imply considerable parental involvement and organisation which automatically bring at least some parents into regular contact with the school.

Parent delegates attend certain school meetings but merely as observers without any discussion power or direct influence. Before children move from primary school into secondary school a parent–teacher meeting is organised to brief parents on the nature of the programme to be followed. In secondary school all parents are invited once a year to make appointments with a maximum of 5 individual teachers with whom they can discuss their child's progress.

Examinations

The European School programme leads to a special diploma, called the European Baccalaureate, which gives access to universities in most countries of the world. Attainment requirements are harmonised across the language sub-sections for many subjects, e.g. mathematics, natural sciences, philosophy, Latin, and the written examinations for these are identical in nature, irrespective of the language in which they are taken. Other subjects, including the languages themselves, are comparable in the nature of the tasks required. The final examination consists of 5 written and 4 oral sub-components, while the compulsory L2 as a subject consists of 1 written and 1 oral examination. In theory the achievement level expected for the L2 is the same as that for pupils who have that language as their L1 in the appropriate sub-section. In practice, however, concessions are made to those taking examinations through the L2 for less complex syntax or slightly less precise or varied vocabulary, though few concessions are made on accuracy.

Examinations do not become an important issue until the semi-specialisation cycle in secondary school, i.e. after grade 8. It is a deliberate policy of the European Schools not to place too much emphasis on examinations or tests until a child has gone through the observation cycle or the first three years of secondary school. Normally most children move up from grade to grade according to age and not according to test scores, at least until the 8th grade.

Social Engineering

Given the presence of 8 linguistic sub-sections in the largest European Schools this leads to a multilingual and multicultural environment. Great care is taken to produce a unified school population by mixing children for as many subjects and activities as possible. These mixtures increase in significance as the children get older and have important consequences on language learning.

One consequence is that within the school everyone interacts regularly in a language that is not their L1 and that inhibitions to experiment in a weaker language are not strong. Interviews with pupils reveal that all are willing to try out a weaker language, that no-one mocks at linguistic inadequacies since everyone in the school has to try out a weaker language at some time.

The social engineering has important linguistic repercussions in that it promotes conversational interactions in languages other than the L1 with both native and non-native speakers of the other languages. Wagner-Gough & Hatch (1975) showed that acquisition is a process which relies on conversational interactions, while Wong-Fillmore (1986) pointed out the significance of peer-group interaction in promoting language competence. In European Schools the social situation has been so designed that there is frequent contact between native and non-native speakers of the languages being learnt.

Research on European Schools

Several investigations have been conducted to measure the linguistic results obtained by the European School system and to explain the processes by which they have been achieved. Bactens Beardsmore & Swain (1985) compared proficiency in French as an L2 as obtained by 13+ year olds in Canadian immersion programmes and those in the European School of Brussels. Standardised test results revealed that highly comparable scores were obtained by the European children after approximately 1300 classroom contact hours with the language and Canadian immersion children after approximately 4500 contact hours. These results in no way showed the superiority of one model over the other but could be explained by the totally different circumstances in which each programme evolved.

In the European School investigated, the L2, French, was the dominant out-of-school language and was regularly used by the pupils in natural interaction. This was not the case in Canada. Given that French was the L1 of some pupils in the European School and also served as the common language for intergroup communication for those who had it as an L2 this led to it being used at least sometimes, and often more, in all out-of-class activities apart from at home and with relatives. Outside classes it tended to be used between friends, at lunchtime, in the wider community, and also figured in recreational pursuits like reading magazines and comics and watching television. Thus unlike their Canadian counterparts who only use French inside the classroom the European children were in a context which provided immediate stimulus for out-of-class use of French as well as in class.

An interesting observation has been made by an investigator of the European School established in Britain (personal communication), where English tends to be the natural lingua franca since it is present in the out-of-school environment. Parents of Italian siblings studying at the European School there were distressed to note that in spite of their children being enrolled in the Italian sub-section and the fact that Italian was the home language their children tended to interact in English. Also, one German teacher in the German sub-section in Britain began to penalise his pupils for using English during his lessons. This anecdotal evidence points to the overwhelming impact of the out-of-school environment on language usage.

A second study in the European School of Brussels examined linguistic proficiency among pupils in the final grade of secondary school (Housen & Baetens Beardsmore, 1987). The pupils had all obtained satisfactory grades both in scholastic achievement and in their different L1s, L2s, L3s and L4s. Their productive competence in L1 and L2 was sufficiently high for them to take equivalent examinations in either language and it was also discovered that competence in all languages varied in function of a variety of factors. The most important factor was the spontaneous seeking out of opportunities to use a particular language in self-initiated interactions, particularly with peers. This factor outweighed attitudinal and motivational dispositions and was clearly dependent on the nature of the social environment in the school. Given the ample opportunities to use a particular language in social interactions the pupils perceived language acquisition as immediately relevant to their everyday needs and not subordinated to either some long-term goal, as is the case with standard foreign language learning classes, or as an obstacle to be overcome in moving on to other interesting activities, as is the case when language learning is totally divorced from other learning processes.

A third study (Baetens Beardsmore & Kohls, 1988) looked into this question of immediate pertinence of the language acquisition process as a causal factor in determining the success of the European School system. Current theories on second language acquisition place considerable emphasis on input as a primary source of progression in competence (Gass & Madden, 1985). Krashen (1981) hypothesises that comprehensible input, where the learner focuses on understanding messages and not on form, gradually leads to the acquisition of structure. For Krashen it is sufficient to provide large quantities of comprehensible input, without grammatical or structural lessons, for a learner to progress in a second language. This practice is what mainly occurs in Canadian immersion programmes to date, but it has been noted that the results in grammatical accuracy leave much to be desired if teaching relies exclusively on the absorption of input. In European Schools, however, lessons on the structure of the L2 precede the use of the language in content-matter lessons and continue throughout the programme, even after the L2 has taken over for the majority of content-matter lessons. This factor probably accounts for the high levels of grammatical precision in the L2 obtained by the majority of European School pupils by the end of schooling.

A second major difference between the European School model and immersion models is that the structure of the European School programme forces learners to interact at peer level in the L2. Unlike immersion pupils who have little opportunity to engage in two-way negotiated meaning exchanges in the classroom (Swain, 1985: 247) European School pupils have ample opportunity, both inside and outside the classroom, to do so. Swain has argued that input alone does not lead to high levels of productive competence and that output is equally important, where the learner is pushed to negotiate meaning by delivering a message that is conveyed as precisely, coherently and appropriately as possible. For a learner to be willing to put in the effort to produce output the attempts must be perceived as immediately pertinent; such is the case in the European School model where use of the target language is immediately rewarding as it is necessary for establishing friendship circles and conducting co-operative activities in mixed lessons.

For learners to be willing to take linguistic 'risks' in attempting to produce accurate output the circumstances must not only be naturalistic but also non-threatening. In Canadian immersion programmes using French in the classroom is non-threatening since all the pupils come from the same background and are not made to feel inferior because of inadequacies in language. In European Schools the situation is the same since everybody has to use a weaker language at some time so that feelings of monolingual superiority cannot easily be maintained. In many American schools where limited English proficient pupils find themselves next to native speakers of English only the former are subjected to the struggle of expressing themselves in a weaker language, which may give rise to feelings of inadequacy and insecurity, thereby impeding the spontaneous arisal of output. Consequently, friendship circles may well form among the in-group of speakers from the same language background, preventing the two-way peer interaction. This is why it is felt important to give all children in a multilingual school the opportunity to learn and use a second language, and to make the process pertinent for all. The constant mixing up of children for group activities provides the natural environment for such pertinence to be perceived, as has been borne out by the study by Housen & Baetens Beardsmore (1987).

A final study by Baetens Beardsmore & Anselmi (1991) looked into the way code-switching operates in a European School, with particular emphasis on its function as a tool for language acquisition among secondary school pupils, once again revealing how the extra-curricular factors, with the design of the programme, the social engineering and the out-of-class peer negotiation influencing language choice and usage.

Conclusions

The fact that approximately 90% of all pupils attending European Schools since their foundation in 1958 have obtained certification leading to higher education clearly indicates that the model is successful both academically and linguistically. This success is not to be attributed simply to the social class make-up of the population or the status of the different languages involved, though they undoubtedly play a role. More important is the care with which the programme has been developed so as to take into account a certain number of fundamental principles which are strictly adhered to so as to give the complex situation a chance to succeed. These principles can be summed up as follows.

(1) All pupils are put on an equal footing as far as language requirements

are concerned and all are led through the same process of transition from instruction through an L1 into that of an L2.

(2) The L1 serves as the basis for instruction as competence in the L2 is gradually built up, while the L1 is never totally abandoned.

(3) Transition to the use of the L2 is a gradual process which moves from cognitively undemanding and context embedded activities in the language to more cognitively demanding and context reduced activities as the student gets older. An examination of the curriculum shows how this process breaks down into three major phases. The L2 is first introduced as a subject while the task of coping with general learning takes place in the L1. In the second phase the L2 is used in naturalistic circumstances that are non-threatening and easy to handle (in European Hours, for example). In the third phase, when more intellectually demanding activities are undertaken in the L2 they are first conducted in areas similar to those that had been previously treated in the L1 (e.g. history and geography) before spreading out into new activities.

(4) Throughout the programme both the L1 and the L2 are taught as subjects in order to reinforce grammatical accuracy and lexical precision.

(5) Testing and examinations are not allowed to determine success or failure until the pupil has had sufficient time to become thoroughly acquainted with a language; ultimate attainment is considered more important than mid-stream progress and there are no unrealistic comparisons with monolingual peers until the very end of schooling.

(6) The programme is organised to promote considerable interaction at peer-group level between both native and non-native speakers of a given language so as to reinforce the formal teaching aspects of language acquisition.

(7) Using a particular language occurs in naturalistic, non-threatening circumstances which are immediately pertinent to the task in hand, making the operation a rewarding one and a stimulus to further effort.

(8) Great care is taken to avoid the formation of linguistic ghettoes by mixing children up for as many activities as possible.

(9) Teachers are all bilingual in different combinations of languages but always teach through their first language, no matter what the subject or the population make-up of the class they are taking. This situation is possible in Europe with a large pool of qualified teachers to draw from.

(10) Attempts are made to eliminate strong ethnolinguistic perspectives by fostering a European identity and a cross-cultural view of the

world while maintaining respect for the student's national heritage. In another context a similar respect for the home language and ethnic heritage could be maintained while promoting a pluralistic cultural identity which reflects the kaleidoscopic make-up of contemporary society.

The positive linguistic and academic results obtained by the multilingual school described in this monograph are not a uniquely European phenomenon based on some supposedly inherent superiority in language acquisition. Similar positive results based on fundamentally similar approaches have been achieved in bilingual education in the United States involving two languages in the curriculum. Krashen & Biber (1988) have posited three requirements as necessary for successful bilingual programmes, namely,

(1) rigorous subject matter teaching such as mathematics, social studies and science in the first language;
(2) development of literacy in the first language;   ˙
(3) English instruction that is comprehensible through daily English as a second language lessons and subject matter teaching geared to the second language acquirer.

Krashen & Biber's (1988) examination of seven schools or school districts in which the above principles were rigorously followed showed that in comparison with pupils not receiving properly organised bilingual instruction five of the bilingual programmes provided clearly superior results, one produced comparable results and in one case there was insufficient data to draw any conclusions. The results also showed that adequate levels of conversational ability in English were obtained after about two years in a given programme but that adequate levels of formal or academic language took from five to seven years. Once the time factor had been taken into consideration the children involved in the properly structured bilingual education programmes investigated in California were comparable to native speakers of English on all tests used. However, this success was determined by the fact that children in the successful programmes were not exited from bilingual education into mainstream, monolingual education prematurely.

The above results reveal certain parallelisms with the practice of the European Schools and reveal similar positive outcomes. The only major difference between Krashen & Biber's findings and those for European Schools is the number of languages involved on the particular school site. The European School model shows that it is possible to operate a multilingual school made up of unequal numbers of pupils with different language and cultural backgrounds. Success is determined by the care which has gone into enabling the transition from one language to another to take place, as well as the continuous efforts to integrate the school population in order to achieve the desired linguistic, cultural and interethnic goals.

As a model the European School should not serve as a blueprint in a totally different environment. On the other hand, many of the features that have been incorporated over the years are well-tried elements that can serve as guidelines for other societies confronted with similar complex linguistic and educational issues.

Note to Chapter 7

1. This paper is a modified version of a study commissioned by the Bilingual Education Office of the California State Department of Education, Contract No. 106B025-05.

References

BAETENS BEARDSMORE, H. and ANSELMI, G. 1991, Code-Switching in an unstable, heterogeneous, multilingual speech community. Papers for the Symposium on code-switching in Bilingual studies: Theory, Significance and Perspectives. Strasbourg: European Science Foundation pp 405–36.

BAETENS BEARDSMORE, H. and KOHLS, J. 1988, Immediate pertinence in the acquisition of multilingual proficiency: The European schools. *The Canadian Modern Language Review* 44, 2, 240–60.

BAETENS BEARDSMORE, H. and SWAIN, M. 1985, Designing bilingual education: Aspects of immersion and 'European School' Models. *Journal of Multilingual and Multicultural Development* 6, 1, 1–15.

CUMMINS, J. 1981, The role of primary language development in promoting educational success for language minority students. *Schooling and Language Minority Students: A Theoretical Framework*. Los Angeles: Education, Dissemination and Assessment Center, 3–49.

— 1984, *Bilingualism and Special Education: Issues in Assessment and Pedagogy*. Clevedon: Multilingual Matters.

GASS, S. and MADDEN, C. (eds) 1985, *Input in Second Language Acquisition*. Rowley, Mass.: Newbury House.

HERNANDEZ-CHAVEZ, E. 1984, The inadequacy of English immersion education as an educational approach for language minority students in the United States. *Studies on Immersion Education: A Collection for United States Educators*. Los Angeles: Evaluation, Dissemination and Assessment Center, 144–83.

HOUSEN, A. and BAETENS BEARDSMORE, H. 1987, Curricular and extra-curricular factors in multilingual education. *Studies in Second Language Acquisition* 9, 83–102.

KRASHEN, S. 1981, *Second Language Acquisition and Second Language Learning*. Oxford: Pergamon.

KRASHEN, S. AND BIBER, D. 1988, *On Course: Bilingual Education's Successes in California*. Sacramento: California Association for Bilingual Education.

Schooling and Language Minority Students: A Theoretical Framework, 1981, Los Angeles: Evaluation, Dissemination and Assessment Center.

Studies on Immersion Education: A Collection for U.S. Educators, 1984, Los Angeles: Evaluation, Dissemination and Assessment Center.

SWAIN, M. 1985, Communicative competence: Some roles of comprehensible input and comprehensible input in its development. In S. GASS and C. MADDEN (eds) *Input in Second Language Acquisition*. Rowley, Mass.: Newbury House, 235–53.

SWAIN, K. and LAPKIN, S. 1982, *Evaluating Bilingual Education: A Canadian Case Study*. Clevedon: Multilingual Matters.

WAGNER-GOUGH, J. and HATCH, E. 1975, The importance of input data in second language acquisition. *Language Learning* 25, 297–307.

WONG FILLMORE, L. with VALADEZ, C. 1986, Teaching bilingual learners. In M. WITTROCK (ed.) *Handbook of Research on Teaching*. Third Edition. New York: Macmillan, 648–85.

8 The German Model of Bilingual Education: An Administrator's Perspective

NANDO MÄSCH

Origins

The 'German Model' of bilingual education originated in the German–French sections of the *Gymnasium* (grammar school), where it was created, developed and tested. At a meeting of European education specialists held in 1990 this by now well-established model was first recognised for its structure and qualities and became known as 'The German Model' due to its specific characteristics.

These bilingual German–French streams have been in existence in German secondary schools since the second half of the 1960s as the offspring of a 1963 treaty of co-operation between France and Germany. The first significant group was established in 1970 and by 1992 there were 49 *Gymnasien* in Germany with a French–German section, as well as two middleschools and one comprehensive school.

In the initial years the spirit behind these establishments, based on the desire for post-war reconciliation, was to arrive via linguistic comprehension at understanding and awareness between neighbours whose roots lay in a common western European cultural background. Former sentiments of hereditary enmity which had historically influenced the relationships between France and Germany were to be replaced the goal of partnership through the conscious fostering of neighbourly goodwill. This objective is also reflected in the language of the treaties. Thus the language of the French neighbour was called, and is still called today, the 'Partner Language', and it is also customary to call the Treaty of Co-operation the 'Treaty of Friendship'.

Events have shown that what may have been thought of at the time as utopian has developed into a reality. The spirit of the treaty has triumphed over difficulties and perceived setbacks.

German–French bilingual sections in German schools are based on the spirit outlined above. They should be seen not merely as historical background but as a living concept. The type of bilingual education provided is aimed at inculcating the language of the immediate neighbour as a language of a partner; as such this goes far beyond using language as a mere means of communication, or 'lingua franca'.

This is also the spirit in which Europe should aim towards further integration. The bilingual German–French sections therefore regard their concept of partnership as orientated towards a future Europe and recommend it as a model. The schools involved see themselves as 'Schools for Europe' with a broader European philosophy.

Current State of Development

At a conference jointly organised by the Commission of the European Communities and the European Council for Cultural Co-operation in May 1990 in Namur (Belgium), the development of bilingual and international education was the focus of attention. At this Namur conference the 'German Model' was declared as 'exemplary for Europe'.

The design is not merely applicable to German–French but potentially to any coupling of a mother tongue and first foreign language aimed at a predominantly homogeneous, indigenous school population, irrespective of where it may be located, including small urban centres. For mixed or migratory school populations, however, other models are considered more appropriate.

The Two Specific Types of the German Model

Of the two types of bilingual education in the German Model, the INTEGRATIVE and the ADDITIVE types, the most frequent is the INTEGRATIVE type.

The Additive type

With the aim of using as many French-speaking teachers as possible, the teaching of French as a foreign language (reinforced by two weekly periods) and of the three bilingual disciplines (Geography, Politics/Civics, History) are shared between two teachers, one German and one French, speaking in their mother tongue.

Advantages

—This distribution allows for a separate and thereby planned period-by-period progression in both foreign language and mother tongue competence in the bilingual disciplines.
—It guarantees an authentic encounter with the foreign language through native speakers which is essential.

Disadvantages

—Sharing between two teachers entails not only a break-up of the themes of the subject matter but a separation between the mother tongue and the foreign language progression in the bilingual subject matters.
—Grading in the bilingual disciplines is rendered more difficult for the teacher because a low level of foreign language competence in the pupil could have a negative influence on the grades within a given subject matter, which would be unfair.
—Often German pupils do not like the generally teacher-dominated style prevalent among French teachers.
—There are difficulties in arranging the consistently higher number of periods per week in the general timetable. Parents legitimately do not want a reduction of hours in other subjects.

The Integrative type

Ideally the teaching here is also done by a native French-speaker, but without any separation of periods between those conducted in German and those in French. Bilingual disciplines and French as a foreign language are each taught integratively by one and the same teacher. The French speaking teacher ought nevertheless to have a German or French qualification for the bilingual discipline as well as a

German teaching qualification (lower and upper secondary) for the subject and for a foreign language—not necessarily French. He must also possess good working knowledge of German.

Since French teachers with such qualifications are rare, frequently German teachers can be found with qualifications in French and the specialised subject; many of them do excellent work.

After an initial period of fascination with the authentic 'language bath' idea, in which French-speaking teachers were either former teachers of German teaching specialised subject without the required credentials or else teachers of history or geography without any competence in teaching a foreign language, the conviction grew that it was more important for teachers to be competent in both the subject matter and the teaching of a foreign language, rather than neglect one of these two aspects and allow the sole domination of the authentic language model alone. If we accept the principle that there should be no lowering of standards in subject matter as a consequence of bilingual teaching, then the programme must avoid producing students with a general foreign language competence at the cost of knowledge of content and methods of specialised subjects. However, teaching which may be correct in specialised content but which fails to come across due to incompetent language teaching is obviously not optimal either.

Advantages

—Progress in content and language are co-ordinated.
—Evaluation is simpler.
—There is no division of content between two languages and two teachers.

Disadvantages

—Mother tongue development in the subject matter covered is not institutionalised but is at the discretion of the individual teacher.
—Since there are not enough teachers of the ideal type mentioned above, pupils may have inadequate authentic language exposure.

Both in the additive and the integrative type of bilingual teaching, it is essential that the subject matter should not be treated by reading the usual in foreign language texts but rather with full attention to the specific methodology of the subject matter, for instance use of source material.

TABLE 8.1

Grade	French	Bilingual Disciplines			
		Geography or History			
13	6	3			
12	6	3			
11 (term 2)	6	3			
11 (term 1)	6 (*3)	3			
		Geography	Politics	History	Art/Ph. Ed.
10	3	—	2	2	
9	3	2	—	2	
8	4	2	3 (*2)	—	
7	4	3 (*2)			
6	7 (*5)				(2)
5	7 (*5)				(2)

Explanation:
To be read from bottom to top
* = instead of normally —
— = indicates that the normal timetable makes no provision for the subject for all pupils at this grade.
No indication = Teaching will follow the normal timetable in German.

Description in Key Words:
— After 4 primary school years the target language is the first foreign language (for instance French).
— Foreign language instruction in the first two years is reinforced. The timetable for grades 5 and 6 explicitly designates two extra periods per week.
— Specific to the bilingual sections are the bilingual disciplines taught through the foreign language.
— By 'bilingual' one means that mother tongue competence must also be promoted. This is a fundamental difference from the Canadian immersion concept.
— Compulsory bilingual curriculum covers three disciplines, usually social sciences, e.g. Geography, Politics (Civics) and History, usually in that order from the 7th grade onwards.
— Provision of periods is accorded to the generally valid timetable.
— Because of slower progress one weekly period is added to the relevant bilingual discipline in the first year.
— Art or Physical Education in lower secondary from grade 6 upwards are optional for each individual school.
— No more than two bilingual disciplines will be taught at the same time.
— Meetings with representatives of the partner language play an important role. Every pupil has a pen-friend in the partner country with whom the first exchange takes place between families in the second year of study. With the possibility of annual repetition these exchanges assume the character of a permanent feature.
— Two conditions are laid down for continuation in the bilingual stream in the upper secondary: (1) *Leistungskurs* (advanced course) in French and (2) an ordinary course in one of the bilingual disciplines.
— At the *Abitur* examination a bilingual discipline is examined either orally or in writing.
— On the *Abitur* diploma a 'Bilingual Mention' is noted.

Structure of the integrative type

Only one type of bilingual education will be detailed here, namely the integrative type. It has become by far the most common type in Germany, and official decrees and the 'Recommendations for the teaching of bilingual disciplines' have moved it, unlike the additive type, from an experimental to a highly developed and consolidated stage.

The structure of the bilingual section is the same for the different foreign languages and is based on two decrees (North-Rhine-Westphalia).

The target population

The target population of the bilingual section is primarily German pupils; that is why the curriculum programmes adopted respectively in the different German *Länder* (states) are taught. The bilingual factors are additional elements. The subject content of the bilingual disciplines and the weekly periods given to other subjects cannot be reduced.

Transferability

With French in the bilingual section and English as the first foreign language in the normal section transferability can be realised in the following three ways :

(1) at the end of the 5th grade, a new beginning in grade 5 (repeating the year) with English as the first foreign language.
(2) At the end of the 6th grade (Orientation Phase) he may change to the *Aufbauklasse* of the *Realschule* (middle school) which starts with English in grade 7. If a school provides both a German–French bilingual section and a normal French first foreign language course, transfer is easy. However, a genuine or alleged problem of 'elitism' arises which can render the work at school more difficult. If a school provides the bilingual German–French course in addition to a normal English first foreign language course, then the bilingual pupils are not doing something 'better' but something merely 'different'.
(3) Without any difficulties at the end of the 10th grade, he may leave the bilingual stream and continue in the normal stream.

Justifying Reasons

A European perspective of the bilingual German–French sections

The bilingual German–French sections see themselves as European in character and ideally as schools for Europe, dedicated to the language policy supported by the European Commission.

Through the in-depth study of foreign languages in bilingual sections, the 'partner language' is seen as something more than a mere vehicle. The different bilingual sections are meant to contribute to a better understanding and awareness of other European cultures and to go well beyond a mastery of their respective languages. The EC aims at being a 'Community', and a community requires partnership and not domination, least of all a linguistic domination.

The concept of a 'dominant language'—which could obviously only be English—does not fit European language policy. Since thought is determined by language, a dominant language suppresses not only other languages, but also impedes the development of other cultures to a point of threatening their very existence. We maintain that Europe cannot find its identity by means of one leading language, but rather through the concept of diversification.

Hence it is to be applauded that, in Germany other forms of bilingual sections are coming into being: German–Spanish, German–Italian, German–Russian and German–Dutch. In this way, support is lent to the official foreign language concept of the European Community through diversification of foreign language provisions.

The German–English sections benefit from the growing recognition of many parents that, after 1992, a knowledge of foreign languages will become ever more important to the future of their children. The arguments in favour of English as the most important world language are easy to explain; that is why these particular sections are at present experiencing a boom after several years of stagnation. Still more parents, however, are also seeing the need for a more intensive foreign language education from the standpoint that 'English is not enough'. A good knowledge of English can be acquired not only through English as the first foreign language, but also through English as the second language after French, especially in the German–French sections.

Given the rapid progress made by German-speaking pupils in the genetically related English language, many teachers, politicians and industrial leaders have doubts about the need for further intensification of the normal nine-year course of English in the German grammar school. In its final years language acquisition is proportionally less efficient. This problem does not arise with a non-Germanic language, since more time is required to bring linguistic efficiency to a comparably high level. There is also the temptation that some German–English bilingual sections may neglect their contribution towards building Europe and transmit the English language merely as 'lingua franca' and not as the language of one or more partners whose cultures should be the object of in-depth study.

Bilingual education is aimed at developing bicultural competence; therefore education in European partnership is fundamentally distinct from an efficiency-based intensive language course which neglects culture.

Selection and didactic functions of the bilingual disciplines

Although other subjects than Geography, Politics and History are conceivable as bilingual disciplines, these social science subjects are particularly appropriate for two reasons:

(1) If in bilingual education the second language is to be understood as the partner language, then these subjects have a particular significance, given their affinity with the partner culture. Natural science subjects have no significant relationship with the culture of the partner country.

(2) Specialised social science language is covered to a far greater extent by general language than is the case with the natural sciences.

The presentation of highly specialised foreign language—i.e. subject-linked discourse and terminology-features—should not exceed the absolute minimum.

Though broad language competence can only be acquired through intensive employment in specific circumstances, it will only remain flexible and productive if it does not get lost in details but concentrates instead on grasping general principles, specifically those specialised elements that are useful and transferable for an educated speaker. It is incontrovertible that a candidate in the bilingual section is also expected to have a certain linguistic competence in the natural science subjects. The 20-year experience with bilingual studies has shown that Geography alone sufficiently covers virtually all the necessary elements from the natural sciences through physical geography and geophysical phenomena, and from the application of methodological skills through its work with figures, statistics, graphs and sketches.

It cannot be sufficiently stressed that the major features of the bilingual streams are the bilingual subjects. The decisive criterion is that bilingual teaching has a different quality of communication when compared with foreign language only as a discipline. Communication in bilingual subjects is fundamentally determined by the imparting of information. Here the language is not just a matter to be learnt, but is more of a vehicle—the original function of language—and is experienced as such by pupils.

A didactic concept governs the choice and succession of bilingual disciplines. They compliment each other and their respective functions.

Art: a concrete situational function

In the early years, activities in the visual arts are not primarily verbal. Therefore verbal communication is relatively free and can be used for conversation accompanying concrete actions. This form of communication works by giving 'hidden exercising' and is particularly effective as a disguised learning process. Such specialist teaching in concrete situations is generally forward-looking in foreign language pedagogy.

Geography: referential, information giving function

In Geography, a relatively simple start is possible through an initially descriptive phase; value judgements are possible at a higher level. This subject has a referential function, since cognition is transmitted. Communication here is subject orientated information and no mere language exercise.

Politics (Civics): partner orientated and affective function

This subject also has aspects of referential functions. Personal and affective functions of education, however, play a larger role based upon the definitions of the disciplines. In the study of Politics pupils are often required to express opinions, feelings or to reactions to feelings (an emotive function) and/or to influence interactions, thoughts and feelings or conversely to be influenced by them (the conative function). The aims of the course in politics suit the bilingual section: an ability to recognise different types of action and a capacity to form an opinion. A further advantage of this subject is that the content is relatively free; what is of concern are attitudes and judgements rather than any specific learning matter.

Particularly in connection with the discipline Politics, it is important to point out that in the bilingual sections the expression of spontaneous opinions in the mother tongue must be allowed, not only in order to maintain general motivation and interest in the subject matter, but also to guarantee the expression of personal opinions in spite of at times inadequate foreign language competence. Moreover, it must be remembered that in bilingual sections—as the name implies—bilingual competence is the aim.

History: a referential, information giving function

This subject is particularly relevant to a deeper understanding of the culture of the partner. The specialised language is even closer than that of Geography to the general language, and this makes the subject less difficult. On the other hand, the understanding of complex historical situations requires great foreign language competence. As with Geography, the referential function dominates in this discipline.

Other subjects are not as appropriate to 'European' bilingual education as the social science disciplines. In Biology, for instance, it is true that referential and concrete situational communication is united-specific content-matter communication in ordinary classroom teaching and personal communication in experimental work. However, Biology has not proved satisfactory as a bilingual section subject for three reasons:

(1) The quantity of indispensable specialised terms is much larger than in Geography, History and Politics. If there are to be no reductions in the level of specialised knowledge, the rich terminological load cannot be avoided.
(2) Biological terms are used infrequently in general language, especially those that are highly scientific.
(3) Biology has little relevance to a deeper understanding of the culture of the partner country.

The structure of bilingual disciplines as practised in the German–French bilingual streams (Geography, Politics, History and, optionally, Art) has been carefully thought out and tested. The didactic function of the disciplines when used together form a harmonious whole in which optimal foreign language pedagogy is combined with the objective of aiming at co-operation and partnership in a European framework.

Aims and Objectives

The aims of the German–French bilingual education programme are firstly to create a continuously developing bilingualism in two vehicular languages, the mother tongue and the partner language and secondly to allow pupils by the end of their schooling to communicate orally and in writing about central objective aspects of history, the state, the economy and culture so as to express personally developed opinions.

Subdivisions of the above aims:

—Candidates should acquire bicultural competence.
—They should become brokers between the German culture and another, preferably that of a European partner.
—The 'Bilingual Mention' on the *Abitur* diploma exempts them from language examination upon entry to further studies in the partner country.
—The 'Bilingual Mention' is a sort of supplementary qualification for non-foreign language professions.
—Beyond the formal aspect of final certification, it leads to a real-life possibility of study and employment mobility.
—It aims at linguistic preparation for cooperation in the EC and throughout Europe.
—Through in-depth understanding of a foreign language, the learner obtains, according to Wilhelm von Humboldt and Sapir Whorf respectively, a qualitatively different view of the world and a broadening of perspectives.

The Mother Tongue

The pedagogically justified inclusion of the mother tongue is based on the principle: 'As much as possible in the partner language, as much as necessary in the mother tongue'.

The use of the mother tongue is legitimate and/or necessary:

—to guarantee a mastery of the technical language in the mother tongue

—on psychological and motivational grounds, through allowing spontaneous expressions

—in discussions where foreign language competence is inadequate, for example, in discussions about topical issues

—as a last resort for testing knowledge of content-matter

—when materials in the mother tongue are used, e.g. textbooks, atlases, sources, but only when sensitivity towards mother tongue phenomena are considered desirable, for example analysing a speech by a German statesman;

—in pursuance of comparative issues

—as a guarantee of comprehension

—when time constraints are necessary;

—when there is a danger of lack of precision.

—to ensure that complex or abstract learning objectives are attained, particularly in lower secondary when the foreign language competence is still restricted

—on thematic grounds, for example career guidance in Politics in grade 10

—in circumstances which require strong personal commitment.

Bilingual education in upper secondary is based upon the principle that unilingual French subject matter should be taught with the simultaneous knowledge of the indispensable specialised terminology and structures.

Evaluation

Administrative Regulations for Bilingual Sections in the German State of North-Rhine-Westphalia states the following:

> In disciplines taught in the partner language the primary concern of evaluation is the pupil's performance in the subject matter . . . It is comparable to evaluation of disciplines not taught bilingually . . . General deficiencies in the foreign language must not negatively influence evaluation as long as communication is guaranteed. On the other hand, positive linguistic performance will be favourably credited as an extra. If during the *Abitur* examination the pupil makes use of German then he will not obtain the 'Bilingual Mention'

Bilingual competence is considered as an extra; if it is found lacking, it should not lead to a downgrading in the final evaluation of the subject in question.

Evaluation of performance in French itself as a subject should be 'externally' and not 'internally' relevant, e.g. bilingual students should be assessed according to the same standards as non-bilingual students. Thus a student who is average in the bilingual class but excellent compared with non-bilingual students would not be assessed as average on the school certificate but as excellent. However, given the reinforced foreign language course and work in the bilingual disciplines, the expectations and demands placed on students in the 'bilingual' advanced course in French are different and build on previous learning. Students are therefore stimulated to raising their performance level without feeling disadvantaged relative to their peers.

Opportunities and Difficulties in the Creation of German–French Bilingual Sections

Initiatives

Establishing a German–French bilingual section in a German *Gymnasium*, which traditionally develops its structure in the proportion of 3:1 (3 normal classes : 1 bilingual class), depends on the following:

—the decisive will of an initiator, usually one of the teachers with qualifications in teaching French and in one of the bilingual disciplines (Geography, Politics (Civics), History)
—the conviction of a small group of teachers ready to acquire the necessary competence for a bilingual discipline
—the persuasive powers and strategic skills of the initiator and the 'bilingual group'
—a benevolent and, even better, committed school director, convinced of the successful outcome.

Resistances

There are those teachers of English who cannot understand that their language is not 'the first'. However, they forgo their resistance when they realise that, by the end of grade 10 the most proficient students in English come from the German–French bilingual section, having experienced and studied a strongly differentiated and orally practised language.

Resistance from Latin teachers also has to be overcome. It may well be true that what one begins to learn at ten years of age is learnt more easily than later. However, teachers and parents who advocate Latin as a first language must ask themselves if they really wish youngsters to neglect their pre-pubescent imitative capacities which are so necessary for oral foreign language acquisition in order to begin cognitive processes which they do not yet sufficiently possess at this age. Whoever begins with a dead language is not using age-specific capacities optimally. The well-known argument that, with a basis in Latin one can more easily learn French (e.g. *fenestra > la fenêtre*, the relationship between adjectives and participles etc.) is only correct in so far as the genetic relationship between languages is a help to learning. But it is equally applicable in the reverse direction (*la fenêtre > fenestra*). However, as a dead language Latin can be learnt equally well later, which is not the case for a living language like French. One only need ask those who take French as a second or third language after Latin about their oral proficiency in French. Apart from some gifted exceptions, the results are deplorable.

For conscientious parents it is not the number or nature of foreign languages to be learnt which is the problem but the order in which they come. A child who begins with a highly distinct oral foreign language, follows it with another oral language, and then builds on this foundation non-spoken Latin, reaches a high level of performance in all three. Latin teachers too become convinced when they experience highly satisfactory results with the order French, English and Latin. They may even be astonished with the often exceptional achievements of pupils who come from the German–French section.

There are some teachers who potentially could be considered as qualified teachers of French and Geography, Politics or History but who are not fully acquainted with the specialised terminology and structures of the foreign language discipline. They may claim that many pupils nowadays are not capable of understanding a given subject matter and its methods even in their mother tongue least of all in foreign language. At first sight this can be a convincing argument, supported by those who lack courage and diligence. But those who go deeper into the matter know that the limitations in specific foreign language terminology and structures, actually mean that knowledge is anchored even stronger. The restricted linguistic competence of pupils demands that their ways of thinking and speaking frequently have to be strictly controlled and reinforced with the same linguistic process so they become ingrained, rather like steadfastly treading the ground until deep and lasting footprints remain. Experience from 14 classes of Abitur candidates (1992) shows that the knowledge of the subject matter learnt in a foreign language is usually very secure and the technical terminology correct.

Generally speaking, the bilingual section will stand or fall on the good will of the school director and the professional, didactic and, last but not least, *human* qualities of the teachers in the bilingual disciplines.

Constitution of the classes

Due to possible cross-disciplinary interaction, it is advisable to set up a separate bilingual class whenever possible, rather than to integrate it with a normal class.

Though separate classes should be the rule, insufficient numbers may warrant a bilingual group being combined with a normal group. This practice has already been carried out and requires no additional organisation other than the type of streaming common to many secondary systems in Europe.

General teaching time

The maximum number of hours per week is an important factor in the structural conception of a bilingual section. Although it may be essential in the interest of the efficiency to increase the number of hours per week of French as a foreign language and to compensate for the slower progression in the subjects taught through the medium of French by a similar increase in contact hours, there are limits imposed by the general amount of schooltime available. The 'integrative' type of the German Model takes this problem into account, as the bilingual programme requires only the following increase in periods:

Grade 5: two periods per week (French as foreign language)
Grade 6: two periods per week (French as foreign language)
Grade 7: one period per week (Geography as bilingual discipline)
Grade 8: one period per week (Politics as bilingual discipline).

If the bilingual education should be extra and should not exist at the cost of other subjects, then no extension of hours is possible in grades 9 and 10, since the natural sciences require their legitimate hours here. In the upper secondary the 'integrative' type requires no extra weekly periods. This has revealed itself as positive for the maintenance of a wide spectrum of optional courses.

Teaching materials

In the bilingual sections, as a rule pupils receive the standard German textbooks which are used in their school and, in addition, an appropriate French textbook, often on loan to reduce costs. Because of its link with the German curriculum and with the local curriculum in each school the German textbook is essential to facilitate transfers, e.g. from the bilingual to the normal section at the end of lower secondary.

In the lower grades teachers often have to adapt their texts linguistically and develop substantial materials of their own. However, since 1993 printed materials for the bilingual disciplines have been published in Germany by Klett Schulbuch Verlag in Stuttgart with the first volume entitled *Espace Africain* which includes *'Aides au travail élémentaire'* and *'Introduction au travail géographique'*. These materials illustrate, in an exemplary manner, the didactic and methodological procedures of the bilingual discipline as they are practised in the German Model.

Information for parents

Each year, the parents of potential pupils in bilingual sections must be informed of what is involved, even if the programme has been long-established. Parents are easily convinced of the importance of foreign languages given the recent developments in Europe and elsewhere. Through written and oral information, they need to understand why 'English is not enough', and that modern European society urgently needs people with diversified knowledge of languages.

Costs

No significant extra costs are involved in running a bilingual section. All schools can procure the necessary materials within their normal budgets if a book loan system is used. A limited extra budget is helpful, though not necessary.

Teacher training and in-service training

There is as yet no institutionalised teacher training for bilingual disciplines. As far as in-service training is concerned, the *Arbeitsgemeinschaft der Gymnasien mit zweisprachig deutsch–französischem Zug in Deutschland* (c/o Nando Mäsch, Stresemannstr. 56. D-5160 Düren) has organised conferences for teachers involved in this field since 1975. Its preparatory work led, in 1988, to the publication of 'Recommendations for the teaching of bilingual disciplines' by the ministry for education in North-Rhine-Westphalia, the first publication of its kind in Germany.

Perspectives

The possibility of simultaneously obtaining both the German *Abitur* and the French *Baccalauréat* is a projected goal. A German–French educational project is at present being tried out in Germany and in France and is to be concluded in the middle of the nineties. Based on the German–French bilingual sections in the *Gymnasien* this project will lead to the simultaneous acquisition of both *Abitur* and *Baccalauréat*. Candidacy for the double qualification is voluntary. Two conditions for admission are required: Two bilingual subjects rather than one are in the ordinary course in the upper secondary (History and Geography/ Civics), one of which must be taken as a written *Abitur* exam. The advanced course in French must be an oral *Abitur* exam. In the French language exam, the French inspectorate is present. The curricula have been and are determined by the German and French authorities together.

Given the developments in European unification presently under way, the time is ripe for the creation of further bilingual programmes in diverse languages. The experiment has been tried and is proving successful and has convincingly persuaded parents and educational authorities as to its worth.

Bibliography

BUTZKAMM, Wolfgang 1992, Zur Methodik des Unterrichts an bilingualen Zweigen. *Zeitschrift für Fremdsprachenforschung* 3 1/92, 8–30
CHRIST, INGEBORG 1992, 1. Bilingualität in der Schule. Chance oder Notwendigkeit im Europa der Zukunft? 2. Bilinguale Züge im Sekundarbereich. *Grensoverschrijdend talenonderwijs/Grenzüberschreitender Sprachunterricht*, Nr. 1, November 1992, Goethe-Institut/Zernike College Amsterdam.

Drexel-Andrieu, Irène 1988, Rapport sur l'enseignement du langage technique propre à la géographie dans une section bilingue franco–allemande. *Die Neueren Sprachen*, 87, 203–14.

— 1993, la documentation pour la géographie bilingue dans l'Oberstufe. *Der fremdsprachliche Unterricht* 26, 1/93.

Krechel, Hans-Ludwig 1993, Spracharbeit im Anfangsunterrict Erdkunde bilingual. *Der fremdsprachliche Unterricht* 26, 1/93

Kronenberg, Werner 1992, Lieber bilingual nach Europa als sprachlos in die Zukunft. *Die Neueren Sprachen* 6/92.

— 1993 Europäische Vergangenheit und ihre Bewältigung – der Beitrag des bilingualen Geschichtsunterrichts zur mehrsprachigen Gestaltung der Zukunft. *Der fremdsprachliche Unterricht* 26, 1/93.

Kultusminister des Landes Nordrhein-Westfalen 1988, *Empfehlungen für den bilingualen deutsch–französischen Unterricht*. Frechen, Verlagsgesellschaft Ritterbach, Politik: Nr. 3441; Geschichte: Nr. 3442; Erdkunde: Nr. 3443.

Mäsch, Nando 1981, Sachunterricht in der Fremdsprache. *Neusprachliche Mitteilungen*, 34, 18–28.

— 1989 (1994), Bilingualer Sachunterricht. In Richard Bausch et al., *Handbuch Fremdsprachenunterricht*. Tübingen, 280–83.

— 1991, Ziele des zweisprachigen deutsch–französischen Bildungsweges. In Raasch et al., *Fremdsprachen lehren und lernen*. Saarbrücken (Uni), 47–56.

— 1993, Grundsätze des bilingual deutsch-französischen Bildungsganges. *Der fremdsprachliche Unterricht*, 26, 1/93.

Wode, Henning and Burmeister, Petra 1991, *Erfahrungen aus der Praxis bilingualen Unterrichts, Informationshefte zum Lernen in der Fremdsprache*. Heft 2, Universität Kiel.

9 Bilingual Geography: A Teacher's Perspective

IRÈNE DREXEL-ANDRIEU

The following report deals with the practical side of Geography lessons given in a *Gymnasium* (Grammar school) in Hamburg. In 1981 the *Gymnasium Osterbek* started a bilingual German/French stream. During the first year of secondary school, the pupils involved are taught 8 hours of French-as-a-subject per week, in the following year 7 hours. In the third year, Geography is taught through French for 3 hours per week— instead of the usual 2 of the standard German curriculum, together with 5 hours of French-as-a-subject. Later in the programme these pupils will learn History and Social Sciences through the medium of French as well. In all they will receive up to 10 lessons per week either on or in French by the 10th grade. If pupils wish to take a *bilinguales Abitur* (bilingual equivalent of an 'A' level course) they carry on with 5 hours of French in a *Leistungskurs* and 2 hours either in Geography or History in a *Grundkurs*, where one of these subjects shall form part of the *Abitur* examination.[1]

The Learners

The majority of the learners in bilingual streams are Germans. Generally they had good marks in the *Grundschule* (primary school) and their parents wanted them to receive an education well adapted to the European future.

Some of them are francophiles merely because of journeys to France or because they appreciate French civilisation. Only about 10% of the learners are French or have one French or francophone parent. But they live in German surroundings, and sometimes these pupils don't even speak French at all at home.

Curriculum

Although the pupils concerned learn Geography in French, they are integrated into the German school system and the curriculum is binding for them as it is for other Germans. In other words they must be able to change to a regular German class at any time. In the *Sekundarstufe I* (Secondary Grade 1) this is no real problem, for the German curriculum prescribes themes where teachers choose the illustrations themselves: for example, treating the activities of a port one can take Marseilles as an example. Nevertheless the danger is that treating only examples from France or in the francophone world (e.g. former French colonies), specifically German aspects of the curriculum might be neglected; I cannot expect the Hamburg pupils to be motivated to study the port of Marseilles if they know nothing about their own port.

However, this aspect will be possible in a later transfer phase. In this second stage of knowledge pupils are eager to compare with the twin city where their pen-friends live and which they have visited.

A second potential danger is the arousal of a feeling among the German children of being turned into French people. At this point of development the pride in learning in an uncommon and original way may give way to suspicion, leading all motivation to vanish. It is up to the teacher to assess the learners' feelings. Often, pupils' willingness depends on the experiences enjoyed in France during the school exchange which takes place in the second year of the bilingual programme.

The First Minutes of the First Lesson

At the start it is advisable to take a concrete topic and to avoid anything abstract, such as the representation of the earth with latitude and longitude. According to the Hamburg curriculum[2] the primaeval forest is a suitable topic for starting the first bilingual lesson in French.

In my case I project a slide showing an overflowing river in a forest composed of high trees with slim trunks. In the blue sky one can see rather large grey clouds. I let the pupils describe what they see. They easily verbalise the river amongst high trees and clouds in the sky.

Then one pupil may ask in German how to say 'flooding', e.g.:

Pupil: Wie sagt man Überschwemmung?
Teacher: Une inondation. Fais une phrase maintenant.

Pupils respond to my request to put the new word into a sentence by making a descriptive sentence. The lesson continues in the same way; every time the learners cannot express themselves in the target language they ask for the missing expression.

Unilingualism/Bilingualism

When the whole matter is too complex pupils ask if they are allowed to carry on in their strong language, German. In most cases this authorisation must be given, since priority belongs to the content-matter, Geography, rather than language learning. At a later stage, and depending on the degree of complexity, it might be possible to encourage other pupils to express the same idea in French, for the teacher to translate the idea herself, or even to leave it in German.

For the teacher working in this bilingual mode it means a permanent evaluation of the circumstances in the class at any given point in a given lesson, in order to avoid frustration. Flexibility is paramount. Tired pupils might be unable to discuss a certain topic in the target language, in which case it is preferable for them to do so in the reactivation phase at the beginning of the next lesson.

According to the teacher's attitude concerning the role of the foreign language, learners quickly understand that the use of their first language remains the exception, even if it is sometimes necessary to speak mainly in German. An introductory comment such as,

Ausnahmsweise heute auf deutsch (Today in German, as an exception)

makes it clear that French is the teaching language, so that quite naturally the learners feel compelled to use it and, if they cannot, to ask if they may speak German.

Teaching Aids

Visual media

Geography is especially suited to being dealt with in a foreign language because visual media play a dominant role in lessons. Standard aids are slides, diagrams, plans, lists of figures and graphs. These can be understood without any, or with very little lexical help.

Geographical films/videotapes which form part of standard geographical teaching aids present some difficulties. In the foreign language these might be quite difficult to understand, since with no plot or story-line to help them pupils may well see a geographical phenomenon but hardly understand the explanations. Making use of French TV programmes is not particularly helpful either, since the density of information is rather low, given that documentary films also aim to entertain, making them less useful for didactic purposes. Since I do not wish to do without films, I find it helpful to show German educational films or German TV programmes which we discuss afterwards, also in German. In some cases I give a written summary in French to make sure pupils have the technical terminology in a suitable context which they will need in other situations.

Texts–documents

The use of authentic texts is at times difficult since these often represent a heavy linguistic task which does not properly belong to the domain of studying geography. Nevertheless, even if the use of texts is reduced it should not be entirely suppressed. Text analysis forms part of an important geographical skill and it provides the opportunity to practise extracting the gist from an authentic text. Reading an article from Le nouvel observateur about farming in the USA is highly motivating in the second Geography year, but cannot be repeated too often as it is time-consuming.

Searching for quite easy texts leads the bilingual teacher to unconventional solutions, for instance the use of literary texts as sources of information (Drexel-Andrieu, 1990). One Senegalese tale I have used reveals the culture of millet. The advantage of this is to make clear that Geography is everywhere: it is an all-embracing subject.

Keeping this idea in mind, there are other visual aids which provide geographical information, although they were originally not intended as such: cartoons, drawings, paintings. Examples are a contemporary cartoon by the artist Plantu in Le Monde about the European Community, a drawing portraying poverty in Calcutta by Günther Grass or a painting of the tropical karst landscape in Guilin (Southern China).

Comics can be very useful too, as when one reads *Astérix chez Rahazade* (Goscinny & Uderzo, 1987) and discovers all the allusions to India. There is no better preparation for a trip to Marseilles than reading very carefully the two and a half pages devoted to Massilia in *Le tour de Gaule d'Astérix* (Goscinny & Uderzo, 1965), where one can find the city's foundation by the Greeks, information on vegetation, fishing, playing *à la pétanque*, local expressions, the mediterranean pronunciation, the typical exaggeration in retelling events and even, Marcel Pagnol with the famous actor Raimu.

In conclusion, what began as an emergency solution has become constructive teaching material.

Books and Didactically Prepared Texts

The German pupils like French Geography books for their beauty as they contain lots of photographs and little text. Being short the texts are, however, concise and not easy for foreign learners to understand. Sometimes they are even written in the *passé simple* which increases the difficulty. So there is no other solution than to write texts oneself.

There are two ways of doing this. At the end of a lesson, pupils may provide a summary. Results of this I write myself on the board to avoid wasting time, because of mistakes, and to give me the opportunity to change or add something. The learners then copy these down in their exercise books.

This procedure is a time-consuming, but useful outcome of the lesson. Another solution consists of pre-preparing the text and distributing it at the end of the lesson. It is formulated solely in French, without any syntactic difficulties, but using technical language.

Vocabulary

At the end of a text or lesson new words are listed with their German meaning. In fact, this list is not only a comprehension aid, it guarantees that the learners know the technical language in their first language as well. I always leave enough time at the end of a lesson for the reading of the text, to guarantee that each pupil fully understands it. This is no longer necessary, however, in the upper classes.

The beginning of geography lessons in French coincides with the start of English lessons, which means in fact that the young pupils are learning vocabulary in three subjects; French, English and Geography. This is definitely a burden. Hence, we may use part of the lesson time to play with new expressions by using crosswords and the usual language teaching games (Drexel-Andrieu, 1988). Needless to say, pupils are very fond of these, and after a while they prepare the games for their classmates themselves.

Assessment Tests

There are two types of assessment. The first one is meant to make sure that the facts have been learnt at home, and where the pupils' performance represents mere reproduction. For instance, a test can consist of completing a map or a diagram.

In bilingual Geography it is absolutely necessary that from the very beginning pupils command the technical language, which makes vocabulary tests indispensable. In these I will give a term in German which has to be translated into French and used in a sentence. Providing a given definition in French would be too difficult and not beneficial for the subsequent use by the pupil.

Example:

Grundwasser: la nappe phréatique. La nappe phréatique est polluée par les engrais chimiques.

In written tasks I correct every mistake, but only the technical terms and the cohesion of the sentence are marked. Pupils have told me that when learning the vocabulary list, they also think of adequate sentences!

The second type of assessment is an *Arbeit* (assignment) which is more complex and usually longer. The first part consists of reproduction, but then the learners must show that they are able to work with geographical documents: i.e. to comment on a demographic pyramid, or some figures. In other words they perform a transfer. The questions and the documents are in French; I always check carefully that the tasks have been understood before pupils start working.

Answers are given in the target language, French, only using the first language if they are unable to continue in French. Usually when correcting I translate the German words/expressions/sentences in the margin without any comment, except when the missing term belongs to the technical language which should have been known. Only this will be taken into account in the final mark.

Experience shows that pupils prefer taking the risk of incorrect French rather than writing in German, which tends to get used as a last resort. They know that a wrong expression will play no role in the final mark. This may sometimes result in a large number of mistakes they would not normally make, since pupils are concentrating on the contents.

Somewhat discouraged at one point because of mistakes like *la précipitation* (precipitancy) instead of *les précipitations* (precipitation) or *la courbe se baisse* (the curve bows down) for *la courbe baisse* (the curve drops), upset about *vertil* instead of *fertile*, *culturation* for *culture* I decided to write a model version of the expected answers, which was distributed after an oral correction and had to be learnt as homework. This again was checked with very positive results: the linguistic and geographical expressions improved greatly and in a short space of time I could suspend the check, so that the investment in time had been worthwhile, though I maintained the use of model versions.

I am in total agreement with the *Empfehlungen für die bilingualen Sachfächer* (Recommendations for Bilingual Content-Matter Subjects) referred to by Mäsch (cf. this volume), that good linguistic performance must be taken into account in the final mark of the *Abitur* examination. Yet to do this in normal assessment tests might lead to privileging certain francophone pupils. To avoid being impressed by only well expressed sentences I merely underline all technical terms which have been well used and can easily find out if idiomatic language coincides with geographical knowledge.

Typical Difficulties

Motivation

Pupils in bilingual sections need not necessarily work more, but do need higher concentration. They must not be distracted too often since they can lose the thread very quickly. Consequently, as already mentioned above, it is of the greatest importance to use all possibilities to retain motivation, e.g. by having an Indian meal together and trying to eat properly with one's fingers; visiting an exhibition about the American Indians in the Prairies and then going straight away to see the film 'Dances with Wolves' are positive pedagogical experiences conducted for the sake of learning Geography.

To a large extent pupils become aware of their geographical

surroundings and they do appreciate the use of unusual media. After a while they start to contribute and bring objects found during trips, e.g. spices and stones, or they report a conversation with a foreigner.

Teaching from the front

More than in a lesson in the first language, in bilingual Geography the teacher comes across as omniscient, both in disseminating knowledge and in the way to express this knowledge. To reduce the predominance of teacher domination pupils should be given opportunities to present certain topics to their classmates. But to carry this out in the target language, French, is the exception. This is because usually documents required for preparation are written in language which is too complex. Nevertheless, presentations are a necessary skill, since learners must look for information themselves, garner the gist, classify it and finally present results to their classmates, with the teacher in the background. Rather than give up this valuable exercise because of language difficulties, papers are presented in German. The procedure is exactly the same as for films mentioned earlier, where the following discussion is in German. Pupils do not miss any potential technical vocabulary even if the subject of the topic only verges on geography; for instance, in the case of biographies of Gandhi or Mao Tse-Tung.

In higher classes (after three years of bilingual Geography) it becomes possible to give a text to prepare as homework: this facilitates inter-pupil communication during the lesson.

Teaching materials

Finding adequate teaching material for working in the upper classes is quite a problem. The reason is a fundamentally different point of view concerning geography teaching in Germany and France.

In Germany one tends to choose a concrete example, e.g. Tourism in the valleys of the Grödner and of the Villnöß (two small rivers in Austria). At the end of studying this topic pupils will have worked out the economic advantages, dangers for the environment and possible measures which take into consideration all interests. At the end of the school year German pupils become specialists in certain topics and are able to transfer their knowledge to similar subjects. If they have studied the specific problems of the North Sea Area they are able to work out, for instance, those of the Mediterranean Area.

The French approach to a similar topic is a more global one. Pupils are given figures concerning overnight accommodation for a given year, the kilometers of sandy beaches, etc. for the whole country, so that at the end of the theme of study they have an overall view of the importance of tourism for France (or any other country). By the end of the school year French pupils have a working knowledge about quite a lot of topics which allow them to see the interconnections between different fields (Drexel-Andrieu, 1991).

It is not my concern to discuss which approach is more efficient, the inductive or the deductive one: it depends on the results which are aimed at. The concrete problem for teaching Geography in French according to the German curriculum is finding suitable information. If I want to study city centres from their historical development to the problems of infrastructure and reconstruction, I can find these aspects illustrated by different cities: i.e. in the chapter on *Les centres-villes* of the French text-book, Lyon, Cergy-Pontoise, Marseilles, Bordeaux, Paris and Stockholm are mentioned on only four pages! (Géographie du temps présent, 1985.) Needless to say this approach does not fit in with the practice of German geography teaching.

The solution is to find university material which is not too complex for grammar school students and, once again, to use unconventional media. Ecogeography—which is supposed to be dealt with during one semester—has only seven pages devoted to it in the French text-book (Géographie, 1987). Fortunately, Greenpeace publishes good magazines with suitable geographical material about problems of the environment.

Many geography teachers everywhere complain about the difficulty of finding up-to-date material, bilingual teachers complain even more, though with imagination and hard work this problem can be solved.

Conclusion

Experience shows that pupils taught bilingually are successful in Geography; the reason is not that they might be more intelligent, the point is they are more attentive and concentrate more, since they cannot just speak for the sake of speaking, whether they have something to express or not. In other words, in this type of teaching we waste little time just 'chatting geographically'.

Although it may sound like a cliché, Europe and the world need linguistic experts. I have noticed that when they apply for a job our ex-pupils are often more successful than others. They may well be preferred either because they were ready to learn something unusual or because their specific geographical knowledge can be put to use by a wider variety of different companies.

My last point is a personal one. I must admit that teaching bilingually is sometimes uncomfortable. On the other hand I experience new ways of co-operating with pupils, and this gives great professional satisfaction.

Notes to Chapter 9

1. For a better understanding of the German system of Bilingual Education I refer to the article by Nando Mäsch in this volume. The *Gymnasium Osterbek* belongs to the 'Integrative Form', despite a few differences: during the first three years we teach three Geography lessons per week, in the upper classes only two.
2. Freie und Hansestadt Hamburg, Behörde für Schule und Berufsbildung, Amt für Schule: Lehrplan Erdkunde, Sekundarstufe I. 1988, p. 7.

References

DREXEL-ANDRIEU, IRÈNE 1988, Rapports sur l'enseignement du langage technique propre à la géographie dans une section bilingue franco-allemande. *Die Neueren Sprachen* 87, 1/2, Diesterweg, 209–10.
— 1990, Geographische Literatur/Literarische Geographie: Ein Bericht aus dem deutsch-französischen bilingualen Unterricht. *Schule und Forschung: Literatur im Fremdsprachenunterricht—Fremdsprache im Literaturunterricht*. Frankfurt: Diesterweg, 92–101.
— 1991, Bilinguale Geographie. In H. WODE & P. BURMEISTER (eds) *Erfahrungen aus der Praxis bilingualen Unterrichts*. Eichstätt, Kiel: EKIB. p. 38.
Géographie du temps présent seconde—Collection Grehg 1985, Paris: Hachette. 188–91.
Géographie seconde, Collection Frémont, 1987, Paris: Bordas. 94–101.
GOSCINNY, R. and UDERZO, A. 1965, Le tour de Gaule d'Astérix. Neuilly-sur-Seine: Dargaud. 30–32.
— 1987, Astérix chez Rahazade. Paris: Albert René.

10 Bilingualism and Information Technology: The Welsh Experience

DAFYDD PRICE & COLIN BAKER

Introduction

The aim of this chapter is to consider how the English language threat posed by the sudden growth in the use of microcomputers in schools has been tackled in the bilingual education system in Wales. The chapter is contextualised in the rapid growth of bilingual primary education in Wales since 1939. Before 1939, primary (first level) education in Wales was English medium. Children from Welsh language homes and communities received their education in English. Since the middle of this century, an exponential growth in provision of Welsh-medium and bilingual teaching has occurred, particularly in the last two decades (Baker, 1985, 1988). There are currently 597 Primary schools in Wales where Welsh and English are both used for classroom learning, many of which are smaller schools. Such schools form 34.5% of all Primary schools in Wales.

Against this revolution in the language of schooling, arrived the potentially anglicising influence of microcomputers in the early 1980s. This chapter briefly details the initial problems of Welsh medium schools being given English language software, and then portrays the solutions that have been adopted to ensure that bilingualism and bilingual education are fostered rather than threatened by use of the microcomputer. The chapter finishes by giving practical advice based on a decade of experience in Wales on the infrastructure and the pragmatic aspects of promoting bilingualism through IT (Information Technology).

The Growth of Computers in Bilingual Schools

In the 1970s in Wales, the provision of English-only television was regarded as the threat to the Welsh language. In the 1980s and 1990s one perceived threat became the IT revolution (Baker, 1985). With many universal IT advances (e.g. microcomputer software, electronic mail across the world, CD Roms holding vast databases of information), the inherent danger is that minority languages and therefore bilingualism will be under threat. With the IT revolution, the status of majority languages, particularly English, rises; minority languages may appear of historical rather than futuristic value in the global village. The balance tilts away from minority languages towards high prestige, high profile international languages. The danger lies in the identification of advanced technological society with English; and Welsh being identified with religion, the home and history (Baker, 1992).

In the early 1980s, the perceived danger was that an IT revolution would be another nail in the Welsh language coffin (Baker, 1985). Following a survey of Welsh medium schools, Baker (1985: 162) found that:

> . . . the microcomputer was being used almost totally in English. Secondary schools reported 97% usage in English; Primary schools 86% . . . In classrooms where Welsh is the dominant medium of communication, English is the dominant language in using the microcomputer.

This led to a conclusion that, unintentionally, the English language had found another Trojan horse to enter the sparse breeding grounds of the Welsh language (Baker, 1985). It was argued that the horse needed to be bridled and used to promote bilingualism. It is the harnessing of the horse to work in the field of Welsh medium education that is now considered.

The introduction of microcomputers and initial responses

In 1983, the British Government provided a 50% grant to enable all interested Primary and Special schools to buy a computer. In Gwynedd, one of the eight counties of Wales, this grant gave schools the opportunity to purchase a microcomputer with colour monitor and cassette player for half price. Included in the government package was a selection of 35 computer programs called the *Primer Pack*. This package was envisaged as a starter pack that would give schools an opportunity to use a computer in the classroom. Today, many of the programs would be seen as naive and unacceptable. At the time, the Primer Pack pioneered the way and provided the stimulus to develop more effective software for classroom use.

In the many areas throughout Wales where there are bilingual schools, the *Primer Pack* presented a problem, if not a threat to the Welsh language. The new technology could prove detrimental to the precarious state of a minority language. In England and in non-Welsh speaking areas of Wales, the package could be introduced into the classroom immediately after introductory teacher in-service education courses on how to use the new hardware that had been largely thrust upon them (Baker, 1983). Generally a period of frustration followed in bilingual schools with the danger of changing overnight the bilingual balance of the curriculum through the introduction of a package of monolingual English software.

The absence of Welsh medium software presented a challenge as well as a concern to those involved in the introduction of computers to bilingual schools. If bilingual education in Wales did not respond to the need for Welsh software, the new technology would place another nail in the coffin of the indigenous language. Welsh educators decided to respond to the challenge of the new technology (Price, 1985). It became important that the computer was made capable of 'talking' to children in the classroom in Welsh as well as in English.

It was also envisaged that Information Technology would present another threat; the powerful presentation through an attractive medium of majority Anglophone culture. The indigenous culture, threatened in this century by the anglicising influences of mass media, communications, in-migration and industrialisation, appeared to have found another threat—the mighty microcomputer.

In response to this challenge, various individuals throughout Wales began to write simple programs in Welsh and to translate available English language software. Many of these early pioneers were teachers working in their spare time trying to overcome the monolinguality of classroom software. There was duplication of effort, variability in translation and little accepted computing terminology in Welsh.

In an attempt to respond to the situation, Gwynedd's Local Educational Authority seconded a teacher (via a central Welsh Office Grant) to translate programs into Welsh. Also, in November 1983, the Director of MEP Cymru (Microelectronic Education Programme—an all-Wales co-ordinating body), brought together the main individuals involved in translating software with the aim of co-ordinating such work.

This small group later became the *Welsh Panel* of MEU Cymru, (the Microelectronic Education Unit (Wales) that superseded the old MEP Cymru). It has since developed to provide a valuable national framework for steering all the Welsh medium IT needs in an efficient cross-county manner (Roberts, 1987). It also evaluates IT applications for Welsh Office funding via the Welsh Language Education Development Committee. The remit of the original small group was to:

(1) Initiate discussions that later led to the right to translate the *Primer Pack*. Initially this permission was not forthcoming because those holding the rights did not understand the need to translate. It is salutary to note that those producing the original *Primer Pack* did not realise that the Welsh language was in living existence in schools. Nor did they realise that the Welsh language is often the main medium of education in a bilingual education system.
(2) Share experiences of effective ways of overcoming computing problems when translating software (e.g. inclusion of accents).
(3) Decide on standard patterns of response within programs so that there was an agreed 'quality control' of translation.
(4) Discuss the need for a new Welsh language terminology to respond to the new technology. IT words have been introduced naturally into the Welsh language by programs, in-service education of teachers courses and program notes. Gradually these terms have become widely used, accepted into the language and given the language a modern vitality.

In the Welsh speaking areas of Wales, the counties were also fortunate in that all those needing translations opted for the same computer—the BBC microcomputer. Co-ordination of the translation of software for the BBC microcomputer ensured that valuable time was not being used 're-translating' the same programs for different machines.

At this stage, there was no talk of writing new, original Welsh language or bilingual programs. It was realistically accepted at this early stage that it would be quicker to fill the void with many good quality translated programs than to write a few time-consuming original programs that would most probably be doing the same type of screen work as their English language counterparts. The act of choosing programs to translate focused attention on the curriculum objectives of those programs. Such selection ensured that Welsh programs were educationally relevant and valuable. The development of new programs came later in response to the need for Welsh programs, mostly based on the Welsh cultural heritage.

From the outset, drill and practice programs were avoided and not translated into Welsh. This resulted in the introduction of translated Welsh software that was, at the time, thought to be among the best software available. The main body of programs initially translated were those within the *Primer Pack* and the many programs written by Anita Straker, who had become the dynamic leader of the National Microelectronic Education Programme Primary Project. Anita Straker wrote programs that were innovative and involved investigative mathematical work. Her programs effectively meet the needs of the new National Curriculum in England and Wales. Anita Straker's vision led to the introduction of a variety of curriculum packages. These packs included not only software, but also included courseware (accompanying materials) to guide the leaders of in-service education of teachers.

The Welsh language focus of IT changed with the setting up of the Microelectronic Education Programme Primary Project for England, Northern Ireland and Wales. The first seconded teacher was appointed to work part time with MEP Cymru (the Welsh Microelectronic Education Programme Unit) as a Co-ordinator with responsibility for Welsh software and for schools working through the medium of Welsh. At that time, very few County IT Co-ordinators or IT Advisory Teachers (English-medium or Welsh medium) had been appointed. The support of the U.K. National Microelectronic Education Programme Primary Project was immediately sought. A National Microelectronic Education Programme Co-ordinators conference, attended by Co-ordinators from England, Northern Ireland and Wales provided the opportunity to gain the support of those working in IT in schools in other parts of the United Kingdom. Arousing awareness of minority language IT issues in non-Welsh speaking people within the field of IT outside Wales was an important initial strategy.

Software translation

The need for the introduction of the computer as a bilingual educational tool with both languages having equal value became recognised by the National Microelectronics Education Programme Primary Project following lobbying. This body agreed to release the English Primary school software packs in their pre-release form, enabling translation work to start as soon as possible. The aim was to ensure that both the English and the Welsh translated programs would appear in Wales simultaneously. This task was difficult to achieve given the slender human resources available for translation. There was always a time lag created by the need to ensure that the final Welsh language pack was correct when compared with the final English language pack. However, the support and willingness of the U.K. Microelectronics Education Programme team provided an effective means of responding to the immediate need for Welsh software.

This support in turn enabled Wales to turn to commercial Software Houses to negotiate the rights to translate their programs. From the experience and expertise gained through earlier translation work, Microelectronic Education Programme Cymru and later MEU Cymru (all-Wales bodies), acting as central brokers for all the counties of Wales, were able to show that:

(a) there was a strong demand for Welsh software;
(b) there was a sufficient market (sometimes the translation work has been financed by a Welsh Office grant, but not always);
(c) the experience and expertise are available in Wales to carry out the translation work to a professional standard that maintained the quality expected by a reputable Software House.

Regional (county) contacts with Software Houses are important so that companies are aware of individual county needs. However, it is now part of the Welsh software framework that the final negotiating stages for the translation of a particular package of software is dealt with centrally by MEU Cymru (acting as an all-Wales body). This method ensures that the rights to receive the translated material belong to all counties in Wales; thus avoiding individual counties spending both their time, and that of a particular company, re-negotiating the same packages. Over time, a valuable sense of trust has been built up with many of these companies and they are willing to enter negotiations and allow either their work to be translated and distributed on the basis of an English version having been bought, or a county licence bought, or that a translated Welsh version is prepared commercially and marketed by themselves or via MEU Cymru as an agent.

The human resources for software translation have been meagre through prioritisation rather than availability. This resulted in a decision to translate only the elements the child encounters. Usually, manuals and teacher handbooks have not been translated. The aim has been to have a computer that 'spoke' to children in both Welsh and English in the classroom. If it was perceived that there was need for Welsh written material for teacher guidance, then shortened versions of the original were produced explaining salient points or changes that had been made. For example, information in Welsh may be given as to whether the initial letters of the Welsh keywords were accepted within a program rather than the original English key letters.

IT Terminology

With the arrival of the IT in the classroom, there arose the need to create new Welsh vocabulary. In 1984–85, under the auspices of the Welsh Joint Education Authority, those involved in the field were brought together. The computer terminology file created by Dafydd Roberts at University College of North Wales was used as the basis for the creation of a Dictionary of Welsh Computer Terms. New terms already in use were agreed upon and standardised. Where necessary, new words were created with the aim of ensuring that IT could be discussed effectively in Welsh, not only in the classroom, but also by those outside education.

New IT words have now become a natural part of the Welsh language. There is a constant need to update the Dictionary of Computer Terms to include new jargon. To be perceived by its younger generation as a language deserving respect and of utilitarian value, any minority language must have the dynamic energy to develop new vocabulary. For a minority language to survive, it needs to retain its historical–cultural language and adopt the developing constructions of each successive decade. the adoption and adaption of an IT vocabulary in any language is important for that language to survive as a living language and bilingualism to flourish.

The evolution and consolidation of an infrastructure

A major step forward in Welsh language IT usage came with the appearance of the Welsh language version of the word processing program, EDWORD (Clwyd Technics, 1983). The Welsh language EDWORD, prepared with the assistance of a Welsh Office grant, responded with the correct accents needed for the Welsh language and enabled pupils to write and draft creatively in a way that was interesting, meaningful and encouraged collaborative work. With a Welsh medium EDWORD came the need to introduce printers into school. The printer became the stimulus for a more effective use of classroom computer resources by encouraging, via hard copies, the discussion of draft work away from the computer, releasing the equipment for other groups to use.

With the introduction of more content-free software to schools, the need for In-Service education of teachers increased. In the early 1980s, the county of Gwynedd appointed a Mathematics/Computer Adviser to develop the new technology appearing in schools. A teacher was seconded to translate software; this teacher being joined by another as the first teacher became more involved in in-service education of teachers and Advisory Teacher work in schools. A programmer was attached full-time to the team from 1985 onwards. The Information Technology team grew in an attempt to respond to the ever increasing calls for technical as well as advisory assistance from schools.

In 1987, based on the recognition of effective IT practice in particular primary schools, 12 'satellite' Computer Centres were set up in the county of Gwynedd at these schools. Such 'satellite' Centres were created alongside a central Unit for IT which facilitates and co-ordinates work in these Centres. The individual teachers appointed as Co-ordinators within these Centres were 'missionary' volunteers willing to spend time outside school hours to help colleagues make better use of hardware and software in the classroom. The new local Co-ordinators attended one to three day residential courses every term to raise their level of understanding of the technology and of its educational possibilities in the classroom. The aim was not to create local 'experts' but to enable an enthusiastic group of volunteers help their colleagues more effectively. Each Centre was provided with a small library of software and, from time to time, was able to lend extra equipment to local schools for evaluation purposes. This equipment included printers, concept keyboards and more recently colour printers. There are currently 21 Primary (first level) 'satellite' Computer Centres in Gwynedd (one within each Secondary School catchment area).

The central Gwynedd Computer Unit consists of the following staff:

Computer Unit Head with responsibility for the Primary and Special Sectors;
Deputy with responsibility for the Secondary Sector;
3 Primary Advisory Teachers;
2 Secondary Advisory Teachers;
1 Half-time Special Needs Advisory Teacher;
1 Full-time Programmer;
1 Full-time Administrative Assistant;
1 Half-time Administrative Assistant.
(The 21 Sub-computer Centres play an important role within this framework).

The opportunity to appoint bilingual Advisory Teaching staff came with a Welsh Office Educational Support Grant, the grant being consistently supported with substantial additional financial funds by Gwynedd's Local Educational Authority. This grant also provided further funding to increase the number of computers in schools. In Gwynedd, the practice of placing computers in bilingual Primary schools without necessary backup support has been avoided. The strategy has been for the three Primary level Advisory Teachers to work in specific catchment areas. When initially arriving in bilingual schools, they brought with them a full computer set-up, including colour monitor, disk drive and printer. The Advisory Teachers visited the schools on a regular weekly basis and worked alongside the teacher in whose class the extra computer had been placed. The Advisory Teachers ensured development in the use of the technology from one week to the next. After the Advisory Teachers' 12 month period in a catchment area, the computer, which had by then proved itself as a valuable educational tool, was offered to each school at less than half price. Not one school refused the offer.

The three bilingual Advisory Teachers currently spend 80% of their time in schools and their pattern of work is as follows:

Monday, Tuesday, Friday: working in bilingual Primary Schools of a designated catchment area.
Wednesday: at the central Computer Unit. In-service Education; preparation; responding by telephone to school and arranging future visits.
Thursday: responding to calls for assistance from schools that are outside the present designated catchment areas

Besides this, the Advisory Teachers attend school meetings to assist with cross-curricular use of Information Technology.

In 1989–90, the county of Gwynedd financed a major scheme to increase the number of computers in schools. This money, alongside monies available through Parent Teacher Associations and various school fund raising activities, enabled the county to reach its short term aim of a minimum of one computer between every two classes. Many of the 194 bilingual Primary schools in Gwynedd have reached a ratio of one computer for each class and that is now the medium term aim for the whole primary sector in the county.

At the computer Unit, a special 'Hot line' has also been set up specifically to assist schools who need help. Schools are encouraged, if possible, to have their computer and software ready by the telephone so that step by step help can be given. This telephone advice system has, in a sparsely populated but geographically large county like Gwynedd, proved invaluable (as revealed in responses from bilingual schools to a questionnaire conducted by the Gwynedd Computer Unit to evaluate their service to Gwynedd Schools).

Bilingual teachers are still coming to terms with the new technology; they are in constant need of support and assistance, not only with old and new hardware, but also with the increasing cross-curricular use of IT. The stage has not been reached when Information Technology is effectively and efficiently used to its full potential. It is felt that through the core subjects (Welsh, English, Maths and Science), and through cross-curricular work, IT aims and objectives may effectively be reached. When one considers the world of IT in the classroom: word processing, desk top publishing, data, LOGO, Microworlds, control, problem solving, art and design, music and sound, a tremendous and fascinating challenge is presented to minority language educationists. CALL (Computer Aided Language Learning) programs can sometimes offer a threat to minority languages as they promote majority languages such as French and English. At the same time, CALL provides models for minority language programs to emulate for the learning of those minority languages (CTI, 1990; Learning Technology Unit, 1990).

Schools in the county of Gwynedd are broadening their use of IT by moving from the short, specific types of computer program to the more open framework type packages that fit cross-curricular work. These programs are sufficiently flexible to be used in either Welsh or English. There is still room for short programs that enhance the understanding of specific concepts or help an individual child with specific educational needs. However, it is often felt that the strength of the computer is in its ability to enrich learning by encouraging interactive and collaborative learning in a bilingual group (Cummins, 1988).

In the early days, the technology was often criticised for hindering the development of language and communication in the classroom (Baker, 1984). As the use of the new technology developed, it was realised that it could provide valuable opportunities for communication, for example, in the language of reasoning, argument, theorising, interpretation and presentation of work. The computer can support, enhance and change what is happening in the binguality of the classroom. The classroom microcomputer affects almost all ages, all children, all aspects of the curriculum and in turn all teachers. It is therefore possible for IT to present invaluable opportunities for bilingual language development at all levels (Sayers & Brown, 1987).

In Gwynedd, it has been found that teachers generally, after the initial stage of using simple programs to gain confidence in the use of the computer, find word processing a good access point to a wider use of IT. Writing is a natural part of most areas of the curriculum. The development from word processing is often to Desk Top Publishing or Data Accumulation and Analysis. Data Analysis blends in well with any project where information is gathered. Further development of IT use in the classroom varies according to the personal strengths and interests of particular teachers. Recently, the following order of preference of use appears to have emerged:

(1) Word processing
(2) Desk Top Publishing
(3) Art, Drawing and Paint packages
(4) An Amalgamation of 1, 2 and 3 (recently combined with 5)
(5) Data/Questionnaire Analysis
(6) LOGO/Control Technology/Problem solving situations.

The most frequently used areas of IT in bilingual classrooms in Gwynedd (Word Processing/Desk Top Publishing, LOGO and Data Analysis), will now be considered to illustrate the possibility of providing opportunities for bilingual language development through the use of IT.

Word Processing and Desk Top Publishing

By their very nature, Word Processing and Desk Top Publishing provide a vehicle for bilingual development across all aspects of the curriculum. There are opportunities from creative writing to factual record keeping in both languages. Children can discuss the content and style of their writing in groups using printed copies, thus making good use of scarce hardware resources by releasing the equipment for use by other groups. Using word processing and desk top publishing software, pupils can become sensitive to the needs of the target audience of their written work. In writing a story for the infants class, they are not only discussing content and language level, but also deciding how best to set out their work in an appealing manner. They may be describing a visit to a local industrial estate as part of their class project. On the other hand, they could be presenting the conclusion of a survey within the local community for an article that will appear in the school's regular bilingual newspaper which is sold to parents and friends of the school. Such school produced newspapers and magazines can be valuable platforms for the sharing of experiences. Bilingualism and biculturalism can be promoted among pupils and parents, in the classroom and in the community by such activity.

There is constant interaction between one language and another in the production of a newspaper. Apart from the normal group work in writing, there are also language interaction processes in the production of each page. The language used is for a specific purpose. It is authentic, meaningful language to engender communicative competence. The written work may be presented in both languages; discussion regarding the presentation of articles and pictures could similarly be in both languages— so long as the children's language experiences are rationally and sequentially structured. There is ample opportunity for problem solving and this means discussion, consensus and possibly a record of the decisions taken in a particular language.

LOGO

Most schools in Gwynedd have the Welsh version of the Longman Logotron LOGO. This provides a situation where children whose first language is not Welsh find themselves using their second language to solve the problems presented. The simple commands needed in LOGO graphics have been used successfully for second language learning. A group of learners with the teacher may discuss in Welsh the problems involved in getting the turtle to respond, or learn to create a certain shape or design. Here again, language is being used purposefully in a situation that demands clear thinking and yet may be at a level that develops functional bilingualism. The listings on screen or hard copy will be in Welsh; the recording of how they overcame the problems might also be in Welsh to enrich authentically a second language.

Data Analysis

A user-friendly and flexible English language database program called GRASS (from Newman College, England) was translated (and called ADDA) and widely distributed early in the development of Welsh language software. A development from this well received conventional database program was the creation of software that was curriculum led rather than computer led. As a result of a visit made to a Gwynedd Primary school where pupils were having difficulty in analysing data collected in a questionnaire, the Gwynedd Computer Unit created a new program. This package, called PONTIO, was one of the first programs which appeared in Welsh that was subsequently, as a result of pressure from teachers involved with non-Welsh classes, translated from Welsh into English.

PONTIO (or ASK as the English version is called), enables pupils to create a questionnaire, collect the data and then analyse the information efficiently in tables, graphs and diagrams, on screen or as print-outs. The program makes good use of IT resources by encouraging and creating group work away from the computer. As a package, its use is cross-curricular. Pupils have to agree on their field of study; create their questions and decide on the order of operations. When the data have been collected and fed into the computer, the theories and hypotheses of the project can be tested. At all stages of an ASK project, there exist bilingual opportunities. Analysis demands effective communication. Results need to be discussed, recorded and effectively presented so that conclusions drawn can be clearly communicated to a wider audience. In many schools, both languages will be used in such intra group and inter group communication.

The ASK or PONTIO bilingual projects undertaken include market research outside supermarkets, a comparison of the lives of three different generations. In the castled town of Conwy, a questionnaire was used in mid-summer to gauge public opinion about the town. Children created bilingual questionnaires to study the personal and social patterns of different generations. A typical questionnaire had the title 'When you were 10 . . .?' The pupils compared their lives at 10 with those of their parents and grandparents when they were 10 year old children. The projects produced interesting comparisons of social, cultural, economic and dual language activity over the years. What exists is a rich opportunity for the development of bilingualism: from computer program to group work, questionnaire production to the execution of a survey. Within a changing Welsh language community, it has been valuable for pupils to find that people have different language, social and cultural needs and expectations but that they do not of necessity have the same cultural backgrounds. Biculturalism is promoted as well as bilingualism.

Recommendations and Advice for the Development of Information Technology in Bilingual Contexts

(1) A minority language must respond to the challenge of the IT revolution to survival. An ostrich 'head in the sand' or 'buried in a bunker' reaction may be part of minority language decline.
(2) The immediate need is for computers in schools to be seen 'talking' the minority language as well as the usual software language. Try to ensure parity between languages.

(3) Co-ordinate the efforts of those in the field when possible. Use or create an organisation that will have this responsibility and perhaps will also be in a position to obtain grants to help with translation costs.

(4) Concerning translation:

    (a) Find out who else is translating or composing software. Be prepared to share your knowledge and work to avoid duplication of effort.

    (b) Translate only the 'best' software available and be prepared for someone else to carry-on with a program that you may have already started to translate.

    (c) When negotiating for software translation, make it clear to the Software House from the start that the majority language version will not be bought if permission to translate is not given.

    (d) All final negotiations best take place through a central body; the software can then be made available to all who need it in the minority language.

    (e) Initially concentrate on translating and not writing new material to ensure a plentiful supply of software. Translation often takes much longer than expected. Initially translate only material that the pupil experiences.

    (f) When choosing programs and packages, consider the cultural implications for the minority language. Beware of accidentally spreading only majority language culture via minority language programs.

    (g) A central body needs to ensure that the standard of translations is satisfactory and to take charge of disseminating information as widely as possible.

    (h) New IT terminology needs to be created and standardised. Produce a booklet of terms in the minority language as soon as possible. Make it available to all (especially those working in education, the media, commerce and industry).

    (i) Obtain the co-operation of experts producing software; their expertise will be useful.

    (j) Invite the representatives of 'software houses' to come and discuss needs. Show them that there is a market; gain their confidence.

    (k) Test translations fully before releasing them. A badly translated program or a translated program that crashes can produce an unwanted backlash against software in the minority language.

    (l) The quality of the programs is important, not the amount. Try to ensure a varied cross-section of software.

(m) Share experiences with others, particularly with those from other language minorities. If you write a successful program, make it available (if for sale, at a reasonable price) for others to translate.

(n) When dealing with commercial companies, they are not a charity, even if you are desperate for their software. You will usually be expected to pay the standard rate. Negotiate the right to supply a translated version free based on the receiver having bought the original 'English' version. By doing this, the company secures its royalties and your translation does not incur them in any financial loss.

(o) Do not give away any translated programs that you do not have the legal right to distribute.

(p) Establish and protect the integrity of a translation operation when dealing with software houses.

(q) Make people aware of what you are doing and why. Be honest, be fair and you'll be surprised how help can come from the most unusual places.

(r) Be tactful—you cannot afford to lose willing translation help, especially voluntary help.

(s) If you do see a translated program that is not up to standard:

—(i) draw the users' attention to the errors tactfully and offer help if you can. Be constructive and not destructive—it might be his/her first attempt and you might just have found a potentially keen translator for you minority language IT team.

—(ii) try to find out who did the translation work. Tell him/her that you also translate and that you find it useful to give your programs to the Central Body for testing by others as it is often difficult to evaluate one's own work effectively and guarantee correctness.

—(iii) try and find out who else has received copies so that they can receive a corrected version.

—(iv) inform the Central Body of your find; they might be able to support and help the translator.

Conclusions

This chapter has considered the experience of Wales in moving away from an English-only computer software solution. The initial move was to translate software from English to Welsh, thus providing an immediate response to an anglophone software invasion. The second and current stage comprises the co-existence of home-grown Welsh language software and the translation of high quality curriculum-based software. Recently, bilingual software has developed, allowing choice of language within a program.

The argument from this chapter is that schools and classrooms throughout Europe increasingly use Information Technology. Unlike language laboratories and programmed learning, microcomputers and their school software are here to stay. English language software is dominant and widely distributed. Bilingual education needs to meet the challenge and turn a danger into an opportunity. Bilingual education in Europe stands to gain by translating and developing software, wherever practicable, into the variety of European languages.

The gains are many. Minority language Information Technology can aid language survival and spread. It is a small but important support to maintain the richness of diversity of European languages. Minority languages become modernised in terminology and technical functionality. Such modernisation aids the symbolic status of the language, particularly among the impressionable young. This ensures that Information Technology is a supporter and not a destroyer of bilingualism in children. The threat to the colourful language diversity of Europe posed by the mighty microcomputer can be turned into a tool to support European bilingualism, multilingualism, bilingual education and multiculturalism. The uniformity of microcomputer monolingualism can be translated into supporting the diversity of bilingualism in Europe.

Acknowledgements

The authors wish to express their gratitude to Alwyn Evans, Chief Education Adviser, Gwynedd LEA, for his valuable constructive comments on an initial draft.

References

BAKER, C.R. 1983, The microcomputer and the curriculum. *Journal of Curriculum Studies* 15, 2, 207–10.
— 1984, A critical examination of the effect of the microcomputer on the curriculum. In C. TERRY (ed.) *Using Microcomputers in Schools*. London: Croom Helm.
— 1985, *Aspects of Bilingualism in Wales*. Clevedon: Multilingual Matters.

—1988, *Key Issues in Bilingualism and Bilingual Education*. Clevedon: Multilingual Matters.
— 1992, *Attitudes and Language*. Clevedon: Multilingual Matters.
CLYWD TECHNICS LTD. 1983, EDWORD. Mold, Clwyd.
CTI CENTRE FOR MODERN LANGUAGES 1990, *ReCALL Software Guide*. University of Hull.
CUMMINS, J. 1988, From inner city to the global village: The microcomputer as a catalyst for collaborative learning and cultural interchange. *Language, Culture and Curriculum* 1, 1, 1–14.
LEARNING TECHNOLOGY UNIT 1990, *Educational Technology in Modern Language Learning*. Sheffield: Training Agency.
PRICE, D. (ed.) 1985, *Y Micro mewn Addysg*. Gwynedd Computer Unit, Caernarfon.
ROBERTS, H.G. 1987, Microelectronics: The Welsh connection, *Education for Development* 10, 3, 55–62.
SAYERS, D. and BROWN, K. 1987, Bilingual education and telecommunications: A perfect fit. *The Computing Teacher* 14, 7, 23–26.

List of Contributors

Josep Maria ARTIGAL was a kindergarten L2 teacher for nine years in Catalonia. At present he is a researcher in applied psycholinguistics at the University of Barcelona. He has been a consultant on immersion programmes in Catalonia and Finland, and an L2 teacher trainer in France, Italy, Finland and the Basque Country. He has given many talks and workshops on theoretical and practical issues of immersion and early L2 acquisition. His publications include, *The Catalan Immersion program: A European Point of View* (1991).

Hugo BAETENS BEARDSMORE is Professor of English and Bilingualism at the Vrije Universiteit Brussel and the Université Libre de Bruxelles. His research covers linguistic, sociological and educational aspects of bilingualism. He has been visiting professor in the University of Berkeley, California and the National University of Singapore and has been a consultant for the European Community and Ministries of Education in California, Singapore and Brunei.

Colin BAKER is currently Senior Lecturer at the University of Wales in Bangor and Director of Research Centre Wales. His current research includes the effectiveness of bilingual education, the national assessment of minority language attainment and a Council of Europe initiative on bilingual education. He has published three books with Multilingual Matters Ltd.: *Aspects of Bilingualism in Wales* (1985), *Key Issues in Bilingualism and Bilingual Education* (1988) and *Attitudes and Language* (1992).

Michael BYRAM is Reader in Education at the University of Durham. He is responsible for the training of foreign language teachers and for courses in comparative education. He has carried out research on minority education in Belgium and Denmark and published *Minority Education and Ethnic Survival* and edited with Johan Leman *Bicultural and Trilingual Education*.

Irène DREXEL-ANDRIEU, a French national married to a German, teaches bilingual geography in a German secondary school in Hamburg where she developed the methodology and materials for teaching content-matter via a foreign language. She has several publications in Germany and French on this innovative issue and has spoken at conferences in Germany and Austria on questions of integrating mixed curricular pedagogic and examination criteria.

Nathalie LEBRUN comes from the Belgian province of Luxembourg and studied language and linguistics (English and Spanish) at the Université Libre de Bruxelles where she produced a dissertation on education in the Grand Duchy of Luxembourg. At present she is working in the international banking sector in Luxembourg City with responsibilities covering France, Spain and Asia.

Johan LEMAN is Director of the Cabinet at the Royal Commissariat for Immigrant Policy in Belgium, Professor at the Centre for Social and Cultural Anthropology and at the Centre for European Studies at the University of Leuven, and President of the Foyer, a socio-pedagogical centre for immigrants in Brussels.

Nando MÄSCH was a teacher of French before becoming headmaster of a grammar school in Düren. In 1971 he created the first bilingual German–French section in his school and became the founder and President of the Federation of Schools with bilingual German–French sections in Germany in 1975. Since 1980 he has published much on bilingual education in schools and from 1991 became a Director with the education authority of North-Rhine-Westphalia in Cologne.

Bent SØNDERGAARD cand. mag. (University of Aarhus, Denmark), dr. phil. (University of Copenhagen) has been Professor of Danish as a foreign/second language since 1973 at the Pädagogische Hochschule Flensburg, Germany. He is a Corresponding Member of the Research Centre on Multilingualism, Brussels.

Index